A Queer Scrapbook

Britain and Ireland since 1945

'A goldmine for anyone seeking to reinvigorate their hearts, minds and toolkits for activism, harvested from beautiful case studies of queer life and love that have been hidden... until now.'

Dan Glass, author and activist

'Proof we've always been here, proof of all we've fought for, proof that we need to keep fighting now more than ever.'

Charlie Craggs, actress and activist

'Our histories are often unspoken or erased, so this lovely treasure trove provides a wealth of fascinating insights into the personal lives, stories, activism, communities, art and desire of queer people that have occurred since the post-war period. Highly recommended!'

Paul Baker, author of *Fabulosa!*

'Leaps energetically from moment to moment, place to place – a book as delightfully idiosyncratic as queer and trans history itself.'

Morgan M. Page, author and activist

'Queer life bursts from these pages, messy and touching and grubby and gorgeous. The voices of *A queer scrapbook* have something urgent to say to everyone: it's a treasure trove of historical sources and community across time, and it will hold you as you hold it.'

Kit Heyam, author of *Before We Were Trans*

'Wonderfully researched and richly illustrated, *A queer scrapbook* is the next best thing to being in a queer archive. Not only a brilliant introduction to queer history but a thoughtful commentary on the future of queer archival work.'

Elizabeth Lovatt, author of *Thank You for Calling the Lesbian Line*

'Queer history is often about lives lived in the margins: notes scrawled on scraps of paper, homemade zines, blurry Polaroids and photocopied posters. *A queer scrapbook* is an ode to this history, an authoritative and comprehensive collection of queer life in Britain over the past eighty years. More than this, it's a love letter to the real queer people of Britain, not just the celebrities or the uber rich. Everyday people who built their own communities from scratch, despite incredible hardship. This book will make you happy, will make you proud, not in a fluffy corporate way, but in seeing real queer people changing the world – one flyer, Post-it note or cartoon strip at a time.'

Sacha Coward, author of *Queer as Folklore*

A QUEER SCRAPBOOK

Britain and Ireland since 1945

Edited by
Justin Bengry, Matt Cook,
Rebecca Jennings and E-J Scott

Manchester University Press

Copyright © Manchester University Press 2026

While copyright in the volume as a whole is vested in Manchester University Press, copyright in individual chapters belongs to their respective authors, and no chapter may be reproduced wholly or in part without the express permission in writing of both author and publisher.

Published by Manchester University Press
Oxford Road, Manchester, M13 9PL

www.manchesteruniversitypress.co.uk

British Library Cataloguing-in-Publication Data
A catalogue record for this book is available from the British Library

ISBN 978 1 5261 6531 2 paperback

First published 2026

The publisher has no responsibility for the persistence or accuracy of URLs for any external or third-party internet websites referred to in this book, and does not guarantee that any content on such websites is, or will remain, accurate, accessible or appropriate.

EU authorised representative for GPSR:
Easy Access System Europe, Mustamäe tee 50, 10621 Tallinn, Estonia
gpsr.requests@easproject.com

Design by Chris Bell

CONTENTS

Introduction	2
Section 1: **Home and family**	6
Section 2: **Socialising and sex**	52
Section 3: **Arts and culture**	102
Section 4: **Activism and community**	152
Conclusion	194
List of contributors and editors	197
List of illustrations	198
Index of places	206
Index of subjects	208

INTRODUCTION

By Justin Bengry, Matt Cook, Rebecca Jennings and E-J Scott

WELCOME TO *A Queer Scrapbook!* This book is a dip into the rich histories of LGBTIQ+ lives in Britain and Ireland from 1945 to the present. Imagine yourself at a table in a library reading room in Dublin, opening up a plain brown archive box to find the treasures within. Or sitting over a cup of tea with an LGBTIQ+ elder, hearing their stories of life in 1960s rural Wales. Or wandering around a local gallery, looking at photographs of trans house parties in late 1970s Sheffield. We invite you to settle in and enjoy the traces of LGBTIQ+ life in the past, reaching out across time to share in the joys and fear, the anger and desire, the love and loss that our queer forebears and near contemporaries have felt.

In this book we zoom in on some of those individual lives and the places where they were lived – from the queer artist inspired by St Ives in Cornwall to the Irish teenager finding her feet in a down-at-heel queer bar in Manchester which became 'like home'. We zoom out to trace larger trends and movements that LGBTIQ+ people have been involved in, from the story of how lesbian feminists took skills in carpentry and plumbing from their London squats and used them to create a thriving LGBTIQ+ community in Todmorden in the Pennines, to the digital map charting Brianna Ghey vigils across the country from Orkney to Redruth. Our eclectic collection is nowhere near comprehensive or representative – instead, it gives a flavour of the richness and diversity of LGBTIQ+ culture and experience across the British and Irish Isles, often at a distance from the notorious queer hubs.

Much of the LGBTIQ+ history that has been produced since the 1970s has focused on major cities and particularly on London. Historically, cities and large towns offered opportunities for LGBTIQ+ people to meet others like themselves, to form communities and establish social spaces, as well as to debate and coordinate struggles for legal rights. These spaces have been hugely important in shaping queer identity, community and subculture; they have been places where individuals in the past have met lovers and friends and found ways to live happily and authentically. They have shaped the society we live in today. But small towns and rural areas have also provided important and valued settings for LGBTIQ+ lives, allowing our queer ancestors to make homes with their lovers, form networks with LGBTIQ+ neighbours and friends and feel connected to a place and to family ties. In this book, we want to decentre London and put it in its place among the rich diversity of queer experience across the country. Those experiences haven't been contained within national boundaries either. *Queer Scrapbook* also shows the ways in which global networks of people and ideas have travelled to and from the UK and how this has enriched our histories.

Queer history is being recorded and brought to life in many different ways and by a diverse array of people. We have tried to represent those different approaches to thinking about queer history in this book. We have spoken to librarians and archivists, curators, journalists, activists, academic historians, local community history groups, LGBTIQ+ individuals and more, asking them to send us the sources they find fascinating and to tell us about their own, their families' and their communities' histories. What we have found is that 'history' can mean many different things to different people. It can be about exploring what life was like for our elders when they were young, or for people we never met who lived long before we were born. In this sense, the past can feel like 'a foreign country', as queer novelist L. P. Hartley put it. 'They do things differently there.'

Successive generations of LGBTIQ+ activists, from the homophile groups of the 1950s and 1960s to the gay liberation activists of the 1970s, have seen history of the long-distant past as an important tool in advocating for LGBTIQ+ rights in the present – showing that queer people have existed across time, often making important contributions to the societies in which they lived. LGBTIQ+ individuals, like the editors of this book, have also turned to history as a way of finding kindred spirits or 'queer ancestors', helping them to make sense of their identities and experiences in the present. But history doesn't have to be a long time ago. Contemporary history, recording events that have just happened or that we are currently living through, is just as important. We would not be able to explore and understand the experiences of LGBTIQ+ people in the past if individuals and groups hadn't recognised the historical importance of what they were doing and preserved records and the personal paraphernalia of their daily lives. In this book, we move between both of these registers, looking back to the early post-war decades of the 1950s and 1960s and charting the actions and ideas of LGBTIQ+ people in the twenty-first century. We have been helped in this by the upsurge in LGBTIQ+ local and community history work since the early 2000s, with projects, many funded by the National Lottery Heritage Fund (more commonly known as the HLF), across the UK and Ireland.

The words we (that is, LGBTIQ+ people) have used to describe ourselves – and the terms others have used to refer to us – have changed many times across the period this book covers. In the 1950s, the word 'queer' was a typically derogatory term applied to homosexual men, but in the 1990s it was reclaimed by activists who wanted to express a range of politically confrontational sexual identities which transgressed social norms. Some of the commonly used words were coined as medical terms, including 'transsexual' and 'homosexual', while others, such as 'dyke' originated in the communities they described. We have chosen to use the acronym LGBTIQ+ to indicate the broad and inclusive forms of gender and sexual identity we hope to capture in this book, but in places we use other terms which were widely used in the historical moment being discussed.

Just as language has changed, so too has people's understanding of what different categories of sexuality or gender mean, complicating our desire to look back into the past and see reflections of ourselves. Individuals in former generations who seem to have much in common with us in their desires or self-expression, may have understood themselves within unexpected categories, or without claiming any identity at all, while others may have claimed different identities at different points in their lives. In the 1960s, the lesbian magazine *Arena Three* hosted a lively debate among readers about how to categorise women who were married to men but desired other women: while they were often referred to as 'married lesbians' at the time, some felt that the category 'bisexual' was a better fit, highlighting the ways in which language and categories can obscure a diversity of experience.

We have organised the book into four broad sections: home and family, socialising and sex, arts and culture, and activism and community. In home and family

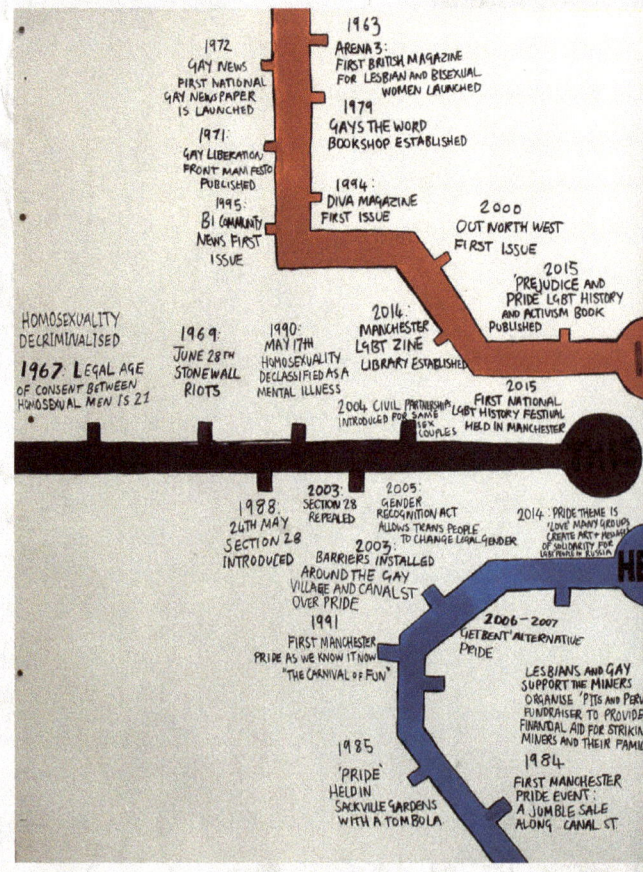

4 | A QUEER SCRAPBOOK

we delve into LGBTIQ+ people's relationships with their families of origin, histories of marriage and LGBTIQ+ parenting, as well as taking a look at the sorts of housing LGBTIQ+ people have lived in and what those homes have meant to them. In socialising and sex we look from home towards other places where people met each other: pubs and clubs, community centres and events, conferences and cruising places where friends, lovers and new forms of family were found. The arts and culture section charts the significance of creative work in forming community and identity, in protesting and imagining different, better futures and in mapping a past which might be sustaining in the present. In activism and community, we march through the rainbow alphabet with lesbians, gay men, bisexual people and the trans and intersex communities all speaking up and acting out. Our struggle for equal rights and justice manifest in multiple forms – direct action, fashion statements, Pride marches, legal battles, unionism and digital activism.

While we've organised this wealth of material into themed sections, queer life of course can't be divided up neatly into boxes, and there are lots of interconnections between the different parts of the book. For example, in the activism and community section we learn about the creative production of a quilt to be carried on political protests, while in the home and family section we hear about the importance of homes as community social spaces and sites of activism. These intersections and crossovers are part of the excitement and richness of what we think of as a queer scrapbook of British and Irish life.

← This mural, titled *This Is How We Got Here*, was a history project researched and created by members of the Manchester LGBT+ Centre youth groups and creative café. It was displayed in the centre between 2015 and 2019.

INTRODUCTION | 5

SECTION 1: HOME AND FAMILY

Curated by Rebecca Jennings

Like many LGBTIQ+ people, I can tell the story of my sexuality through homes. I spent my closeted teenage years in my family home in 1980s semi-rural Surrey, escaping to Manchester to come out in the mid-1990s. Those early years of finding myself and a community took place against the backdrop of a succession of rented flats across south Manchester. Nights out began at friends' concrete-floored housing association flats in Whalley Range, waiting for everyone to get ready – and ended in the early morning, collapsed on someone's sofa as we all talked over the night, reliving the music and the gossip about who had gone home with whom. When I started my first long-term relationship, my girlfriend and I sealed our commitment with the purchase of tealights and a new (second-hand) sofa and made a home.

As the sources in this section show, homes and access to housing have played a central role in LGBTIQ+ people's lives since the 1950s. After the Sexual Offences Act 1967 decriminalised homosexual acts between men in private, access to a private home of some kind allowed gay men to pursue sexual and loving relationships in relative security and, for much of the period explored in this book, trans people have created 'safe houses' to express and share their authentic selves. For LGBTIQ+ youth, living with parents or other family could significantly impact on their ability to express their sexual or gender identity and, at any life stage, LGBTIQ+ people's access to a secure home has been constrained by hostile neighbours, the unaffordability of housing and failure of council and other tenancy agreements to recognise queer forms of kinship. Some LGBTIQ+ people have responded to these challenges by creating squats or living in house shares, while others have lived more or less discreetly with partners in suburban homes. Homes have often been the setting for family life, and this section traces the diverse ways in which LGBTIQ+ people have interacted with their families of origin – coming out to and seeking support from parents and siblings – as well as constructing families of their own. We will delve into the rich histories of queer and trans parenting and the formation of families in all their forms.

Rebecca Jennings

QUEER SQUAT ON GRAND PARADE, BRIGHTON, 2013.

Here and overleaf is a taster for the section, which includes spreads on coming out to family; queer family; marriage; marriage equality; lesbian, gay and trans parenting; housing; domestic lives; and housing activism from across Britain and Ireland.

MANCHESTER SOCIAL SERVICES POSTER ADVERTISING FOR LESBIAN AND GAY CARERS, PROBABLY CIRCA LATE 1990S.

← Kathy Sells and Daniel (her son) on a Positive Images march through Haringey in May 1987, protesting against the banning of educational books about homosexuality in schools.

1: HOME AND FAMILY | 7

LESBIAN MOTHERS BANNER AT LESBIAN STRENGTH MARCH, LONDON, 27 JUNE 1981.

Danish children's author Susanne Bösche's book *Jenny Lives with Eric and Martin* was published in English in 1983 to help children learn about non-traditional families. It became a focus of the media and political outcry surrounding education about homosexuality which culminated in the passing of Section 28.

↑ Scottish poet Jackie Kay with her son, Matt Kay, at her installation as Chancellor of the University of Salford in 2015.

Sketch of the Families and Friends of Lesbians and Gays (FFLAG) banner at Pride 1995, probably produced by a member of the Manchester Parents Group. FFLAG grew from parents' groups across the country from 1986 onwards and was officially launched as a national organisation in 1993. Four national conferences were held: in Leicester (1993), Manchester (1995), Cambridge (1997) and London (2000).

→ Bryan Bale grew up in Cardiff in the 1940s and 1950s, before moving to London and coming out as a gay man in the 1960s. His cousin's son, Anthony, tells his story as part of a reflection on queer family on page 16.

Poster created by Out For Our Children for use by early years centres and primary schools to depict 'the complexity and infinite diversity of ordinary families'. Out For Our Children was created in 2004 by lesbian mothers to work with parents, childcare workers and teachers to create a positive environment in education for the children of same-sex parents.

HOMOSEXUALITY AND THE FAMILY IN THE 1950S AND 1960S

DURING THE 1950s and 1960s, medical 'experts' and cultural commentators produced a growing body of literature about homosexuality, frequently identifying problems in the family environment as a primary factor in a person growing up homosexual or bisexual. From the 1960s onwards, lesbian and gay publications and groups were challenging these ideas through activism and satire.

Anthony Storr, Sexual Deviation (Harmondsworth: Penguin, 1964), p. 83

'Research into the family background of male homosexuals has already yielded results which tend to show that certain specific family patterns are particularly likely to produce a homosexual son. Of these patterns, by far the commonest is one in which the father is detached from, and either shows little affection for, or is actually hostile to the son in question; combined with a mother who is extremely intimate and over-emotional.'

'There seems to be one childhood pattern which is, as it were, the archetype, and everyone who goes into the subject has to remark on it before long: over and again it is found that a homosexual person has had an intense relationship with the mother and a deficient one with the father. When I say a deficient relationship with the father I am referring to the deficiency of the relationship, not the deficiency of the father, who may be an adequate and well-adjusted person. Of course, it may be that a man has a deficient relationship with his child because he is a weak character, but it may also be that he is a strong character who is so tied up in his job that he has only a weak contact with his children, or with one particular child. He may not be on hand much – he may be someone whose job keeps him travelling most of the time. He may be away at war. He may be a chronic invalid. He may be in hospital. He may have gone off with another woman. The parents may be divorced. The father may be absent for any one of a hundred reasons – he may even be dead (and this of course makes him an exceedingly deficient father from the child's point of view).

Similarly, the intense relationship that is so commonly found with the mother may be due to the fact that the mother is a loving, warm and affectionate woman; but there is almost

Cartoons by Jo Nesbitt, published together with Sue Cartledge and Susan Hemmings, 'How did we get this way?', *Spare Rib*, no. 86 (September 1979), p. 45.

always more to it than this. A woman who is all these things will normally pour out her feelings towards her husband and children alike, and her relationship with one child will not be intense in the possessive or exclusive way that seems to be so dangerous. What one very often finds when one goes into it is that there is something wrong with the mother's relationship with the father, and because of this her warmth and affection all go into her relationship with her child. So the child has an abnormally intense relationship with its mother precisely because there is a deficient relationship between mother and father. So one can now begin to see the different ways in which a child may become homosexual because of a pattern of relationships in which the entire family is involved.'

Bryan Magee, *One in Twenty: A Study of Homosexuality in Men and Women* (London: Secker and Warburg, 1966), pp. 30–1

COMING OUT TO FAMILY

From the early 1970s, feminist and lesbian and gay politics emphasised the importance of 'coming out' and embracing a positive and visible identity; but long before that, queer and trans people found ways to talk to their families about their gender and sexual identities.

Helen Hallam interviewed by Alys Duggan for West Yorkshire Queer Stories (2019). Between 2018 and 2020 the project collected 200 stories from all kinds of people of all ages and backgrounds. For more stories and background on the project, visit https://wyqs.co.uk

'I am a trans woman but I've always been a woman; the whole of my life I've been a woman. It's very difficult to explain, but I've always felt I was female, from/through childhood ... When I got to about fourteen, maybe – yeah about fourteen – I said to my parents this is how I felt, and this is in the 1950s, and my parents said, 'Oh you'll grow out of it, you know, you've got a sister, you've got brothers, we know about these things, you'll grow out of it'. So I got to fifteen and – bit more than fifteen – and I said 'Look, this is how I feel. I'm not growing out of it.' And, my parents obviously didn't know much, well, in the fifties you didn't know much about those things and they said, 'Look, if you keep saying these things, we'll probably have to take you to the doctor's. The doctor will probably refer you to a mental hospital, and, what's gonna happen then is you'll get electric shock treatment – now is that what you want? Is that what you really want?' Well at that age I got really very scared. Nobody wants that. I don't think they did it out of any, I don't think it was a bad thought on their part, I think it was just the way that things were.'

'Well, a fairly conventional family. I had two parents, one brother. Grandparents living with us for much of the time. And I went to a Church of England primary school ... Excitement wasn't really the overriding feature of the place, but it was a pleasant enough upbringing in its way ... Yes, I was eighteen in '68.

'How many more times, Son, before you win your bet?', cartoon sent in by a reader to the *Beaumont Bulletin*, magazine of Britain's first trans organisation, the Beaumont Society. *Beaumont Bulletin*, vol. 2, no. 9 (May/June 1970).

I don't think [my parents] were [aware], no. I mean my mother, who is ninety-four, still isn't aware, although I think she must know, at some level. She just chooses not to acknowledge it. My father never did and he was fairly homophobic. 'It's not natural is it' – that's what he would say. I had friends who knew, yeah, very close friends, one or two, not many. But they did know because I told them. And my brother, who was seven years younger than I am, he knew as well. But it didn't help them knowing because none of them was interested in doing anything about it and I obviously couldn't.

Yeah, it became clear to my brother certainly and to my best friend that I was not after the girls and was not interested in sport, I was interested in arty things and painting and all that sort of stuff and he said 'Are you um, er?' 'Yes', I said. So that was that conversation. That was coming out circa 1968 ... There was no problem with that. I mean, they were all perfectly friendly, not happy about it, I wouldn't say necessarily, but friendly about it. But it was difficult because the West Wight, and the Isle of Wight generally, are a wee bit on the backward side and they were then, too and we're talking of church schools and all the rest of it ... I mean coming out there, against that background, I mean forget it, you wouldn't. You'd be damned to hell and back. So they took me to the doctor. My mother, my father sort of thought, 'There's something strange going on here'. Doctor said 'Are you interested in women?' 'No'. 'Interested in men?' 'Not especially.' 'Oh good!' And that was that. He was an ex-army doctor.'

'It would have been around this time that I told my mum I thought I was bisexual. I remember saying 'I think I'm like David Bowie', and she said 'What do you mean?' I said 'I think I'm bisexual'. She said 'Let's have a cup of tea.' All these things were happening at the same time. Suddenly you had this music and fashion and club scene and it was ok to be bi. I don't think it was ok to be gay necessarily but you had people in bands who actually, you know, Boy George was coming on the scene, Marc Almond was coming on the scene, Small Town Boy, Bronski Beat, you know, it was suddenly all changing.'

MY PARENTS are typical Asian parents, wanting the best for their daughter, especially as I was the only daughter they had, and I was the eldest in the family. They were in the process of arranging a marriage for me, and I got fed up of having to lie every time I wanted to go out, so it became urgent to tell them.

My father was told first as I can communicate better with him and feel close to him, and I'll never forget the look in his eyes. The look of failure, the fear of what people will say. He immediately thought that I was ill and arranged for me to see a psychiatrist through the family doctor. My mother was totally shattered; she cried for a month continually, not once looking at me in the eyes or speaking to me. Their hopes of me being an ideal woman, getting married, having children and holding a respectable position in the community were shattered, and I had to pay for it. That terrible feeling of guilt will never leave me.

I was torn. What was I supposed to do? Should I return to their expectations or lead my life my way, or find a compromise? ... I made my decision, I 'chose' to live my life my way – as a lesbian – and I started to explore into the great big world.

Madhu Patel, Birmingham, *Spare Rib*, **no. 136, November 1983**

Extract from oral history interview with Robert Jones, collected by Franko Figueiredo-Stow for StoneCrabs' Out On An Island project (2019)

Interview with Berkeley Wilde, OutStories Bristol (OH416): https://outstories bristol.org.uk

FAMILY SUPPORT

FAMILY SUPPORT FOR LGBTIQ+ loved ones could come in a variety of forms, from unspoken acceptance to a range of groups such as Parents Enquiry and Families and Friends of Lesbians and Gays (FFLAG) which provided public demonstrations of allyship as well as private advice.

Amanda Russell, who grew up in Essex in the 1960s, described the support she received from Parents Enquiry when her mother struggled to accept her sexuality:

Interview with Amanda Russell by Evelyn Pitman, 21 October 2019, From a Whisper to a Roar project, Bishopsgate Institute Archives

'My parents moved out to Essex when I was quite young. So I grew up there. And I was always attracted to girls ... I worked as a kennel maid. I worked in a factory. So I wasn't really expected to look terribly feminine, apart from by my parents. That was the thing, really. And I suppose the thing about those early days was keeping quiet about it. I didn't feel ashamed, but I knew if it came out it would cause a lot of problems, and finally it did come out. My mother took me, straightaway, to see the doctor, who referred me to a psychiatrist, whom I saw for ages. I can't really remember a lot, but she said, 'Don't worry about it,' and told my mother it was a phase. ...

Parents Enquiry was about helping parents come to terms with their kids being gay, basically. And this woman, she was an elderly woman, her son had come out and his friends had had problems coming out to their parents. I spoke to her quite a lot

Two parents with placards from the Manchester Parents Group on the Clause 28 march in London, 30 April 1988.

14 | A QUEER SCRAPBOOK

and she was really helpful, and she wrote a letter to my parents saying that she'd come and talk to them with me, and help them to understand everything. And my mother just went up the roof. 'I'm not having a woman like that coming here.' Even though she was a grandmother, this woman.'

In his semi-fictionalised autobiographical novel, *Rid England of This Plague* (Paradise Press, 2006), Rex Batten describes how the hero, Tom, became the subject of police interest after a former boyfriend, Ashley-Jones, was arrested for gross indecency. Tom's mother wrote to describe a visit that Dorset police made to his family home in search of him:

'*Dear Tom,*
The weather here is a lot better and your father can get on with the garden.
This morning three policemen came to the door and they said they wanted you, so I said you were not here. Then the one that did all the talking asked me where you were.
What odds is that of yours where he is? I said to him.
Then he went on about you being mixed up with Ashley-Jones so I wanted to know how he knew you was mixed up in it.
We have our ways of finding out he said.
I think they were going to come into the house. One of them try to push past me. He is not here. I said, and they looked at me as if I were telling a lie. Well I were not having none of that. The one standing behind him took out a pad and pencil all ready to write. I looked at him.
Go on and he said it again. Go on he said. Well nobody says go on to me. Not the way he said it.
Tell us his address. He talked to me as if I were a kid. I said not a word. We have our ways of finding out he said. Well that was it so I said. You go on and you use your ways to find out where he be. Good morning to thee. An I shut the door in their face.
Your Mum.

Tom could hear his mother. She must have written the letter immediately the police had gone. He bent his head and kissed the letter mistakes and all. She must have been in a real temper to misspell or misuse any word in a letter. That letter told him everything he wanted to know. He did not have to fear for his mother. She was protecting her family as fiercely as any tigress would.'

UNDATED LETTER SENT BY THE MOTHER OF A GAY MAN TO FFLAG.

QUEER FAMILY
By Anthony Bale

THE FACE ON THE SCREEN is beguilingly familiar. His top lip is the same as my dad's. His eyes have the same direct, clear stare as my dad. His thin, fine wrists are precisely the same shape as my dad's. He reads the *Guardian* exactly as my dad did, holding it away from him and peering down his straight nose – the same shape as my dad's – at the pages. And the accent – soft Cardiff Welsh under a long veil of middle-class England – is the same as my dad's. He looks into the camera and says: 'You can't misbehave in Cardiff. To this very day you can't, because everybody knows everybody else. You have to be on your best behaviour, shall we put it like that?'

The man on the screen is Bryan Bale, cousin of my dad, John, and he is talking in a prize-winning short film, *Bachelor, 38* (dir. Angela Clarke, 2017). 'I didn't like ladies. I liked men,' he says, with a cheeky grin. The film is a revelation for me: a gay relative, quite a close one, who had grown up in Cardiff in the 1940s and 1950s, living across the road from my dad. An eloquent, out gay man with the same surname as me, talking about moving to London and coming out and having sex in the early 1960s with candour, humour and great insight. I'm moved and proud to watch him talk on screen, but ashamed too that I hardly knew him.

I only met Bryan twice, at family funerals. The first time, at my granny Alice's funeral in 1995, he had been one of dozens of relatives – there are many Bale relatives in south Wales – who came to St Augustine's Church, in the respectable Cardiff suburb of Rumney where my father grew up. The second time I remember him more clearly; also at a funeral, this time in 2011, for my dad's brother Keith. At this funeral, Bryan made quite an impression on me: he turned up with his partner (whom my mother recalls as 'a short man in a belted raincoat and beret, like a glamorous French spy'). At the wake, Bryan immediately made a beeline for my dad, and he fondly reminisced about Alice, whose home he remembered as a refuge when things were difficult with his own family. Bryan's father had been a heavy drinker and had committed suicide, and people whispered about how unhappy the household was. But Bryan had left Cardiff, moved to London, come to terms with himself, and had a full and successful life. At this point, he was living back in Wales, and was an urbane, fun presence.

It was only after this meeting that I learned about Bryan's life, about which he speaks so eloquently in *Bachelor, 38*. He had moved to London, aged nineteen, in 1963, around the same time as my father moved from Cardiff to London to become a teacher. Bryan developed a successful career in fashion in high-end Mayfair stores and threw himself into London's still-illegal gay underworld. He was, by all accounts, a hugely social man with a gift for language, an avid traveller, an authentic person who loved red wine, all things Danish and telling stories. All these traits were shared with my father.

And yet Bryan and my father had no contact when they both lived in London. Part of my dad's self-mythology was that he had left working-class Cardiff – his father was a marine fitter at the docks, Bryan's was a tug-boat pilot – and in doing so had left the rest of his family behind. But it didn't seem to occur to my dad – at the London School of Economics studying sociology and listening to jazz with his exotic Jewish fiancée – that other relatives may also have come to London and built entirely new lives there.

BRYAN IN NAPLES, 1970.

They lost touch as young men and then again as older men after these family funerals. My dad was shortly afterwards diagnosed with dementia, and time passed. Bryan died of cancer, on St David's Day 2020, during the COVID-19 pandemic so his funeral was online. I watched a recording of it; it was a joyous and moving event. I was struck by how Bryan had established a wide and loving chosen family around him, a new family I only uncovered in Bryan's death, but I was also saddened by the thought that I, a relative, didn't know him better. If only I had known about these queer connections – wonderful, fabulous, exciting people – when I was growing up, and I believed myself to be utterly isolated as the first and only queer person in my family.

The heteronormative lifecycle celebrates births and christenings, hen nights and marriages. In contrast, it mourns divorces and funerals, even though these are no less common or, in the case of death, inevitable. Can we rethink the funeral, queerly, as a chance not only to say goodbye to the dead, but as an opportunity to revisit past relationships in new ways? In my experience, the queer potential of each funeral has been joyfully realised in recovering people whose lives and identities the past had not been able to accommodate.

Anthony Bale is Professor of Medieval and Renaissance Literature at the University of Cambridge and a Fellow of Girton College, Cambridge.

CHOSEN FAMILIES

Poet and journalist Zenka Bartek with her girlfriend, Wyn Cooper, in the 1940s. She later formed a long-term relationship with Countess Judith Karolyi and the couple lived in Vence and Tourrettes-sur-Loup, France, before returning to London in the 1990s.

↑ Manchester-based indie singer-songwriter Jasmine.4.t speaking to fans at the Green Man Festival, Brecon Beacons, August 2025, and with fellow band members, Eden, Phoenix and Emily, after performing at BBC Radio 6 live in November 2024. The songs on Jasmine.4.t's debut album, 'You Are The Morning', describe the pain of coming out as trans to friends and family in Bristol, divorcing and finding herself homeless, but the music conveys the power of friendship, warmth and chosen family in bringing the trans community through dark times.

In the news reporting following the murder of Terry Sweet in Plymouth in November 1995, interviews with friends and family revealed that he had been surrounded by a loving extended circle. Lisa Hay from the Evening Herald reported: 'Mr Sweet, who was divorced in 1984 from Patricia, his wife of 13 years, had lived with Albert Priaulx for six years … [he] had a daughter Audrey in America, [and] was known to Mr Priaulx's children Nick, Selwyn and Elizabeth as "Uncle Terry"'. His friends, Hay said, 'have many memories of a gentle and friendly man who smoked a pipe or cigars and regularly went shopping for a pensioner in her 80s.' Dave Banner, landlord of gay pub The Clarence in Stonehouse, told the Herald, 'Many of our customers have been married in the past for 10, 20 or even 30 years and are now out-gay – but many were not sure even until their 50s that marriage was right for them.'

Plymouth Evening Herald, 6 March 1997.

MARRIAGE

WHEN BRITAIN'S first lesbian magazine, *Arena Three*, was launched in 1964, a significant number of letters to the editor came from married women. They described having married due to social pressure, in the hope it would 'cure' them of their lesbianism, as a way to have children or because they did not yet realise they were attracted to women. The letters showed the challenges of living as a married lesbian.

'In the years before my own marriage I used to worry about my lack of interest in the opposite sex. The emotional posturings of my friends over romances either just beginning or just broken off, struck me as completely ludicrous. Surprisingly, I had no difficulty in attracting boyfriends. So, not wanting to be 'different', I indulged in the same amusements and made the same silly noises as everyone else. There was no-one in whom to confide about my 'abnormality', and I had reasoned out for myself that I must be 'frigid' – a condition I could successfully hide by 'good acting' and which would miraculously disappear when I met the right man, married and had children.'

Mrs E. J. S. (Cheshire), Arena Three, vol. 6, no. 4 (April 1969), p. 5

"This is not Mommy's dress, its mine"

↑ *Beaumont Bulletin*, (March/April 1970), p. 12.

'I was married for 12 years and have five children. I could never find real satisfaction with my husband, and he tormented me with this for a very long time. I was lucky enough to become friendly with a gay boy ten years my junior who has been my helpmate ever since I divorced my husband. Although the eldest children understand the position, as I think they should, we maintain an outward appearance of 'normal' family life for the sake of the children.'

Mrs M. D. (Bromley), Arena Three, vol. 6, no. 3 (March 1969), p. 6

'Dear Esme Langley – I live on the borders of Kent and Sussex, and should so much like to hear from other married readers, especially those with children, as to how they cope with the problems they inevitably must have if, like me, they only discovered their innate homosexuality after several years of marriage and children, and then realised all that their relationship with their husband lacked.'

Mrs R. (Sussex), Arena Three, vol. 6, no. 2 (February 1969), p. 5

'Dear Editor, I am married but have always deep down, known that I am lesbian, but it didn't really come to me until I fell in love with my best friend after I was married. I have suffered mental torture because I know I can never tell her how I feel; she could never accept me as a lesbian. Being a married lesbian is just as lonely as being a single one. Another thing is I have no children: not because I don't like them – I love children – but if my marriage eventually came to an end (which I expect it will, due to obvious reasons) I don't think children should have to suffer because of me. I hope I don't give you the impression of myself as a miserable married lesbian. I am happy-go-lucky and always live in the hope of meeting someone I can have a long and happy association with.'

Anon, (Worcestershire), Arena Three, vol. 8, no. 3 (1971), p. 12

DON'T OPEN THOSE LIPS!!

Now, I was aware of gender oppression, but to me it felt more like something that was unjust and unfair to me personally and to some other women, rather than the clear-cut oppression that affected lots of different peoples.

Anyway, from early childhood I declared very, very firmly that under such circumstances I wasn't going to marry. Initially my family thought it was amusing and kept telling me that it was 'a stage I was going through' as they gave knowing smiles among themselves and laughed at my naivety. However, of course my family was quite determined to marry me off to some suitable man. It didn't help that my mother is the matchmaker in our community (we came from a long line of matchmakers). When I later travelled through India, if I ever said to anyone there, 'No, I don't wish ever to get married' it was like I might be saying that I wasn't going to grow old. That's perceived as an inevitable part of life. And people would look at me and think 'Oh! She says she won't marry, but what she means is that no-one will marry her!'

Part of the reason that marriage seems inevitable is because there are no alternatives, because we women find it even more difficult to get jobs, nor is it possible for us to live on our own. Anyhow, it appears to me that if there is no discernible reason for a woman not to be married then our people assume there is probably a hidden disability, or even 'madness'.

Uma, 'Don't open those lips', Mukti, no. 3 (spring 1985)

A CATFORD COUPLE
By Alison Oram

IN DECEMBER 1954, Vincent Jones and Jean Lee were each fined £25 at the local magistrates' court for making a false statement to obtain a marriage certificate. Three months earlier the couple had wed at a church in Catford, an ordinary working-class district of south London. They had met and fallen in love when they both worked at the local telephone exchange.

NEWS OF THE WORLD, 19 DECEMBER 1954.

DAILY HERALD, 14 DECEMBER 1954.

When interviewed by the police, Jones said: 'I am a man but if you mean physically I still possess female organs ... I have been to doctors to alter my sex completely but I was sick of waiting.' The press reported that the couple intended to carry on living together and save from their wages for Jones to 'go abroad for treatment. Then I shall apply for an alteration of my birth certificate.' Jones told a reporter: 'We both love each other and when everything is put right we intend to get remarried. We shall have a public ceremony. We have nothing to be ashamed of.'

DAILY EXPRESS, 14 DECEMBER 1954.

THE PEOPLE, 24 OCTOBER 1954.

Alison Oram is a Senior Fellow at the Institute of Historical Research, University of London and author of Queer beyond London *(2022) with Matt Cook, and* Her Husband Was a Woman! Women's Gender-Crossing in Modern British Popular Culture *(2007)*

MARRIAGE EQUALITY
By Peter McGraith

I WAS EXPERIENCING a joyous whoosh from fantastic sex, while I was coming to the gradual realisation that I was that thing that some people loathed or pitied, precisely because of the sex I was having. It was 1980. I was sixteen. That blast of life-changing sexual liberation made me question everything I had been taught about gender, class, politics, religion, right and wrong, the primacy of 'the family', mainstream sexual morality and marriage.

A poster celebrating the history of human rights advocacy group LIBERTY (National Council for Civil Liberties), featuring the first gay marriage in the UK, between Peter McGraith and David Cabreza.

↑ Royal Mail 'Smilers' stamps of McGraith and Cabreza moments after being married at Islington Town Hall.

The first draft of history now endures, uncorrected, with all its factual errors, misrepresentations and journalistic assumptions intact, online. Numerous articles state that I fought for marriage equality, regardless that I was never actively involved in the campaign. And however consistently I have critiqued the institution of marriage in media interviews, the weight of hackery declares that marriage is what I'm about. The media loves a wedding, and ours was big news; therefore, we were congratulated for winning the fight and living the dream. I have never been comfortable with the social and legal hierarchy that elevates married couples above the status of single people, unmarried couples and others who organise their personal lives differently, and I am glad that I came to sexual maturity outside of the models of living and loving that were clearly laid out for my heterosexual contemporaries.

If marriage had not existed, I wouldn't have wanted to invent it, but ultimately I was keen for the same-sex marriage legislation to succeed, because I believed that equal access to marriage could and should be used as a lever for progress on the broader agenda of LGBTIQ+ rights around the world, and that, in part, is why I chose to marry first. Otherwise, I imagined that a couple of de-gayed men with nothing to say about the ongoing global struggle for LGBTIQ+ rights might seize and squander that media moment on talk of wedding cakes and dickie bows.

As the Marriage (Same Sex Couples) Bill 2013 was working its way through Parliament in the UK, same-sex marriage had already been introduced in much of Western Europe and the Americas, plus South Africa and New Zealand. Hundreds of thousands of not-so-gay Parisians and the riot police took to the streets of the French capital over *le mariage homosexuel*, though things were far worse elsewhere. Putin was cracking down on 'the promotion of distorted nontraditional sexual relationships'; India's highest court reversed the decriminalisation of gay sex; Robert Mugabe, Goodluck Jonathan and Yoweri Museveni competed to be Africa's top homophobe. Meanwhile, other ultra-religious states in Africa, Asia and the Middle East more quietly continued the torture and killing of LGBTIQ+ people under the penal code, by sharia law or extra-judicial means. I wasn't in the mood to talk about finding 'the one' and happily-ever-after.

As 29 March 2014 approached, I chose Peter Tatchell as my witness and took a TV news crew to an LGBTIQ+ demonstration at the Uganda High Commission. I refused to be photographed clinking champagne glasses, and I invited the media to a lecture I gave at Middlesex University, warning of a possible future in which younger lesbians and gay men, and others, might take the veil of respectability offered by marriage and parenthood, as their means of living openly and finding social acceptance. A big, self-indulgent wedding might garner approval for the marrying gay or lesbian couple, but buying into an off-the-peg heteronormative life before discovering what you want, without firstly experiencing the emancipating power of sex seems to me an unnecessarily risky and costly way to assuage your family's or community's fears about your soul and your hole.

The focus of my activism, during the AIDS crisis of the 1980s and more so the 1990s, was not only on building an effective community response to the threats to our health and our lives, but also on promoting our civil rights and retaining the sexual culture that had politicised me, even before AIDS. Then, similarly, in the advent of gay marriage, I was concerned about the possible downsides of the coming shift for gay culture and community.

Out gay men and lesbians of the 1980s, 1990s and early 2000s approached marriage as outsiders, many of us contentedly unaffected by the norms and strictures which governed heterosexuals' relationships. Then, why marry at all? We certainly felt no need for a stamp of approval to legitimise our coupledom when we adopted our children. However, it seemed that marriage might simplify our dealings in relation to joint responsibilities and resources, bolster our children's sense of permanence and belonging, and how LGBTIQ+ people were recognised, both in the UK and abroad. Crucially, my partner had asked me, years earlier, to marry him and I had said yes as I intended to grow old with him.

If we the LGBTIQ+ community had completely rejected legal registration of our relationships on the grounds that we disapproved of marriage's history of misogyny, its gendered expectations and the cringeworthy traditions of weddings, we could still be stuck with that problem we faced during the HIV epidemic, of bereaved gay men being stateless, without next-of-kin rights, at the mercy of the biological family, as distinct from our 'pretended' families as defined by Section 28. This eventually became our motivation to demand legal recognition of our relationships, not any desire to structure our sexual and domestic lives like those of heterosexuals.

Many gay men had had no choice but to lie about their sexuality and pretend not to be living with a partner when applying for life insurance and mortgages. One half of a gay couple would officially be the mortgage-holder. Hence the precarity of surviving partners, in the middle of an already stigmatised bereavement, being treated as undocumented lodgers in their own homes, in rare but real cases.

The Tories' distaste for Ken Livingstone's pro-LGBTIQ+ policies, when he was Leader of Greater London Council, 1981–86, and their fear of angry 'gay plague'-era queers led to Section 28. In that climate, Livingstone, as Mayor of London, in 2001, introduced a gay Green councillor's suggestion for a London Partnership Register, which opened the door for Tony Blair's tentative Civil Partnership Act 2004, that in turn led to the coalition government's Marriage (Same Sex Couples) Act 2013, which passed only with Labour votes, though, of course, has gone down as David Cameron's great achievement. Meanwhile, Ken Livingstone's role is largely forgotten.

I was present in City Hall for the first two London Partnership Register signing ceremonies, as a member of the press. Linda Wilkinson, who joined the register with her partner Carol Budd, said, 'We are not doing this to ape heterosexual marriage. We are doing this because we believe it is another nail in the coffin of the prejudice that denies us our fundamental rights as human beings and makes us second class citizens in our own country.'

Peter McGraith is a confidant, carer, creator and communicator.

↑ McGraith and his younger child, Ashley, on the first occasion he and his partner took their children out of their foster home, during ten days of 'Introductions'.

LESBIAN PARENTING

↑ Pauline Heap, Plymouth Campaign for Homosexual Equality's Women's Convenor, in her kitchen with children Joanne and Yvonne.

IN THE 1970s, women in lesbian relationships began to use reproductive technologies to conceive children. In 1978 the London *Evening News* broke a story about the practice, and a media scandal erupted, which began over a decade of negative reporting on lesbian and gay parenting.

Feminist and lesbian and gay theatre groups staged several plays exploring lesbian parenting in the 1970s and 1980s, including Gay Sweatshop Women's Company's *Care and Control* and the Women's Theatre Group's *Double Vision*. Both plays toured around the country. *Double Vision* was first performed at the Old Bull Arts Centre in Barnet in 1982 and subsequently at the Pavilion Theatre, Brighton, and Cambridge Arts Theatre. *Double Vision* included a storyline about lesbian self-insemination.

DAILY EXPRESS, 11 JANUARY 1978.

JEAN ROOK
Don't be fooled by this cosy 'family' image

Evening News
LONDON: THURSDAY JANUARY 5 1978

EXCLUSIVE: The Belgravia man who helps lesbians have babies

DOCTOR STRANGE LOVE

EVENING NEWS, 5 JANUARY 1978.

28 | A QUEER SCRAPBOOK

CHUM: You know Anna – she's pregnant.
SPARKY: Fucking hell! Who's the father?
CHUM: It's a friend. A gay man. They didn't do it or anything. They did self-insemination. Well Julie did it actually – put it up her, sort of.
SPARKY: What?
CHUM: The sperm! It was in a syringe, the bloke had, er, donated it.
SPARKY: I feel sick.
CHUM: Anyway, it worked. She's pregnant.
SPARKY: Good for her.
CHUM: And she's asked me if I want to be involved in it.
SPARKY: How are you going to be involved in it? Too late – she's already done it.
CHUM: No, listen, listen – she's going to have a home birth and me and Julie and Sandy are going to be there. She said to ask if you'd like to be there too. Would you like to?
SPARKY: I would not.
CHUM: We're going to create a really good environment, not all clinical like a hospital.
SPARKY: And what's wrong with hospitals?
CHUM: We're going to make it a social occasion and Marion, you know Marion, the radical midwife, we're hoping that she can deliver it. She's going to do natural childbirth. Leboyer.
SPARKY: It sounds appalling.
CHUM: You're only saying that because it's a bit alternative. I think it's going to be lovely. I'm really excited.
SPARKY: Why? What's so special about it? Oh, of course, it's the pinnacle of a woman's existence, isn't it, having a baby?
[*Music* Where do we go from here?]
CHUM: ... So how it's going to be is that all four of us are going to be involved in bringing the child up, so it's not just Anna's responsibility.
SPARKY: How? How are you going to do that? Where, for a start? Where will it happen?
CHUM: Well, that would have to be sorted out. I suppose sometimes it would be at Anna's and Julie's and sometimes with me.
SPARKY: It's not coming here, no way. I don't want a baby here. I don't understand what it is that you're so thrilled about.
CHUM: I think it's really important – it's an opportunity to work out in practice some of the ideas that we talk about ... and I think it's a challenge, to try and bring up a child without that element of possession that's so destructive.

The Women's Theatre Group with Libby Mason, Double Vision, in Lesbian Plays, selected and introduced by Jill Davis (Methuen, 1987)

When Wolverhampton couple Natalie and Denise conceived by self-insemination, using sperm from a donor they met in a nightclub, it was widely reported in the press. *The Sun*, 19 August 1994.

TRANS PARENTING
By Stephen Whittle

IN 1991 SARAH said she would like to try to have a baby, which meant we needed to get fertility treatment. We spoke to our GP, who suggested that he would have an affair with Sarah so she could get pregnant. So he was dumped. The NHS provision wouldn't even answer our GP's letters. We went to three different fertility services. Finally, one of them agreed to treat us. That was the British Pregnancy Advisory Service, which had just started a service providing fertility treatment to single women. As we were about to start treatment, the *Sun* newspaper had a big headline saying 'BPAS provides woman with sperm to have virgin birth'. Apparently, she'd not had a sexual relationship with anybody, and this was a scandal. The BPAS had to close the service immediately.

The second service was run by a biochemist. He talked about 'My babies, my ladies and my mums'. He made it clear he didn't like me in the room when he was doing the insemination, which was a bit freaky, and we had one of our biggest arguments ever on the way home. Finally, we went to see a nice guy. Dr Stanley Lieberman ran the Manchester Fertility Services. He saw us, he listened to us, he asked us to go back a week later. We returned to find he had read everything possible there was about trans people. He knew all about

TRANS MAN PROFESSOR STEPHEN WHITTLE WITH HIS WIFE AND THEIR CHILDREN (1996).

my hormone treatment, everything, and he said: 'I'm absolutely happy to treat you two. You've taken time over this decision, you've had counselling. Yeah, I'm all for it, but it will have to go before my ethics committee.'

By this time I'd actually finished my law degree and started a part-time PhD at Manchester Met. I was aware there were people I was working with in the department who sat on the ethics committee for Manchester Fertility Services. I'm sure if you'd said to them, 'Should Stephen and Sarah be allowed to have a baby?', they'd say, 'Yeah sure, they'd be great!' But because we became Miss A and Mr B, Sarah received a letter in due course which said, to paraphrase, as a woman you will never be good enough for us to allow you to become a mother while you continue to live with 'it'.

I was so angry. You can thump me, that's fine, but thump my partner and I will fight back. I could not believe the manner in which they'd cut her off – not me, *her* – just because she loved me. That was unbelievable. I remember thinking hold on a minute, I've just spent five years doing a part-time law degree, I've done a master's, I'm now doing a PhD, surely I ought not to take this lying down? I remember us going to the library and getting the books out – pre-computer access of course – and ploughing through *Archbold*'s and other legislative and case law textbooks, until I found that the human fertilisation laws actually afforded us a right to appeal the clinic's decision. The clinic had no idea of that right and responded 'No you haven't'. We said, 'We'll see you in court'.

However, their barrister had fortunately done his homework and realised there was a court decision that related to fertility treatment access, which states you cannot cut off a group of people. It's like saying we won't treat people who are Jewish. It's exactly and precisely the same. And a month later Sarah had treatment and conceived the first of our four children.

Stephen Whittle is a legal scholar and trans activist.

Freddy McConnell: This is me, my kids, SJ and LB, and their grandpa, my stepdad. Taken by their nana, my mum, in Spain. Before becoming a dad, if I'd been asked to describe my dream life, it would have been this: picking olives as a family in the hot evening sun.

1: HOME AND FAMILY | 31

LESBIAN AND GAY CUSTODY

DURING THE 1970s and 1980s, a growing number of married lesbians and gay men were spurred on by gay liberation and feminist politics, and by growing social awareness of homosexuality, to leave their marriages and begin new lives with same-sex partners. For those with children, divorce could end up in a battle for custody, and the courts were frequently hostile to lesbian and gay parents. It is hard to know how many lesbians and gay men lost custody of – and even access to – their children in this period, but some were reported in the media. Activist groups, including Action for Lesbian Parents and the Rights of Women's Lesbian Custody Group, worked to challenge negative stereotypes in the courts and support parents going through custody battles, while several conferences on lesbian and gay parenting were held across the country in Manchester, Leeds, Bristol and elsewhere.

THE PINK PAPER, 15 JULY 1994.

Stranger than fiction? The issue of lesbian relationships and parenting hits the stage as part of the London New Play Festival: Julie throws her husband out and moves her best friend in, but with no job and two kids, it's hard to re-invent yourself. Julie Johnson runs at the Gate Theatre, 11 Pembridge Road, London W11 from 27 July-7 August. Box Office: 071-229 0706.

COVER OF 'ACTION FOR LESBIAN PARENTS' LEAFLET, 1977.

Homosexual father wins adoption fight

A homosexual father yesterday won an Appeal Court plea to prevent his son being adopted against his wishes by his ex-wife and her new husband.

The boy, referred to as 'D', is eight years old and lives with his mother and her husband.

Last April, a County Court judge made an adoption order after dispensing with the consent of 'D's natural father. The judge held that the father, a practicing homosexual, had been unreasonable in withholding his consent. In the judge's view, the father had 'nothing to offer his son at any time in the future.'

Yesterday, three Appeal Court judges quashed the adoption order – but granted the mother leave to appeal to the House of Lords. Lord Justice Orr, sitting with Lord Justice Stephenson and Sir Gordon Willmer, said that the mother and her husband wanted 'D' to be a full member of their family and to break the ties with his father.

The judge who made the adoption order described the father as perfectly honest, frank and straightforward.

The father admitted he was living in a homosexual relationship with an 18-year-old youth and that he had, at different times, lived with four other men.

In the view of the county court judge, a reasonable father would have decided: I must protect my boy, even if it means parting from him forever so that he can be kept free from that danger.

Sir Gordon Willmer said the county court judge had substituted his own view for that of a reasonable parent 'and that is something a judge should not do.'

The father had not been unreasonable in withholding his consent, Sir Gordon ruled. The father had said that he loved his son, wanted to see him and was willing to support him. And he said that he would ensure that the boy was not subjected to homosexual influences.

The judges gave the mother and her husband leave to appeal to the House of Lords on the question of whether the test in this case should be what a heterosexual father would consider reasonable.

**Liverpool Daily Post,
10 February 1976**

Cartoon by Lyn May, illustrating a Rights of Women 'Lesbian Custody Leaflet', c.1980.

GAY MEN AND PARENTING

ALTHOUGH THERE is evidence of lesbians and gay men fostering and adopting children in the 1970s and earlier, carers' sexuality was largely unspoken or hidden. In the late 1980s, the topic of lesbian and gay parenting was brought into the open, when Section 28 of the Local Government Act 1988 framed same-sex families as 'pretend', giving impetus to discrimination against lesbian and gay parents. Gay men were often seen by agencies as unsuitable carers, having a negative effect on the developing gender or sexual identity of the child or even posing a risk of sexual abuse.

At the same time, however, Section 28 and its related debates mobilised community activism and support groups, leading to the formation of the national Lesbian and Gay Foster and Adoptive Parents Network in 1988 and, in 1990, the Positive Parenting Campaign in Manchester, which worked to challenge these unfounded assumptions. By the mid-1990s, a small number of gay men had been approved as carers. Paul described his long struggle, beginning in the 1970s, to be approved as a foster carer or adopter with his partner. Eventually, in the early 1990s, a child was placed in their care.

'I have a clear memory of when it hit me as a teenager that I would not be able to have children of my own. Embarrassing as it is to admit it, I remember crying about it on one occasion in bed at night ...

Collage of media headlines about lesbian and gay adoption in *Adoption and Fostering News*, no. 46 (January/February 1991).

I'm not sure when it first dawned on me that I might one day be able to join the ranks of foster carers. I suppose there were two parallel developments going on in the world [in the 1970s] – one to do with fostering and adoption, and one to do with the identity and expectations of gay men and women. Both ended up affecting me very personally ... The two parallel developments finally came together in 1987 when a London-wide working party was set up ... to look at fostering and adoption policies and practice, throughout the capital, as they affected lesbians and gay men ...

Just prior to this, Paul and I had already started telephoning agencies that were seeking permanent foster carers or adopters for particular children. It felt like we were doing something unacceptable and you had to take more than a few deep breaths before dialling each number. Mostly, we had embarrassed responses. One outer-London council said that they had difficulty enough getting their fostering and adoption panels to accept single carers let alone gay carers. Another council wanted us to explain, when we responded to an advert for a particular boy, why we were interested in fostering boys.'

Paul, in Stephen Hicks and Janet McDermott (eds), Lesbian and Gay Fostering and Adoption: Extraordinary Yet Ordinary (Jessica Kingsley Publishers, 1999)

Since the 1970s many gay men have donated their sperm to lesbian friends or contacts, with varying agreements on how much involvement they would have in raising the child. Pierre told Lisa Saffron about his experience in the early 1980s.

'My lover and I were asked by a friend if we would consider donating sperm in order that her girlfriend might become pregnant. It was explained that we would not be required to have any involvement or access to the child. I remember my lover agreeing immediately, citing the action as an act of solidarity between lesbians and gay men (though he subsequently dropped out). Whilst I agreed with this principle, for me it was a much harder decision. Looking back, I think I wondered what kind of world the child was coming into, what kind of mother Toni would turn out to be, how I would feel when the child was born knowing I could never see him or her.

Having been brought up by my mother as a single parent, I had no problems with Toni's plan to do the same. I did wonder, however, what would happen if the child wanted to know about her/his biological father, and for that reason, I think I was glad the arrangement was not strictly anonymous. I figured Toni and I had friends in common, and if she needed to, she could always track me down. In the end I think I agreed because I liked Toni, respected her wish to be a lesbian and a mother and didn't think it would be that easy for her to find another Jewish donor.'

Pierre, in Lisa Saffron, Challenging Conceptions: Planning a Family by Self-Insemination (Cassell, 1994)

CHILDHOOD HOMES

'IT WAS THE 1980s, it was completely homophobic, they saw you as slightly different, effeminate, whatever it was and into drama which was alien ... I was also getting really badly bullied at home – at Norris Green – like I couldn't walk the streets ... Also, my mum and dad had divorced. They'd had a really bitter divorce, which was a relief 'cos they'd always been, you know, they were always fighting and arguing our whole childhood, so my dad had left. We were at home with my mum, my mum was working. They'd had another baby, I was twelve, thirteen when she was born, so I used to look after my baby sister while my mum was at work, 'cos I just used to sit at home writing. I'd be at home on my own with my baby sister in bed and we'd have bricks coming through the window and the police were involved. Basically, we got offered police protection ... I was told by the police that I had to call them if I wanted to go to the bus stop or the youth theatre, but you would just get beaten up in the street. Like I remember if you turned the wrong corner.

And also I didn't help matters. I was slightly alternative in my appearance, you know. I loved the Smiths. I'd be going to second-hand shops and be wearing big overcoats and trilbies. Now I look back and think, you know, you could have tried to sort of camouflage yourself more and try to be less conspicuous. But you know, you have to be yourself, don't you ... But there was incidents I remember ... I'd just left school at sixteen. I left school, I signed on the dole and the deal was I could keep on the dole if I looked after my young

Three year-old Vicky in the living room of her childhood home in Stockton-on-Tees, on Christmas morning, c.1978. Around 8 years later, Vicky would confide in her best friend that she was 'heterosexual', only to discover that that wasn't the correct word for a girl who loved other girls – prompting her to come out all over again.

➔ Story shared by a contributor to a West Yorkshire Archive Service digital community project, funded by the National Lottery Heritage Fund, in which LGBTIQ+ residents of West Yorkshire were invited to share a personal story on a 'memory card'

> My memory is...
>
> I grew up on a large sixties-built council estate in east Leeds. It was a great place to be as a child as it was right on the edge of Leeds with fields only a short walk away.
>
> In the mid-seventies when I was sixteen I met a boy about a year younger than me. I suppose we were boyfriends but more in lust than in love! But we wouldn't have dreamt of being able to tell our parents. We kept our relationship hidden as life wouldn't have been worth living if people knew. But we would take advantage of the countryside on our doorstep to go off + spend time together. We would get an illicit thrill holding hands together as we walked alone through a farmer's field, never giving much thought that anyone in the nearby tower block would be able to see us!

sister for my mum, so she was only a toddler in a pram and I used to go and get all the shopping and I remember pushing my sister in the pram and getting jumped by a gang of lads and getting beaten up and literally just turning the pram so my sister couldn't see me, you know, being beaten up. She was oblivious, which was good. And then, as they all ran off, just having to carry on walking with my sister ... But eventually we got moved from there under police protection to a quieter street. And then, not long after that, I left home anyway and moved into a house, like a shared house with some friends.'

Interview with Shaun Duggan by Matthew Exley, 11 February 2016, courtesy of Liverpool Voices Archive, Museum of Liverpool

'Smalltown Boy', the debut single by 1980s all-gay synth-pop band Bronski Beat, describes the experience of gay youth leaving home in search of a new gay life. Vocalist Jimmy Somerville moved from his hometown of Glasgow to London in 1980, where he joined the London Gay Teenage Group and lived in squats. 'Smalltown Boy' includes the following lines:

> You leave in the morning with everything you own in a little black case
> Alone on a platform, the wind and the rain on a sad and lonely face
> Mother will never understand why you had to leave
> But the answers you seek will never be found at home
> The love that you need will never be found at home
> Run away, turn away, run away, turn away, run away
> Run away, turn away, run away, turn away, run away.

Bronski Beat, 'Smalltown Boy' (1984). Lyrics reproduced by permission. For more on Jimmy Somerville, see the activism section

1: HOME AND FAMILY | 37

MAKING A HOME IN POST-WAR BRITAIN

IN MAUREEN DUFFY'S 1966 novel *The Microcosm*, Cathy arrives in London having run away from her home in Yorkshire to make a life for herself as a lesbian. She finds a job on the buses and looks for a room to rent.

Maureen Duffy, The Microcosm (London: Virago Press, 1989), pp. 159-60

Lynda Blyth, Hall-Carpenter Collection, BL. C456/114, discussing her involvement in Scottish Lesbian Feminists in Edinburgh in the 1970s

'She wasn't all that surprised when she found a newsagent with one side of the window full of all shapes, colours and scripts with everything for sale, wanted, small removals, lady will baby-sit, lady will, repairs undertaken to electrical installations, let us quote you a fair price for a fair job, all the rag and tag of the district displayed and among them half a dozen or so suit two business gentlemen sharing, good home and food for working man, no coloured, quiet house and finally bed-sitting room, own cooking, use of bath, suit single, £3-10-0 p.w. apply inside.

'No dear, it hasn't gone to my knowledge and anyhow it's always worth a try. Just round the corner, 26 Dorset Crescent, Mr. Gregory; he's a very pleasant gentleman.'

'There are two things first I must tell you why the room is so cheap. That is because it is right at the top of the house and is a very small room ... There is one other lady up here and you have the bathroom between you ... This is the room. You see, each one has its own yale lock so inside it is altogether private and your own business. As I tell you, it is very small.'

But it was very bright too she saw at once and although the furniture wasn't the very latest from House Beautiful it was the kind she was used to and there was plenty of it including a very useful cooker top with a grill and burner, a good quality Axminster on the floor and cheerful matching curtains and bedspread.'

'I mean we did discover that there were women living in as couples, or having relationships with other women in the area where they lived but they weren't out in any way, they were isolated, but as a couple.'

38 | A QUEER SCRAPBOOK

In an oral history interview with Matt Cook, Rex Batten described moving from a bedsit in London to a house with his partner, John, in the late 1950s.

'Well, we were offered this house, with four rooms in it! Living in a bedsitter then to have four rooms. [It] might have been a working-class street but ...

When we moved here in the first fortnight, we had half a dozen bread puddings delivered by neighbours because two young men... well, we were in our twenties; we would either live on baked beans or fish and chips.

We never had any, it was very much a south London working class street, but we never ever had any harassment here at all. In fact next door, if they had a party, we would join in. We would provide some of the food. It was real South London party it was good fun. ...

Not long after the '67 [Sexual Offences] Act, [we] said let's go and buy a double bed. Well that was a hell of a statement to make! Because everybody would know what came in. Now, if you buy furniture the neighbours wouldn't take much notice, but then everybody would though. [whispers] 'They bought a double bed!' [laughs] We never had any comment about it or I don't know whether it was, we just wanted to fit in with the street, and we were accepted. ...

[The Act] really did make a difference 'cos ... one was safe 'cos it was private – it was our home we were living in ... The great thing moving here was it was you had a house you could make a home out of. I think that was it – we found somewhere we could make a home. We didn't discuss it but I'm sure we felt we were both making a home.'

➔ **Andrée and Grace at home in Cornwall with a friend, 1960s.**

TRANS SAFE HOUSES
By Leila Sellers

FOR TRANS FEMININE people living in Britain in the 1970s and 1980s, safe places where they could comfortably explore and express their gender non-conforming identities were hard to find. Spaces used by other social groups, such as restaurants, pubs or clubs, were often unwelcoming, and the threat of public exposure, arrest or physical violence was never far away.

Some trans femmes found opportunities to experiment at home, trying on clothes and make-up behind a locked bathroom door. However, the risk of being discovered by a family member, and the desire to feel part of a community, led many trans feminine people to seek out (and in some cases create) trans-specific social spaces where they could meet others, access support and guidance and, perhaps most importantly, celebrate their trans identity. Here I look at Rose's House, a space that emerged during this time specifically for transfeminine people who – in the language of the era – mostly identified as transvestites or transsexuals.

Photos of one of Martine Rose's parties in Sheffield. *Rose's Repartee*, no. 1 (September 1989), p. 2.

ROSE'S HOUSE

Martine Rose, a trans woman who describes herself as 'a pioneer' within her generation, created a trans social space and support network within her own home in Sheffield in the early 1980s. Known as Rose's House, Martine's home offered visitors a safe place to meet other trans femmes, and she regularly organised themed parties, which people would travel from across the country to attend. At the end of the night Martine would produce blankets and bedding for those who wanted to stay. As well as hosting social events, Martine offered one-on-one support to those struggling to make sense of their trans identity, often speaking to people on the phone at length before they came to her home, and it would sometimes take several attempts for particularly nervous visitors to overcome their fears and enter Rose's House. They would disappear back down Martine's garden path to the safety of their car, unable to summon the courage to ring her doorbell. Once they crossed the threshold, Martine offered emotional support as well as practical advice, including dressing and make-up tips and, crucially for some, a safe place to store clothes between visits.

Martine was not alone in opening her home to others. Around the country, members of the Beaumont Society, a UK trans support group, were similarly providing opportunities to dress and meet others within the privacy of a domestic space. However, it was the atmosphere in Rose's House – the fun and inclusivity of the parties, the care Martine took with new people and the effort she made to improve the space (doing much of the DIY herself) – that put the house on the map and ensured its long-lasting popularity among trans feminine people. Although Rose's House no longer exists in the same capacity, Martine, now in her eighties, continues to hold occasional parties in her home.

Leila Sellers is a Wellcome-funded PhD candidate at Birkbeck whose research explores the everyday lives of trans women through a history of the Beaumont Society.

↑ An advert for a party held at Rose's House. *Rose's Repartee*, no. 1 (September 1989), p. 18.

1: HOME AND FAMILY | 41

SQUATS AND HOUSE SHARES

DURING THE 1970s and early 1980s, as well as more recently, some LGBTIQ+ people in cities around the UK experimented with living collectively in squats and house shares. Squats were partly a response to housing need, allowing queer people to live in cities they would not otherwise have been able to afford. For some, living collectively also provided an opportunity to live out political ideals about sharing possessions and domestic labour, as well as to explore new forms of intimacy and family structures, such as non-monogamy.

Boy George described his experience of squatting in the 1970s:

Boy George, Karma: My Autobiography (London, 2023), pp. 33-6

'I'd originally left home to move to Walsall to live with Martin Degville. I met him in Bournemouth one Bank Holiday in 1977 ... I walked up to Martin and told him he looked amazing. He was wearing stiletto heels and had a massive bleached quiff and huge padded shoulders. He gave me his number and some weeks later when I visited my Auntie Teresa in Ladywood, I met up with him and his fellow freaks. They were all so much friendlier than the London equivalent. In Spring 1979, when I was seventeen years old ... I wanted to leave London and Martin offered me a room and a job working on his clothes stall. We shared a passion for music and dressing up though we both had very different personalities. ...

Cover of the Advisory Service for Squatters' 'Squatters Handbook' (6th edition, 1979), featuring a photograph of Olive Morris climbing onto the roof of the squat where she lived, at 121 Railton Road, Brixton, during one of the attempted evictions of the squat.

42 | A QUEER SCRAPBOOK

I wrote to my friend Hilda in London asking if I could live there until I found a squat ... Late one night we scoured the streets for vacant properties. Squatting was a viable alternative to renting in the seventies and eighties until the law changed. Many a creative was able to develop their art without the stress of forced labour and rent. We found a flat in a council block over the road in Kentish Town but it was padlocked like a fortress. So I borrowed a few screwdrivers and a crowbar from Dad's tool kit and we were in. The décor was evil. I claimed the living room and covered the walls with gay porn and cut-up headlines, shoving my mattress in the corner.'

See pp. 104-6 and 134 in the arts and culture section for more on homes.

Dear Feminaxe,

I really enjoyed reading the paper. It wasn't full of self-congratulatory rants as anarchist papers often are, but had some really interesting articles. I liked the layout too. The point of my letter, however, is not just praise. I have recently moved into a communal house in Birmingham known as 'The Z to A Project'. It is a place set up 2 years ago to promote alternative education and ways of living. We treat education in its broadest sense – learning to take control of our own lives as much as possible – by setting up housing co-ops, workers co-ops and learning skills from each other in an informal non-hierarchical way. There are currently 2 women, 3 men, and 2 children living here. We would really like another woman to move in. So if there is any woman out there who is at all interested and would like to know more, please get in touch with the address below. Single parents are welcome and DHSS preferred. We are shortly opening a vegan cafe and radical bookshop and desperately need more members, particularly women, to join this workers co-op, either as a full-time member (20 hours a week) or part-time. Work is unpaid at the moment, but good for your politics and can be fun too! No experience needed, just enthusiasm. Love, Teress

Letter to **Feminaxe** *magazine, c.1980*

Happy Families

Many but not all of us have been active in GLF [Gay Liberation Front] since the beginning. We didn't know each other then, but through involvement we got to know each other as friends whilst still living within the artificial framework of our own particular flats (territory). One other artificiality was that we related to each other as friends whilst being aware of the growing love that existed between us.

Coming into the commune and sharing everything, our material possessions of course, our ideas, our energy, our minds and our bodies meant that we had to change ourselves from being friends to being lovers.

The best way of describing it is for you to imagine making it with your best friend, the one you call 'sister', and remove the taboo of incest from exploring sexually. You know you love your best friend, but expressing and exploring that love physically! It is not important you say, but what is more important than love?

'Happy Families', Come Together, *no. 15 (June 1972), p. 2*

SMALL-TOWN DYKES
By Victoria Golding

'YOU LEAVE IN the morning with everything you own in a little black case' sings Jimmy Somerville in the video to Bronski Beat's 'Smalltown Boy' (1984). 'You were the one that they'd talk about around town as they put you down.' Portraying a classic queer experience of small-town life in the 1980s, the video fades out as the band finally reach their final destination: the bright lights of the big city.

What the video might also have shown, though, was the train on the return journey: packed with dykes leaving London, Leeds and Manchester for the joys of a small town on the Yorkshire–Lancashire border.

During the early 1980s, lesbians began to move to the small mill town of Todmorden, and later nearby Hebden Bridge, with the aim of making a community for themselves outside of a city. Some were part of the anti-nuclear protests at Greenham Common women's peace camp, inspired by communal outdoor living and wanting a more sustainable way of life. Some were part of the radical lesbian separatist squatting movement in London and had been living in and

MOORS ABOVE TODMORDEN.

renovating squats in Hackney. Swirling around the movement were ideas of rural space as a place where women could make their own rules and live separately from male influence. Other lesbians were simply attracted to the opportunity to form a lesbian community in the countryside, with open moorland and more affordable housing. Why Todmorden in particular became the place to move to is a question I set out to answer by conducting oral history interviews with many of the first queer migrants to the area.

> 'A really big driver for me in getting out of London was that I wanted to be near the hills, and particularly hills. It was that combination of countryside and lesbians, I didn't want to move to somewhere where there weren't other lesbians. I was very happy living in a lesbian ghetto, I wanted it. I wanted to be in a lesbian ghetto but in the country.'

LAMBETH WOMEN'S WORKSHOP POSTER.

Jay, who moved from Hackney squats to Todmorden in 1985

Lying at the bottom of the Calder Valley with vast expanses of moorland above, Todmorden and Hebden Bridge had once been at the heart of the local textile trade. As the mills closed and people left in search of work, the amount of empty housing grew. By the late 1960s, over 20 per cent of the houses in Todmorden were classed as 'unfit dwellings'.

The original lesbian and lesbian-feminist community centred on Todmorden rather than Hebden Bridge. Hebden had been invigorated by an alternative 'hippy' community in the 1970s, and while this undoubtedly added to the appeal of the area for some lesbians, property was cheaper in neighbouring Todmorden. Lesbians who had learned building skills in the squats of London saw an opportunity for a different way of life. Some had taken part in the building and carpentry courses that had been funded by Ken Livingstone's Greater London Council and used these skills in renovations. Barbara, a carpenter from the Hackney squats, recalls buying two boarded-up houses next to each other in 1985, paying the local council £4,750 for both.

'Todmorden got repopulated by manual tradeswomen, and we came in and we took over some of the very, very poor housing stock... you know, roof, stairs, floors, everything needed doing, but if I couldn't do it, I knew people that could.

When we bought that house, I'd been made redundant from [a women's building scheme in] Haringey, ...I'd kind of had enough, I suppose split up with somebody or something. It's a bit like that, isn't it? And then realised that actually I could afford to buy here, and renovate it, in a way that I couldn't in Manchester.'

Judith, who moved to Todmorden in 1987

Lesbians brought with them the community cultures they had developed in London, Manchester and Leeds. The monthly Todmorden Women's Disco was started in a local church in 1986 and attracted women from farther afield, who began to spread the word of this lesbian enclave. This led to some unlikely cultural juxtapositions, as the lesbian disco expanded to Todmorden Working Men's Club and Todmorden Cricket Club, where it is still held today. The community made its own newsletter, had its own telephone tree and put on a yearly all-lesbian Christmas pantomime. Systems of communal care, such as a babysitting rota to help lesbians with children, developed a strong sense of queer family.

Above: Doorstep of lesbian home in Hebden Bridge.
Left: Todmorden Cricket Club, location of the lesbian disco.

Key to this was the role of lesbian domestic space – not only in creating and building the homes people lived in but in creating spaces for lesbians to socialise. The Todmorden lesbian newsletters of 1990 show that lesbian homes functioned as meeting spaces for singing groups and games evenings. A group for lesbians with disabilities and long-term illnesses, a group for older lesbians and even a lesbian library were held in queer domestic spaces. Housing was crucial to both why lesbians moved to Todmorden and how they then built a community there. By 1991, the 'Todmopolitan' lesbian newsletter suggests, this was 'probably the largest lesbian community outside a city'.

Lesbians in the area still experienced hostility and homophobia: this was not some kind of queer utopia. There were ongoing discussions and disagreements within the community about the best ways to live their lesbian and feminist values and about how factors such as class affected this. As more and more lesbians moved to the area, the community spread into the more gentrified Hebden Bridge, and changes in both the size of the community and in lesbian politics meant it lost some of its cohesiveness going into the late 1990s. It was then Hebden Bridge that became known in the media as the 'lesbian capital of the UK' in the twenty-first century. However, the origins of this lie in the previous decades: in the building skills and community spirit of these first women who left the city behind.

Victoria Golding holds a PhD in queer history and has worked at several UK universities. She is currently writing an oral history of queer migration to Hebden Bridge and Todmorden.

The Observer UK news

OBSERVER HEADLINE, 29 JULY 2001.

Lesbians the toast of the Two Ferrets

Hebden Bridge in Yorkshire has been outed as the Sapphic capital of Britain. And no one's complaining

Amelia Hil

In the gay-friendly Yorkshire mill town of Hebden Bridge, everyone feels at home

i HEADLINE, 22 JULY 2017.

HOUSING ACTIVISM

LGBTIQ+ PEOPLE have often faced barriers to finding safe and suitable housing, including hostile landlords, abusive neighbours and housing stock that was designed for the needs of heterosexual nuclear families. By the late 1980s, LGBTIQ+ people were beginning to get together to resist the discrimination they faced in relation to housing, forming tenants' associations and lobbying groups.

Jayne Egerton, Chair of Stonewall's Housing Association, 'Out but not down: lesbians' experience of housing', Feminist Review, no. 36 (autumn 1990), p. 76

'I once advised a Glaswegian lesbian in her seventies who had been driven from one squalid and impermanent home after another as a result of harassment from neighbours. Her family would have nothing to do with her and her only friend had been her lover who had recently died. She had never experienced the pleasures of a genuine 'home' in her entire life and had taken tranquillizers for 'depression' for twenty years.'

'There are priority homeless and there are non-priority homeless, but the council locally recognised in Lewisham that there were people for whom life was harder. So they had a public meeting to say we've set up groups ... around race, gender and disability – this homelessness, non-priority homeless scheme. Believe it or not – this is hard for you, I know – there were hard-to-let properties on Pepys Estate and Crossfields, Tanners Hill up the road where Peter and I lived. ... at the end of the meeting I meant to go up and say, 'Haven't you forgotten some people?' I'm afraid it didn't come out like that – I exploded and was vitriolic. And the guy didn't run from the room.

Cartoon by David Shenton, Roof, no. 78 (November and December 1988).

48 | A QUEER SCRAPBOOK

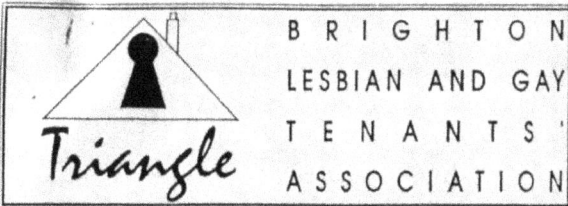

Flyer from Triangle Lesbian and Gay Tenants Association, Brighton, c.1990.

He said, 'OK, go away and write me a ten-thousand-word statement in the next ten days on what the issues are and why it's important what you face.'

So I did that – well, we probably both did it. Typed it up – you had to type it up in those days – took it in to him. And we'd come up with a name – we were drunk enough one night to come up with a name – because if you called it by a name that was obvious, people would not come, on the whole, even if they were desperate, even if they had been thrown out of home and told never to darken their parents' doorstep again, even if they had been thrown out of their accommodation because they were queer or lesbian. We called it DYFAH. So he said, 'I get DYFAH, because you differ. Why have you spelt it like that?' So I said, 'Oh, it's an acronym.' He said, 'What is it?' 'Dykes and Faggots Housing.' Over the next two years, we housed about three hundred people, which I am very proud of.'

Geoff Hardy in conversation with Justin Bengry, 'Glad to be Gay', Goldsmiths, University of London, 9 October 2018, https://soundcloud.com/goldsmithsuol/geoff-hardy-glad-to-be-gay

CONCLUSION

HOME AND FAMILY were a focus of activism from the 1970s, highlighting the difficulties LGBTIQ+ people faced in accessing and affording suitable housing and in keeping their homes after the death of a partner. Attempts to raise awareness about the discrimination faced by lesbian mothers in custody cases in the 1970s and early 1980s expanded into a broad movement arguing for the rights and value of LGBTIQ+ families in the wake of Section 28.

Histories of LGBTIQ+ family formation and life since 1945 are richer and more diverse than a focus on rights and legal frameworks would suggest, however. While families of origin and hostile neighbours could constrain the possibilities of LGBTIQ+ expression in domestic settings, homes – from urban squats to private suburban houses – have also provided a space for experimenting in new family forms and articulating new identities. LGBTIQ+ people have been raising children and creating families in a variety of forms throughout this period, sometimes openly and often discreetly. In doing so, we have contributed to a re-evaluation and expansion of what it means to be a family in twenty-first-century Britain and Ireland.

LGBTIQ+ homeless charity AKT [Albert Kennedy Trust] banner at the Manchester Pride Parade, August 2022.

SECTION 2:
SOCIALISING AND SEX

Curated by Justin Bengry

I'VE NEVER BEEN to Heaven. I feel like a bad gay for admitting this. A former student of mine was at the iconic London dance club's opening night in 1979, and more recently another student has even DJed there. For both, the experience was transformative. The club's historical weight and significance confirmed to them something about their queerness. They participated in the now generations-long queue of people who have danced all night under the arches at Charing Cross. But I've never been.

I have been to Halfway to Heaven, the pub a block or so away towards Soho, London's best-known gaybourhood, at least in the 1990s and 2000s. Still home to a range of venues, especially on and around Old Compton Street, Soho's pull on our collective imagination remains powerful, so much so that it's commonly assumed always to have been queer. Older focal points for socialising such as Earl's Court and King's Cross are falling out of our shared queer memory, even as their heydays overlapped with Heaven's launch. Redevelopment, gentrification and London's spiralling housing costs all mean that those former centres for queer community and possibility are now primarily commercial and elite residential areas in a city where LGBTIQ+ people must look elsewhere to find and build community.

By migration, I'm a Londoner, but even I know that queer socialising and community extends well beyond the M25 ring road that encircles the capital. We queer people have long created our own spaces for meeting one another, catching up with friends for a drink or a dance, finding somewhere for sex or, alternatively, we have subverted existing places to use for our own purposes on our own terms. Socialising, or 'the scene', however we understand it, has been crucial for so many of us to see and be seen, recognising our own lives and desires in the lives and desires (or desire for) those around us. But the commercial scene, influential as it is to queer and non-queer people alike, doesn't alone define LGBTIQ+ life and possibility, not least because it too often excludes so many people within our communities. Queer youth, lesbians, trans people, disabled queers and LGBTIQ+ people of colour have all created other spaces far removed from London's Soho, Brighton's Kemptown or Manchester's Canal Street in some of the incredible range of groups and events you'll find in this section of the *Queer Scrapbook*.

What we all share is the need to be with others, and all of us experienced losses of community and contact with those we care about during the COVID-19 pandemic. Isolation has long been a concern in our communities, but we have always found creative ways to combat it, some of which feature in the half century or so found across these pages. Then, everything changed in 2020. By taking away so many community spaces and opportunities to be with each other, the pandemic reminded us how much we need each other. This section of the *Queer Scrapbook* dances through the decades from a night of clubbing in Plymouth to sex off the A4 in Shirehampton, going out in Dundee and staying in in Leicester. From Belfast to Banbury, Cork to Chester, queer people always find ways to find each other.

Justin Bengry

Nigel Young and Derek Cohen outside 267 Old Brompton Road, London. See p. 92.

OLDER LESBIAN NETWORK STICKERS, CARDIFF, 1990s.

A Lesbian is for life not just for Mardi Gras

Older Lesbian Network Wales (35+), PO Box 239, SWANSEA SA3 4XN

The Older Lesbian Network (Wales) was established in 1993 for women aged thirty-five and over defining themselves as lesbian and committed to anti-discriminatory principles. The group produced stickers that they distributed from their stall at events such as Mardi Gras, a forerunner of Cardiff Pride, now Pride Cymru.

Rhian Diggins is a senior archivist at Glamorgan Archives.

A Lesbian is for life not just for Mardi Gras

Older Lesbian Network Wales (35+), PO Box 239, SWANSEA SA3 4XN

A Lesbian is for life not just for Mardi Gras

Older Lesbian Network Wales (35+), PO Box 239, SWANSEA SA3 4XN

A Lesbian is for life not just for Mardi Gras

Older Lesbian Network Wales (35+), PO Box 239, SWANSEA SA3 4XN

A Lesbian is for life not just for Mardi Gras

Older Lesbian Network Wales (35+), PO Box 239, SWANSEA SA3 4XN

A Lesbian is for life not just for Mardi Gras

Older Lesbian Network Wales (35+), PO Box 239, SWANSEA SA3 4XN

FINDING OTHERS IN THE SMALL ADS

IN THE 1950s AND 1960s, contact ads in magazines allowed queer people to meet each other, discover social groups in their own cities, build communities around the country and even communicate across the seas. *Films and Filming*, launched in 1954, was queer from the beginning. Despite being an important magazine for film enthusiasts sold openly on any high street, producers didn't try particularly hard to hide its queerer interests. Amid features like one salivating over the 'beefcake invasion' in Italian films and plenty of male bodies on display in its photographs, homosexual readers could also find personal ads sent to the magazine. Unlike *Films and Filming*, the lesbian magazine *Arena Three* was not such a widely distributed commercial publication. Launched in 1964 by the Minorities Research Group based in London, *Arena Three* was a subscription magazine designed to address isolation and help lesbian women to meet each other. It also printed contact ads and notices for social groups around the country in addition to book reviews, short stories, features on lesbian interests and reader letters.

Michael O'Sullivan, who worked for *Films and Filming* in the 1970s, remembers first finding the magazine aged sixteen in 1962 and even writing to it from his home in Ireland a couple of years later.

↓ Joint membership card, Mary McIntosh and Elizabeth Wilson, Minorities Research Group, 1965.

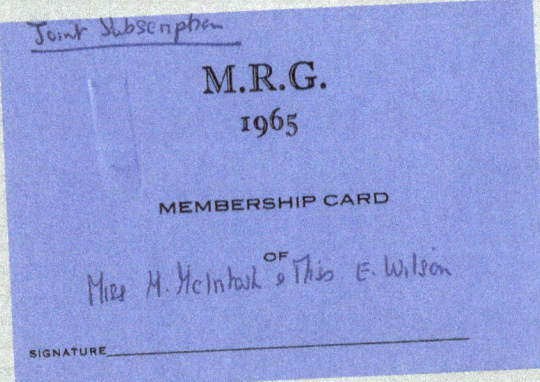

'I had an advert of my own in it when I was seventeen and still living with my parents in Ireland and I got replies from all over the world including Hollywood, Australia, Malta, as well as England, and I made a few lifelong friends from it – one of whom I am still in contact now who now lives in San Francisco. I also replied to some of the ads when I moved to London when I was eighteen in 1964 and again met several very good friends that way which led to sharing apartments, so it did have a considerable influence on my life. There were also those fifties and early sixties ads for the new men's fashions – including a young Sean Connery in one of them!'

Michael O'Sullivan interviewed by Justin Bengry, 2010

ANNOUNCEMENTS, *ARENA THREE* (DECEMBER 1967).

ANNOUNCEMENTS – December, 1967

(6d a word, Box No. 5s. For regular long-term subscribers only). We reserve the right to refuse or amend any copy submitted and to check all box replies.

"I'm from the West Country, I'd like to meet more people. I'm 37, just ordinary – varied interests – sense of humour, I hope! Anyone else in the same boat?"   (Miss) S.T. (Somerset) BOX DEC/1

Member, 23, would like to hear from others in or around Bristol. Car owner.   (Miss) L.G. (Bristol) BOX DEC/3

Wish to meet friends, Cheshire area – Wirral.   M.J. (Cheshire) BOX DEC/2

   (Miss) P.

Very lonely member, 47 – lost friend of 18 years' duration – would appreciate sympathetic pen-friends. Most interests, and animal-lover.   (Miss) C.B. (Devon) BOX DEC/4

Member (33) seeks pen-friend. Interests lean towards arts. Vigorous walks and winter swimming definitely out. Indoor type!

CHESHIRE PEN CLUB ADVERT, *ARENA THREE* (JANUARY 1970).

CHESHIRE PEN CLUB

Many thanks (writes Margaret C.) for forwarding the replies to my letter about a correspondence magazine. I had almost given up hope – having received only one reply previously – but I do understand how madly busy you must be and I do appreciate all that A3 does and the work that goes into it. It has made a great difference to my life.

I have written to the three people who replied and I am hoping to get the mag. off the ground quite soon but we do need more members and would be pleased if you would mention it in future A3's. There will always be a few who drop out. Enclosed a small donation to cover costs!

"Do you like writing and receiving letters?
"Do you like friends dropping in for a chat?
"Why not join our correspondence magazine? A round robin of letters from penfriends".

For more information – or write an introductory letter to – Margaret C. (Cheshire), c/o BCM/SEAHORSE, LONDON, W.C.1.

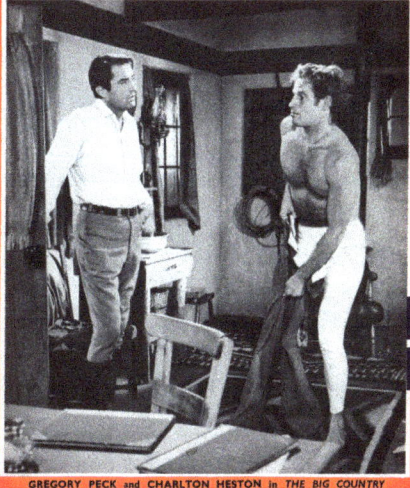

COVER OF *FILMS AND FILMING* (AUGUST 1958).

PERSONAL ADS IN *FILMS AND FILMING*.

FILM—Market Place
Continued from p. 35

MOTOR-CYCLIST (32) ex-Navy, seeks another for riding weekends. Box 241F.
BACHELOR, public school, early thirties, interests: films, theatre, cine photography, seeks similar in London, view friendship, possible holidays, etc. Box 249F.
YOUNG MAN, central London, seeks companion(s) 25-35 for summer holiday, also week-ends etc. Usual interests, also weight training and camping. Sylt, Montalvert, or other suggestions? All answered and photograph returned. Box 250F.
MOTORCYCLIST (28) seeks girl friend in twenties. Should like pillion riding (PVC/Leather kit) films, have broad interests. Box 251F.
YOUNG MAN (28) interested in films, theatre, music, travel, wishes to meet another similar interests. Photo appreciated and returned. Box 252F.
BACHELOR (36) living near Salisbury, interested in motor cycles, etc., seeks similar minded neighbours. Box 253F.
PENNILESS young athlete seeks rich female patron. Photo please. Box 254F.
YOUNG MAN (22) bored with life in general, seeks companion to go tramping round the world. Write fully Box 255F.
YOUNG MAN interested films, motor cycles, travel would like to hear from others (20-30) anywhere, with same interests. Photograph a help. Box 256F.
SMART MOTORCYCLIST (500cc)

YOUNG VERSATILE EX-MATELOT wishes to meet young men in London area. Interests: films, photography, motor-cycling and music. Photograph appreciated. Box 266F.
YOUNG MAN (London) wishes meet sincere male pal (20-39). Interests, films, history. Enclose photo (returned). Box 267F.
HIRSUTE young man 25 wishes to meet, correspond with similar males. Interests: films, music, theatre, Physique. Photo appreciated. Box 268F.
BACHELOR buying house (London) seeks male friends/possible tenants (20-36). Photo appreciated. Box 269F.
BROADMINDED BACHELOR seeks friends of both sexes anywhere. Interests include travel, films and swimming. All letters answered. Box 270F.
BACHELOR (32) living NW England wishes meet/correspond others. Wide and varied interests. Box 271F.
LONDON BACHELOR (31) wishes correspond/meet others. Interests, music, theatre, ballet, cinema. books etc. Photograph appreciated and returned. All answered. Box 273F.
MR PENNY you omitted address from your reply. Box 248F.
BODYBUILDER (27) with good physique seeks others keen on motor bikes, wrestling, photography. Photo please. Box 272F.
TWO MALE MODELS (blond/dark) available for artists' and photographic work. Mid-twenties. Duos and singles, reasonable rates. Send 1/3d PO for sample picture to Messrs Hayes & Pooley, 220 Cavendish Road, Balham, SW12.
PHOTOGENIC young man required

INTRODUCTIONS ARRANGED for all ages with similar interests – details free—Josephine's Marriage Bureau, 51 Wheelwright Road, Birmingham 24.
YOUNG GENTLEMAN (25) ex Public School compiling anthology of civil and military Corporal Punishment, requires assistance. Please write giving details. Box 282F.
THE PETER COXSON Typing (Dup.) Service. Books. TV Plays. KNI 5566 Anytime.
GENTLEMAN living close London Airport keenly interested films would like to contact similar (25-40) living coast/country who would like to exchange weekend visits. Box 283F.
GENTLEMAN seeks correspondence, having experience governess; private school, interest books. Box 284F.
VISITING LONDON? Male pen-friends (18-30) requested by London Bachelor (young 38 with sense of humour). Free week-end accommodation offered. Interests: theatre, cinema, music, tape-sponding, photography. Photograph appreciated and returned. Every letter answered. Hieroglyphics accepted – letters welcomed. Genuine offer. Box 285F.
TWO BACHELORS (26, 29) live Ealing, seek male friends. Interests include cinema, wrestling. Age 25-30. Photo essential, returned. Box 286F.
TWO BACHELORS, late twenties, North London, wish to meet other males, pairs and singles, for outings etc. Interests cinema, music, records. Photo please. Box 287F.
FOREIGN BACHELOR (34) wants male correspondents. Interests: cinema, sun-bathing, photography. Box 288F.

ACTIVE young bachelor (26) music lover interested most things wishes correspondence with similar anywhere. Peter Bonsall-Boone, Flat 1, 2 Rae Court, Windsor, 51, Victoria, Australia.
BATH/BRISTOL. Bachelor (30) emigrating from London to West Country, seeks friends in the area. Letters with photograph appreciated. Box 291F.
MOTOR-CYCLIST (30) wants enthusiastic pillion companion, camping holiday home/abroad, any date. Box 292F.
ONE OR TWO MEN (Twenties) wanted for canal cruising holiday May. Box 293F.
QUIET YOUNG MAN (24) with car wishes to meet another, either Australian or British (25-30) in London for genuine friendship. Varied interests. Photo required. Box 294F.
BACHELOR (39) resident Leeds, seeks general male contacts – view friendship. Box 295F.
UNCONVENTIONAL BACHELOR (42) ex-Navy, own flat in London seeks new male friends especially West Indian or Jamaican for genuine friendships. Usual interests. Photo helps. Box 296F.
COMMERCIAL TRAVELLER (50) Bachelor, covering entire West Country would meet others any age. Interests: swimming, athletics, films. Also seeking B.B in quiet establishment. Box 297F.
BUSINESS MAN, middle 40, frequently travelling would like to rent room in bachelor's flat or house. Hobbies: riding, music. Box 298F.
YOUNG MAN (22) wishes to meet others in London/Manchester areas,

OUTLAWS IN THE LIVING ROOM
By Daisy Asquith

THE FIRST DOCUMENTARIES about homosexuality on British television were broadcast in 1964 and 1965 as part of ITV's *This Week* strand, presented by Bryan Magee. At the time *This Week* was the tenth most popular programme on television, with an average audience of six million viewers, while the most watched, *Coronation Street*, had an average of between eight and nine million.

These broadcasts were followed in 1967 by a pair of BBC *Man Alive* documentaries, 'Consenting Adults: The Men' and 'The Women' on 7 and 14 June, just a month before the Sexual Offences Act 1967 brought in partial decriminalisation of homosexual acts between men.

These four documentaries, the first factual representations of queerness on British TV, give us an extraordinary insight into attitudes of the time. Many of the interviewees' identities are concealed by dark shadows, and the medical experts authoritatively construct homosexuality as an illness and a social problem. The courageous people who appeared on screen, even in silhouette, were of course immediately identified by their friends, families and colleagues anyway, becoming queer outlaw celebrities overnight.

SCOTLAND
THIS WEEK: 'HOMOSEXUALS', ITV, OCTOBER 1964

Homosexuals usually live two lives, one of which is completely concealed from their family and colleagues.

No-one knows, no.

How would they react if they did?

They'd be tremendously shocked. The reason is that I live a very normal life back home. I really live two lives – one here and one up north.

One can tell from your accent that you're a Scot. Did being homosexual have anything to do with coming to London?

Well, I suppose it did have something to do with it, because the bright lights and the company and the certain amount of freedom while here, which we don't have back home.

THIS WEEK: 'HOMOSEXUALS', ITV, OCTOBER 1964.

Has it affected the course of your career at all?

Well, it has, in as much as I have just lost my job because of being homosexual.

Tell me about that.

Well, my company received an anonymous phone call from a friend, and I was summoned into the office and told they had received a phone call saying I was homosexual ... did I deny this? And of course I didn't deny it. Because living a lie is one thing but living an even bigger lie is even more ... so I said no, I was homosexual, and they said they no longer wished for my services. And I was fired as from tomorrow.

NORTH MIDLANDS
THIS WEEK: 'LESBIANS', ITV, JANUARY 1965

Well, it's really that I want to love and be loved by another woman.

How can you find such a woman?

Well, that's the difficulty. In a way it means that I have to keep making friends with people because I can't find out unless I make friends with them. And then, if they are lesbian, there's hope for me. But even then there isn't hope unless they happen to take to me.

Can you tell by looking at a woman whether she's lesbian or not?

Not at all.

THIS WEEK: 'LESBIANS', ITV, JANUARY 1965.

You think that's a complete myth?

Absolute myth. Because I've been looking out hard enough! For years and years and years I've fallen in love with various women, but they've never reciprocated my feeling. Not until I was thirty-six did anyone reciprocate my feeling. And, er, I used to fall in love and then feel quite happy about it at first and then think, 'Oh, but it's hopeless, she won't reciprocate my feeling', and I was right, she didn't. I quite often remained very friendly with that person, but of course I was very disappointed.

What do you do when men make advances to you?

I try to keep quite calm about it. I have been out with boyfriends; in my early twenties I went out with a few. And I didn't find the lovemaking repulsive – I'd say that it was fun in its way. But I never fell in love with the men like I fall in love with women. And with one particular boyfriend, I fell in love with his sister! And I used to enjoy going to the house to play games, because I loved the company of his sister, who incidentally was married. But I enjoyed her company in a mild sort of way you see.

Did she realise that this was how you felt?

Oh, I don't think so, I think she just thought that I found her jolly, because she was married and expecting a baby, but I enjoyed the happy atmosphere that she created.

OXFORD

THIS WEEK: 'LESBIANS', ITV, JANUARY 1965

Most lesbians in Britain are not open about it. They're afraid of shocking their family, scandalising the neighbours, endangering their jobs. All over the country there are lesbian couples living together whose true relationship is unsuspected by others.

At one end of the spectrum is the girl who seems to feel an equal sexual response to both men and women.

THIS WEEK: 'LESBIANS', ITV, JANUARY 1965.

My first sexual experience was when I was a student at Oxford. I fell in love with a woman and had an affair lasting for a year with her. Then after leaving Oxford, I had a very brief affair with a man, quite a casual affair. Since, I've had an affair with another woman, and a lasting affair with a married woman. I was also very emotionally involved with a man, a married man.

Now most people think that to be sexually involved with both sexes like this is perverted. What do you say to that?

It seems perfectly natural to me. I always find it strange that people are attracted exclusively to one sex. I've always been, since I can remember, attracted to both sexes equally.

Is it the same for you when you're sexually attracted to a woman as to a man, or is it different?

I'm not conscious of any differences at all.

But don't the anatomical differences between men and women mean that the sexual relationship can't be the same?

No. They make very little difference. It's the person that matters and not the sex.

A SMALL MARKET TOWN
MAN ALIVE: 'CONSENTING ADULTS', BBC, JUNE 1967

Most homosexuals don't live in big cities. They go to the large towns looking for others like themselves. Desperately lonely men, scared of discovery. Men like this clerk from a small market town, the sort of man the present laws seem designed to protect us from. For him, how did it all start?

Well, I met someone in a gents' toilet when I was about fifteen. I had no idea what was going to happen at all. It was somebody in uniform. And I just got talking to him. We came out and just walked along, walking and talking. And to me, well, it was something. We eventually went somewhere, and things happened. He made love to me and held me and similar things. And we came out and talked about several things, films and music and just enjoying friendship actually. And we arranged to meet a week later. I went home and the next night, when I went to bed, my mother came into the room and said 'I hear you've been with a soldier?' And I couldn't deny it. And she said, 'Well, tomorrow you better pack your things and go, because', she says, 'I don't want anything like that.' So, the next morning I just asked her if I could stay and she said yes. Eventually the police came to where I worked and told me I ought to go to the police station and give a statement of what happened. I didn't know the person's name or anything, well I can't remember the name now, it's a long time ago. I made a statement and where we'd agreed to meet the next week, I think the police were waiting in the doorways of shops for him to come but he never came. That was the beginning of it all.

`For more, see p. 122`

Can you describe what it is about another man that makes you feel at home with him?

With someone of my own sex I feel secure. As I say, I feel at home with someone of my own sex.

Daisy Asquith is an award-winning documentary filmmaker and head of the Department of Media, Communications and Cultural Studies at Goldsmiths, where she convenes the MA in Screen Documentary.

MAN ALIVE: 'CONSENTING ADULTS', BBC, JUNE 1967.

BELFAST AND BEYOND

THE SEXUAL OFFENCES ACT 1967, which partially decriminalised homosexuality in England and Wales, did not extend to Northern Ireland. Gay men there continued to be criminalised until the Homosexual Offences (Northern Ireland) Order 1982. It was in this context that Cara-Friend was founded in 1974 at Queen's University Belfast by members of its Gay Liberation Society to support the well-being of lesbians and gay men across Northern Ireland. Modelled on London Friend, the UK's oldest such charity, which was founded just two years earlier, Cara-Friend offered information services and a helpline, a weekly Lesbian Line, and befriending services in Belfast and beyond.

Between 1977 and 1983, Cara-Friend, along with other organisations, was housed at 4 University Street. 'Number 4' was a vacant house 'loaned' to the Gay Liberation Society by Queen's University Belfast that operated as a focus for the city's gay and lesbian community. Cara-Friend's history demonstrates the importance of university-based gay liberation organisations in some cities to the building of LGBTIQ+ community and activism beyond the ivory tower.

4 UNIVERSITY STREET, BELFAST, HOME OF CARA-FRIEND, 1984.

CARA-FRIEND LESBIAN LINE POSTER, 1980.

Michael Workman answering the Cara-Friend helpline, mid-1970s.

UNIVERSITY LIFE: TOWN AND GOWN

BRIGHTON

Flyers for Brighton Polytechnic's Lesbian & Gay Society show some of the concerns that engaged its members in the late 1980s. While the words 'Lesbian & Gay' took up nearly a third of one poster, text at the bottom reassured students that bisexuals and supporters were also welcome. The other poster playfully engaged with a major issue of the day: the unequal age of consent for sex between men. While the age of consent for heterosexual sex had long been sixteen, it had been set at twenty-one for homosexual male sex in 1967. It would only be lowered to eighteen in 1994 and then finally equalised in 2000.

Even as 'lesbians, gay men, bisexuals + our supporters' were welcome at Brighton Poly, Melita Dennett reflects on membership debates at the nearby University of Sussex.

↑ Brighton Polytechnic Lesbian & Gay Society flyers c.1988.

'In 1991 I was asked to chair a meeting of the University of Sussex Lesbian & Gay Society. This sounds unbelievable, but they were having a debate ... about whether bisexuals should be allowed to join the Lesbian & Gay Society. ... So I chaired this debate and of course everyone assumed that I would be very anti-bisexual, which I wasn't. And we had a lengthy debate of about an hour about whether bisexuals could be trusted, whether they should be welcomed in, whether they would go away from the Lesbian, Gay & Bisexual meeting and, you know, talk to people of the opposite gender. If you have a partner of the opposite sex and you're a bisexual person, are you to be trusted? Should you be a bisexual person who only has same-sex relationships? All these kind of weird, weird debates that seem odd to us now. But they were the currency. [The outcome of the meeting was that] they agreed. It became the Lesbian, Gay & Bisexual Society.'

Melita Dennett interviewed by Justin Bengry for the Queer Beyond London project (2017)

OXFORD AND CAMBRIDGE

'Queer' Oxford was as dead as the proverbial dodo after the war right through the 1950s and 1960s. Things changed quickly through the emergence of student activism in the early years of the 1970s as Oxford's students began to organise and campaign in a major way. The front cover of the student magazine *Isis* from 19 May 1973 always makes me smile.

Ross Brooks is a historian of queer Oxford. For more: https://queeroxford.info/

Throughout the 1970s and 1980s, there was a flurry of organising in the medieval university city of Cambridge. However, the well-known town v. gown trope was not as rigid among the queer population of Cambridge as it was elsewhere, with students and non-students socialising and campaigning together. By the autumn of 1989, Cambridge was home to some twenty different lesbian and gay organisations ranging from political groups such as Cambridge Scrap Section 28 and a local Campaign for Homosexual Equality (CHE) group, to self-help groups like the Lesbian and Gay Teacher Support Group and the Gay Health Education Group, to recreational societies like the East Anglia Bikers and the Cambridge Gay Outdoor Club.

↑ Cover of Oxford student magazine *Isis*, 19 May 1973.

Gay discos were held in college cellars, very much in line with the traditional college 'bop' (a party, whose name is an acronym of 'breach of the peace'). More commonly, though, they were held outside university premises. The Anchor pub played host to many of Cambridge's queer discos, with admission of 60p. The discos are recorded as sweaty, smoky, ale-fuelled evenings of dancing, talking and making friends. They were also largely, though not exclusively, male spaces. This is not surprising. By 1990, males made up 61 per cent of the student body, which, though down from 87.5 per cent in 1970, still made Cambridge a male-dominated institution.

CAMBRIDGE GAY GROUP EVENT, c.1985.

George J. Severs is a historian of modern Britain, activism, sexuality and religion at the Geneva Graduate Institute and author of Radical Acts: HIV/AIDS Activism in Late Twentieth-Century England *(Bloomsbury, 2024).*

BUILDING COMMUNITY

COMMUNITY CENTRES have been at the heart of LGBTIQ+ life and activism for decades. In the early 1980s, Black lesbians and gay men who had started to organise separately in London came together to form the Gay Black Group. With funds from the Greater London Council (GLC) they established the Black Lesbian and Gay Centre in 1985, which eventually found a permanent home in Peckham, south London, in 1992, making it Europe's first Black lesbian and gay centre.

The London Lesbian and Gay Centre, based in Cowcross Street in Islington, was likewise funded by the GLC. It hosted numerous community, outreach and entertainment events, ranging from the Gay Teachers Group to Lesbians and Gays Support the Printworkers. Both the Black Lesbian and Gay Centre and the London Lesbian and Gay Centre were profoundly affected by the abolition of the GLC in 1986 and subsequent loss of funding.

LGBTIQ+ people have worked hard to create community centres around the country that serve the needs of diverse communities. Manchester may hold the record for Europe's first publicly funded and purpose-built gay centre. And the same year that saw the demise of the GLC and the resources it offered queer community groups also witnessed the launch of the country's first Transsexuals/Transvestites (TV/TS) centre in London.

Of course, LGBTIQ+ people build community in all kinds of places and these are just a few of the centres and groups that have offered support and community since the 1970s.

BLACK LESBIAN AND GAY CENTRE FLYER, LONDON 1998.

LONDON LESBIAN & GAY CENTRE
DIARY—AUGUST 1986

FRIDAY 1
- 12.00 PLAY POOL! (CENTRE GAMES GROUP) — 3rd FLOOR
- 9.00 FIRST OF THE NEW LOOK FRIDAY DISCOS! UP FRONT SOUNDS... SOUL THROUGH TO EUROBEAT WITH D.J. MEGA MIX — BASEMENT

SATURDAY 2
- 12.00 PLAY POOL (CENTRE GAMES GROUP) — 3rd FLOOR
- 8.00 AL ANON — 2nd FLOOR
- 8.00 NEW BEGINNINGS — 3rd FLOOR
- 9.00 BELOW STAIRS THE SATURDAY DISCO FOR WOMEN SENSATIONAL SOUNDS FROM D.J.s: LITTLE SISTER

SUNDAY 3
- 12.00 BODY POSITIVE — 2nd FLOOR
- 1.00 VIDEO
- 3.00 YOUNG LESBIAN GROUP — 1st FLOOR
- 8.00 GRAND AUGUST CABARET with THE FAERIE CAKE CONSORT FOLLOWED BY A HITS OF YESTERYEAR DISCO PERFORMANCE STARTS 8.45. — BASEMENT
- 8.00 VIDEO — 3rd FLOOR

MONDAY 4 CENTRE CLOSED

TUESDAY 5
- EXHIBITION OF ORIGINAL BY STEPHEN MAYLOR — CAFE
- 6.00 AL ANON — 2nd FLOOR
- 6.15 PACE MIXED YOGA CLASS — 3rd FLOOR
- 7.00 BEARDSLEY SKETCH CLUB — 3rd FLOOR
- 7.30 L.C.C. HOT TOPIX BODY BUILDING — 1st FLOOR
- 8.00 FLAGS
- 8.00 FULHAM + HAMMERSMITH YOUNG LESBIAN GROUP BENEFIT DISCO — 2nd FLOOR / BASEMENT

WEDNESDAY 6
- 6.00 PACE ADVICE SURGERY
- 8.00 THE PEOPLES MULTI RACIAL GROUP GRAND DISCO — 2nd FLOOR / BASEMENT

THURSDAY 7
- 12.00 PLAY POOL! — 3rd FLOOR
- 6.00 LESBIAN THEATRE GROUP — 1st FLOOR
- 7.00 LESBIANS IN SPORT — 1st FLOOR
- 8.00 THE PEOPLES MULTI RACIAL GROUP — 3rd FLOOR
- 9.00 UNDERGROUND WOMENS CLUB CABARET WITH PENNY WOODS — BASEMENT

FRIDAY 8
- 12.00 PLAY POOL! — 3rd FLOOR
- 9.00 FAB FRIDAY DISCO UP FRONT SOUNDS SOUL THROUGH TO EUROBEAT DJ RANKIN JOSIE — BASEMENT

SATURDAY 9
- 12.00 PLAY POOL! — 3rd FLOOR
- 3.30 FEELING GOOD — CRECHE
- 8.00 NEW BEGINNINGS — 3rd FLOOR
- 8.00 AL ANON — 3rd FLOOR
- 9.00 BELOW STAIRS WOMENS DISCO DJ JULIA — BASEMENT

SUNDAY 10
- 12.00 BODY POSITIVE — 2nd FLOOR
- 1.00 VIDEOS
- 8.00 L AND G. GREEN GROUP — 3rd FLOOR
- 8.00 VIDEOS — 2nd FLOOR
- 8.30 LLGCC IS PROUD TO PRESENT DAVE DALE PLUS DISCO WITH DJ MEGA MIX PERFORMANCE AT 10PM — 3rd FLOOR / BASEMENT

MONDAY 11 CENTRE CLOSED

TUESDAY 12
- 10.00 YOUNG LESBIAN MUSIC WORKSHOPS — 1st FLOOR
- 6.15 YOGA CLASS MIXED — CRECHE
- 7.30 L.C.C. MEETING — 1st FLOOR

WEDNESDAY 13
- 10.00 YOUNG LESBIAN MUSIC WORKSHOP — 1st FLOOR
- 6.00 PACE ADVICE SURGERY — 2nd FLOOR
- 7.00 VOLS. MEETING — 3rd FLOOR

THURSDAY 14
- 10.00 YOUNG LESBIAN MUSIC WORKSHOP — 1st FLOOR
- 12.00 PLAY POOL! — 3rd FLOOR
- 6.00 LESBIAN THEATRE GROUP — 1st FLOOR
- 8.00 THE PEOPLES MULTI RACIAL GROUP — 3rd FLOOR
- JUMBLE SALE & SOCIAL
- 9.00 UNDERGROUND WOMENS CLUB CABARET WITH OUT OF THE BLUE DIERDRE CARTWRIGHT AND FRIENDS JAZZ SOUNDS — BASEMENT

FRIDAY 15
- 10.00 YOUNG LESBIAN MUSIC WORKSHOP — 1st FLOOR
- 12.00 PLAY POOL! — 3rd FLOOR
- 7.30 ITS JUST A PHASE PRODUCTIONS PRESENT OVERCOMING HOMOSEXUALITY! CONFESSIONS OF TWO DEVIANTS — BASEMENT
- 9.00 FAB FRIDAY DISCO UP FRONT SOUNDS! SOUL THROUGH TO EUROBEAT D.J. MEGA-MIX — BASEMENT

SATURDAY 16
- 10.00 YOUNG LESBIAN MUSIC WORKSHOP — 1st FLOOR
- 12.00 PLAY POOL! — 3rd FLOOR
- 7.30 OVERCOMING HOMOSEXUALITY PRODUCTION CONTINUES — BASEMENT
- 8.00 NEW BEGINNINGS — 3rd FLOOR
- 8.00 AL ANON — 2nd FLOOR
- 9.00 BELOW STAIRS WOMENS DISCO DJ LITTLE SISTER — BASEMENT

SUNDAY 17
- 12.00 BODY POSITIVE — 2nd FLOOR
- 1.00 VIDEOS
- 7.30 OVERCOMING HOMOSEXUALITY PRODUCTIONS LAST PERFORMANCE — 3rd FLOOR / BASEMENT
- 9.00 VIDEOS
- 9.00 CABARET with TONY FREY SINGING FRAGMENTS OF HIS LIFE FOLLOWED BY HI ENERG DISCO — 3rd FLOOR

MONDAY 18 CENTRE CLOSED

TUESDAY 19
TODAY MARKS THE START OF LESBIAN AND GAY CARIBBEAN WEEK ORGANIZED BY BLACK PEOPLE— FOR YOU CARNIVAL EVENTS ALL WEEK ASIAN AND BLACK FOOD ALL WEEK FROM CAFE
- 6.15 YOGA MIXED CLASS — 3rd FLOOR
- 7.30 L.C.C. HOT TOPIX—FAME — 1st FLOOR
- 8.00 FLAGS
- 8.00 LAUNCH OF CARIBBEAN WEEK FOOD, DRINK AND SENSATIONAL DISCO — 2nd FLOOR / BASEMENT

WEDNESDAY 20
- 6.30 PACE ADVICE SURGERY
- 8.00 SM GAYS — 2nd FLOOR / BASEMENT
- 8.00 SURPRISE EVENT FOR CARIBBEAN WEEK — 3rd FLOOR

THURSDAY 21
- 12.00 PLAY POOL! — 3rd FLOOR
- 6.00 LESBIAN THEATRE GROUP — 1st FLOOR
- 8.00 THE PEOPLES MULTI RACIAL GROUP SOCIAL AND BAR-B-Q. — 3rd FLOOR / CAFE AREA
- 9.00 UNDERGROUND WOMENS CLUB CABARET WITH MOONLIGHTERS MUSIC — BASEMENT

FRIDAY 22
- 12.00 PLAY POOL! — 3rd FLOOR
- 9.00 A CARNIVAL AFFAIR! MEGA DISCO & COSTUME EXTRAVAGANZA DJ RANKIN JOSIE — BASEMENT

SATURDAY 23
- 12.00 PLAY POOL! — 3rd FLOOR
- 3.30 FEELING GOOD — CRECHE
- 8.00 AL ANON — 3rd FLOOR
- 8.00 NEW BEGINNINGS — 3rd FLOOR
- 9.00 BELOW STAIRS WOMENS DISCO DJ LITTLE SISTER PLUS CARIBBEAN FESTIVITIES IN, AND OUT OF DOORS ALL EVENING. — BASEMENT

SUNDAY 24
- 12.00 BODY POSITIVE — 2nd FLOOR
- 1.00 CARNIVAL AFFAIR VIDEOS ALL DAY — 3rd FLOOR
- 8.00 L. & G. GREEN GROUP — 2nd FLOOR
- 8.30 JAZZ NITE WE PRESENT THIS MONTH MAGGIE NICHOLLS AND FRIENDS PLUS CARNIVAL MUSIC, FOOD, DRINK ALL DAY — BASEMENT / CAFE AREA

MONDAY 25 CENTRE CLOSED

TUESDAY 26
- 6.15 YOGA CLASS MIXED — 3rd FLOOR
- 7.30 L.C.C. MEETING — 1st FLOOR
- 8.00 VIDEO—WOMEN AND THE WISH STRUGGLE — 1st FLOOR

WEDNESDAY 27
- 7.30 LESBIAN AND GAY GREEN GROUP WITH GUEST SPEAKER JONATHAN PORRITT—DIRECTOR OF FRIENDS OF THE EARTH — BASEMENT

THURSDAY 28
- 12.00 PLAY POOL! — 3rd FLOOR
- 6.00 LESBIAN THEATRE GROUP — 1st FLOOR
- 8.00 THE PEOPLES MULTI RACIAL GROUP — 3rd FLOOR
- 9.00 UNDERGROUND WOMENS CLUB CABARET WITH ELLEN POLLOCK'S ONE WOMAN SHOW FIGHT LIKE A TIGER — BASEMENT

FRIDAY 29
- 12.00 PLAY POOL!
- 7.30 FIGHT LIKE A TIGER CONTINUES — 3rd FLOOR / BASEMENT
- 9.00 FAB FRIDAY DISCO UP FRONT SOUNDS SOUL THROUGH TO EUROBEAT — BASEMENT

SATURDAY 30
- 12.00 PLAY POOL!
- 7.30 FIGHT LIKE A TIGER CONTINUES — 3rd FLOOR / BASEMENT
- 8.00 AL ANON — 2nd FLOOR
- 8.00 NEW BEGINNINGS — 3rd FLOOR
- 9.00 BELOW STAIRS WOMENS DISCO DJ JULIA — BASEMENT

SUNDAY 31
- 12.00 BODY POSITIVE — 2nd FLOOR
- 1.00 VIDEOS
- 2.00 LESBIAN & GAY PARENTING GROUP — 2nd FLOOR
- 5.30 TWO VIDEOS ON LESBIANS GAYS AND PARENTING
- 7.30 FIGHT LIKE A TIGER CONTINUES — BASEMENT
- 8.00 VIDEOS

CENTRE OPENING TIMES
CENTRE CLOSED MONDAYS
TUES & WEDS 6.00–12.00
THURS & SUN 12.00–12.00
FRI & SAT 12.00–2AM

CRECHE OPEN
THUR & SAT NIGHT 7.30pm TO 11.30pm
SUN AFTERNOON 2pm–10.6pm
PLEASE BOOK IN ADVANCE

London Lesbian and Gay Centre, programme of events, August 1986.

2: SOCIALISING AND SEX | 67

NEVER GOING UNDERGROUND:
MANCHESTER'S LGBTIQ+ COMMUNITY CENTRE

By Emily Crompton

'WHEN IS OUR birthday?' asked Ali, the LGBT+ Centre manager. A simple enough question, or so I thought. The answer took four months of archival research, knee-deep in 1980s gay magazines and patchy council meeting minutes and records. I unearthed an intriguing story of how Manchester (potentially) became the first place in Europe to have an entirely publicly funded, purpose-built centre for the gay community.

1970S: THE FIRST MANCHESTER GAY CENTRE

↑ Advert for the new Gay Centre in Manchester, published in *Gay Life*, July 1987.

The place considered the first 'Gay Centre' in Manchester was a small, dank 65 m² (700 sq. ft) basement on Oxford Road occupied by a group known as Manchester Gay Alliance. The Alliance consisted of Manchester Lesbians Group, the TV/TS group, the Manchester Homophile Society (the university gay soc), the Campaign for Homosexual Equality (CHE) group and Friend. In 1978 a successful grant application was subsequently supplemented by funding from council rates to help support its services, including general information phone lines, counselling and befriending groups. The Gay Centre's first annual report (1978/79) set out the rationale for the centre and the need for alternative premises as their current space was damp, cramped and, literally, underground.

1981-88: THE SECOND MANCHESTER GAY CENTRE... STILL UNDERGROUND

In 1981, yet another basement, at 61A Bloom Street, became the new home of the Gay Centre. It provided several phone lines including Lesbian Link, Manchester Gay Switchboard and Friend, as well as meeting rooms. In response to a huge number of phone calls from

THE ORIGINAL INTERIOR AND RECEPTION OF THE MANCHESTER GAY CENTRE.

younger people, it also ran a youth club and launched a late-night café called SNAX, which provided much-needed revenue.

In 1984 the staff, supported by the local council's newly formed Equal Opportunities Committee, searched for new premises, as the groups had outgrown another basement home. There was much debate about the new location. Should it remain within the presumed safety of the gay area of Canal Street or relocate somewhere more neutral and anonymous? A site was selected on Canal Street, and in December 1986 the council approved the necessary capital funding of £118,000 for the building. Unfortunately, that site on Canal Street fell through as the seller objected to its intended use. The location eventually became a bar called Manto. So, in the early months of 1987, sites already owned by the council were considered.

1988: NEVER GOING UNDERGROUND, AGAIN

A site on Sidney Street was identified and, from May 1987, open meetings were held to discuss the new premises. Unfortunately, the Covenant Community Church launched a campaign against the proposals as it reached the planning stage. They galvanised support and sent around twenty members of the Gospel Outreach Team to oppose the application, armed with a petition signed by 147 people and letters of opposition from businesses. The Gay Centre obviously had no idea they would face such opposition as the steering group sent only two volunteers to attend the planning committee! Despite this opposition, the committee approved the application.

It is important to place the funding and building of the centre in a national context: in June 1987, *Gay Life* reported that a little-publicised bill had passed through Parliament. Section 28 of the Local Government Act 1986 (Amendment) Bill 1987-88 included a now infamous section:

2A – (1) A local authority shall not – (a) intentionally promote homosexuality or publish material with the intention of promoting homosexuality; (b) promote the teaching in any maintained school of the acceptability of homosexuality as a pretended family relationship;

The Conservative government introduced the amendment at a time when it was alleged that some Labour local authorities were spending money on actively promoting homosexuality over heterosexuality. During 1988 a national campaign against the bill took place and was headquartered at the Gay Centre on Bloom Street. On 20 February 1988, twenty thousand people marched through the streets of Manchester to protest against Section 28. The march was organised by the Northwest Campaign for Lesbian and Gay Equality and culminated in Albert Square outside the Town Hall. This national

> Alcoholics Anonymous (AA) meetings have run continuously at the centre since 1989. One AA member spoke about their first experience of attending a meeting and how they got to know everyone's shoes as they were looking down so much. Many have cited it as a life-saving group to attend.

context makes the decisions of Manchester City Council to continue to fund a purpose-designed building for the gay community at this time all the more fantastic.

Construction work on the new centre started in 1988 around the same time that Section 28 became law (May 1988). But having already approved grants to build a new gay centre, that September the council refused an application to increase the core funding for the services. Sadly, this may have been a consequence of Section 28, along with city's worsening economic situation.

Graham Stringer, leader of the council and long-term supporter of the centre, opened the building on 27 November 1988. In the decades since, the centre has been through many managerial changes, funding cuts, almost getting thrown out, but each time it was under threat, it was the long-term volunteers, dedicated staff and the users who loved the centre who fought for its survival.

2022: THE PROUD PLACE

In 2012 the centre again lost funding and was under threat of closure. Some long-term youth workers set up an independent company called LGBT Youth North West, which later rebranded as The Proud Trust. The charity delivers youth groups, peer support, training, events and campaigns, undertakes research, creates resources and manages the building.

The centre building was difficult to maintain and repair, and in 2015 The Proud Trust commissioned a feasibility study to consider its future and how it could continue to meet the needs of the growing charity and wider LGBTIQ+ community. Due to the cheap and inflexible construction of the premises, rebuilding proved to be necessary and unavoidable. An estimated five hundred people – including staff, members of the public, volunteers and young people – got involved throughout the briefing and design process. Over five years, the charity raised £2.4 million to rebuild the centre.

The new centre has a joyous golden façade which glints in the Mancunian rain and shines out, calling in the next generation of activists to continue demanding LGBTIQ+ rights. Just as its predecessor, but updated for the twenty-first century, the building complements its physical surroundings of shiny new university blocks, providing a cautiously proud exterior affording anonymity as well as hopeful pride.

Emily Crompton is an architect and senior lecturer at Manchester School of Architecture.

COMMUNITY NEWSLETTERS

From the 1970s a range of community newsletters proliferated, demonstrating both the geographical extent of LGBTIQ+ groups but also their interests. Where people might not have felt seen in broader activist or community organisations, or where they might even have been actively excluded, newsletters were vital organs of communication, networking, support and visibility. The Brighton and Hove Disabled Dykes Club, for example, was a social support group that published the *Disabled Dykes Newsletter*. BLACKOUT was produced from 1986 by the Black Lesbian and Gay Centre discussed above. *Gemini* was the newsletter of the Leeds Transvestite/Transsexual Social Group. The *Older Lesbian Newsletter*, *Gay Christian* and the London Bisexual Group's *The Bi-Monthly* all spoke to specific community concerns not sufficiently addressed by other mainstream lesbian and gay organisations, while *GIMS: Gays in Mid Sussex* and *CHEW*, the newsletter of the CHE group in Wigan, both focussed on their communities' local issues and interests.

Above: Cover of *Disabled Dykes Newsletter*, 2004.
Right: Cover of the first issue of *BLACKOUT: A Black Lesbian and Gay Magazine*, 1986.

72 | A QUEER SCRAPBOOK

Top left: The inaugural issue of *Older Lesbian Newsletter*, August 1984.

Top right: Cover of *Gay Christian: Bulletin of the Gay Christian Movement*, no. 15 (November 1979).

Centre left: The newsletter of the *Campaign for Homosexual Equality Wigan Group*, no. 12 (January 1976).

Centre right: Cover of *Gays in Mid Sussex*, no. 5 (August 1982).

Left: Cover of the first issue of *The Bi-Monthly: The Newsletter for Bisexuals*, January 1984.

BUILDING TRANS COMMUNITY SPACES
By Leila Sellers

THE LONDON TV/TS Centre in French Place in Hoxton, Hackney opened in 1986 and was the first trans-specific community space in the UK. Home to the London TV/TS Group, which originally operated out of the offices of gay support group London Friend in Islington, the centre was the brainchild of group organiser Yvonne Sinclair. Recognising the need within London for a permanent place where trans people could safely meet, Sinclair fundraised over the course of several years, before finally securing the premises – a former warehouse next to a 'rag-trade-sweat-shop' – in East London. The property, when Sinclair first took possession, needed significant renovation, and members of the group volunteered their time and skills to make the space habitable.

Known simply by its location, 'French Place', the centre, which was open at weekends as well as one afternoon in the week, provided visitors with lockers to store clothes, counselling services, a kitchen area and, at its heart, a social space furnished with sofas and comfy chairs in the style of a suburban family living room.

Even before its move to French Place, the London TV/TS Group attracted people from all over the UK and was firmly embedded in the city's network of trans spaces. Individuals visiting London for the weekend would come to the centre, often meeting friends, or making new acquaintances there, before going out as a group for a meal in a local restaurant, a night out at a Drag Ball at Porchester Hall or a nightcap in the bar at the Philbeach Hotel.

THE PHILBEACH HOTEL

The Philbeach, which first opened its doors in 1981, was, according to the adverts that appeared in trans newsletters from the time, 'London's only Gay Hotel that also caters for the TV/TS community'. The hotel had an international reputation, particularly among those visiting the city for business, and was often suggested as a safe place to

↓ The second issue of *Gemini*, the newsletter of the Leeds Transvestite/Transsexual Social Group, May 1975.

stay for trans feminine people who were unfamiliar with the city.

The Philbeach was a place where gay and trans people comfortably inhabited the same space, with visitors reporting mingling with 'homosexuals and [trans] girls' in the bar. It also had a reputation among gay men for cruising. Those who did not wish to be propositioned were advised to lock their bedroom doors and avoid the shared bathrooms. 'Admirers' (a term used to describe cisgender men attracted to trans women) could also often be found in the hotel's bar and there is sense that the Philbeach offered its guests a level of social and sexual freedom they struggled to find elsewhere.

By entering the sanctuary of the hotel, visitors were instantly part of a secure network of trans-inclusive people, places and spaces stretching across London. The receptionist at the hotel could, on request, book a taxi directly to the TV/TS Centre, whisking a guest from one safe space to another, almost without having to set foot outside. Similarly, at the end of the night, guests were returned to the safety of the hotel where they could transform back into their masculine selves and resume their other, more conventional lives.

Leila Sellers is a historian of Britain's trans communities.

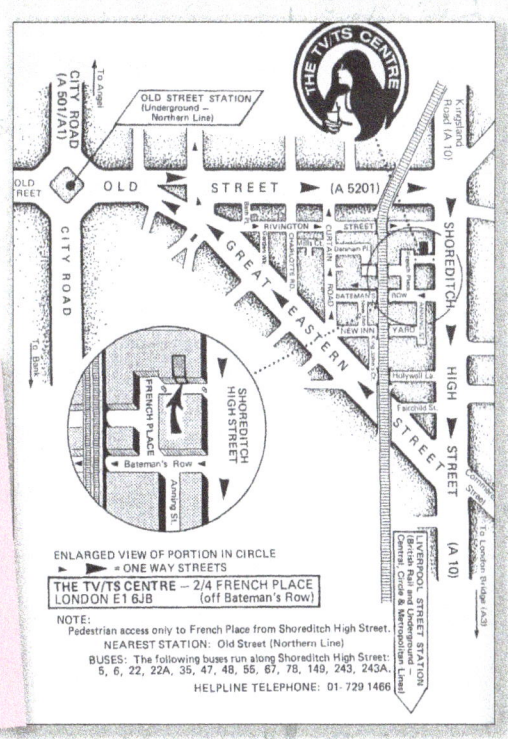

Top right: An advert for the Philbeach Hotel in *The Glad Rag: Journal of the TV/TS Group*, no. 14 (1984).

Bottom right: A map providing directions to the TV/TS Centre in French Place, printed in *The Glad Rag: Journal of the TV/TS Group*, no. 36 (1987).

OUT IN THE NORTH: *LEEDS OTHER PAPER*

ISSUED FOR THE first time on 20 January 1974, *Leeds Other Paper* announced its arrival with a mission statement: 'It is our intention to support all groups active in industry and elsewhere for greater control of their own lives.' Over the next twenty years, the *LOP* provided a lively, subversive and sometimes angry slant on life in Leeds as, for the first time, readers found LGBTIQ+ event listings, reviews and advice alongside items aimed at a wider readership. Even more significantly, the newspaper quickly established itself as a voice for – and by – the region's queer community. Individuals found a central contact point from which to meet and mobilise, forming new support groups and influential local chapters of campaigning organisations like ACT UP and CHE.

The following oral histories were collected as part of the West Yorkshire Queer Stories project (2018–20). For more stories, visit https://wyqs.co.uk.

'At that time there was a paper called the *Leeds Other Paper*. It was a lefty, bohemian, sort of *Time Out* kind of publication. It had lots of things in – it had gigs, it had all sorts of community activities and of course that sort of thing would be on the internet now. But we used to advertise the group in there. And that's how we got more people in. ... At one time we were meeting twice a month, on a Monday. ... We had a period where it

LEEDS OTHER PAPER, NO. 19 (AUGUST 1975).

76 | A QUEER SCRAPBOOK

was fairly enthusiastic, and lots of events, but unfortunately it tailed off towards the end. And eventually it collapsed ... somewhere between '92 and '93. It didn't collapse totally but what happened was the group split...'

Chris, founder of Leeds Bi Group

'I was living in Leeds and ... I put an advert in *Leeds Other Paper*, a box advert, saying West Yorkshire Gay Bi Lesbian Youth Network, and we'd meet in – I think we met in Bradford the first time, but anyway, I can't remember, it's a very long time ago; and I would've been eighteen, and seven people responded. There was a Muslim guy from Bradford, there was a bisexual woman from Leeds, a milkman from Ilkley, a young man doing some sort of technical college work in Dewsbury ... oh God, there was a couple of other people, I can't think now. Anyway, we met in Bradford, and we used to alternate between Bradford and Leeds so that, because, people, most, everyone apart from me lived at home.'

Kellan, founder of West Yorkshire Gay Bi Lesbian Youth Network

'We advertised in the *Yorkshire Evening Post* but they were expensive ... And there was another publication, an independent one called *Leeds Other Paper*, L-O-P, that was on the go in the eighties into the early nineties I think, and we did have ... an advertisement in there [that] we met ... on a Friday evening ... in the [MESMAC] building ... so they could come quite anonymously to that, and they did. Maybe they looked around to see if anybody was worth chatting up [*laughs*] then that would be it.'

Eric, CHE

Ross Horsley was a community development worker with West Yorkshire Queer Stories. He is an archives and museum professional based in Leeds.

The 'Out in the North' column in *Leeds Other Paper* (10 November 1989) contained information about LGBTIQ+ events and groups.

A CLUB FOR HUMAN BEINGS

IN THE 1960s, leading homophile organisations sought to create safe spaces away from the dangers of mainstream pubs and clubs, but which were also more accessible than the few exclusive gay members' clubs in London. In 1964, the lesbian magazine *Arena Three* called for venues it characterised as 'decent surroundings' for 'decent people'. By the late 1960s, gay men seeking to organise Esquire Clubs – member-owned social clubs modelled on continental examples and working men's clubs – likewise sought to create a 'high restrained tone'. Even though these sentiments might not align entirely with our own priorities today, they nonetheless demonstrate that creating safe, often non-commercial, social spaces for the LGBTIQ+ community has been an active concern since at least the mid-twentieth century. These initiatives might seem quaint in their worries about respectability, or even exclusionary in their policing of their own membership. At the same time, however, they speak to concerns that remain relevant today, particularly for those members of our communities who feel excluded from mainstream venues. Esquire Clubs, for example, would not require patrons to buy alcohol. Neither initiative succeeded, but a range of LGBTIQ+ venues and socialising opportunities would emerge in the coming decades.

← An article in *Arena Three*, vol. 1, no. 1 (1964), proposing the need for 'a club for human beings'.

ESQUIRE CLUBS LIMITED

Gaddum House,
16/18, Queen Street,
MANCHESTER 2.

INFORMATION ABOUT ESQUIRE CLUBS LIMITED.

1st July, 1968

(1) The North West Committee was formed in 1964 to promote law reform in the north along the lines of the Wolfenden recommendations. It consists of an informal committee and has a large number of members, homosexual and non-homosexual who support it. Its patrons are Neil Pearson (President), The Dean of Manchester, Professor Colin Adamson, Dr. R. W. Burslem (Vice presidents). It is affiliated to the Community Council of Lancashire.

(2) When the law on homosexuality was changed in July, 1967, the North West Committee was faced with a difficult decision - should it disband? or should it continue and work towards a solution of the many and varied social and personal problems which remain. It was decided to do the latter.

(3) For some time the Committee has provided a Counselling service for people with problems, homosexual and other. A permanent centre is needed in the North for this service.

(4) Through this work we also found many people needing a place to meet. This is a minority which like all minority groups needs its own special facilities without trying to cut off from society. This need for a place to meet we found particularly so in the smaller towns.

(5) The need is not for exclusive queer clubs but for intimate clubs with a gay informal atmosphere where homosexuals could meet, bring their sister to, their friends both homosexual and heterosexual. It would also be a place <u>where they are not obliged to buy a drink</u> - as is the case with most of the bars where they meet now.

(6) Most homosexuals are perfectly normal ordinary citizens. In the past they have had to resort to all sorts of undesirable places as meeting points, public lavatories and dingy seedy bars where they have been ashamed to take their friends and frightened to be seen by their enemies. On humanitarian grounds alone, they have the right to be able to meet in decent surroundings.

(7) On psychological grounds too it is healthy that people who would otherwise lead lonely isolated lives should have a place to meet. We believe that good psychiatric advice is often to "accept your homosexuality and mix with your own kind". In the present state of affairs this is just not possible except in mainly undesirable surroundings.

(8) As for the argument that such clubs will be dens of vice, dating centres and so on, why should it be thought that homosexuals are more promiscuous more wicked than heterosexuals? The quality of the relationship not the physical side is the important aspect - in both homosexual and heterosexual affairs. There would be strict rules of behaviour - no gambling for example - and a high restrained tone throughout.

(9) To bring this about the N.W. Committee has encouraged the formation of Esquire Clubs Ltd. This independent company has been formed for :-

    (a) The provision of food, friendship, drink, dancing and entertainment, cultural activities, discussion groups etc.

    (b) The provision of a counselling service*for homosexual people, members and non members alike.

* the money to pay for the counselling service would come from profits on the clubs other activities, especially the bar.

    (c) Other work in co-operation with bodies like the Board for Social Responsibility, the Lancashire Community Council and a panel of doctors and lawyers. The Company would also work with the N. W. Homosexual Law Reform Committee.

(10) For EsquireClubs Ltd. to fulfil its social purpose it must have and be seen to have the support of well known and responsible citizens who are willing to be vice presidents of Esquire Clubs. There will be opposition from the usual sources - people who see the clubs as further evidence of decay in our society. Such voices might be sufficient to deter authorities from granting licences or potential supporters from joining So we need your support as a vice president.

REMEMBERING DUNDEE'S GLASS BUCKET
By Bob Cant

'Remembering Dundee's Glass Bucket' was originally printed in the Scottish Review, 24 February 2016, and is reprinted with permission.

I DISCOVERED THE GLASS BUCKET by chance. I had just missed a bus, and I didn't fancy hanging around in Dundee bus station for an hour. So, I walked up St Andrews Street and within a few hundred yards I found a pub; no music; no pictures on the walls; lots of small tables with uncomfortable stools; a subdued atmosphere. Because it was so close to a bus station, the Glass Bucket, unlike most pubs in the seventies, lacked any regular local clientele. What the customers here had in common was a desire to catch a bus to their own small town. Or so I thought.

Once I had been in there a few minutes, I realised that some of the men there did seem to know each other; some of them displayed considerable curiosity about other male customers as they walked through the door; sometimes conversations were struck up between men who had previously given every indication of being strangers. There was a steady choreographic flow of men as they moved around the pub to position themselves next to other men with whom they imagined they might have something in common. Surely discussion of the intricacies of the timetables of buses to Alyth or Carnoustie was not worthy of such precision, such finesse?

Gradually, I realised that I had stumbled into a place that was the nearest to what could be described as a gay pub in Dundee. If you had asked the bar staff if this was a gay pub, they would have denied it; all the unaccompanied men could have told you a different story, but many of them would have denied it as well.

The very concept of coming out had not yet reached this part of Scotland. It was rather different from the louder, more ostentatious bars and politically contentious meeting places that I was becoming used to in London. But, in Dundee, in 1972 this was the place for gay men to go to if they wanted to meet other gay men. Quietly!

The law criminalising all male homosexual activity was, of course, a factor in intimidating gay men. Some years after my first visit to the Glass Bucket two men in Dundee were sentenced to a year's imprisonment for committing sodomy in a cubicle in a public convenience, but that was an isolated incident. While a handful of men knew about legal persecution, everybody who experienced any desire for other people of the same sex knew about shame; There was the inner shame that you might feel about having an inferior sexuality; there was the more public shame that would pursue you and your family if your sexuality became public knowledge. Shame was found in other countries, but Scotland was particularly noted for the unforgiving nature of its Presbyterian shame.

At first, I thought the silent, ultra-cautious behaviour of the men in the pub was indicative of their shame but over the years I changed my mind about that; there were no helplines in those days and, if you had got through the door of the pub, you had, somehow or other, come to terms with the implications of shame; you might find the atmosphere rather more constrained than you would like but you would accept it because you didn't want to rock the boat; you didn't want to be barred from going there. Far clearer examples of unresolved shame were to be found on the street outside, among the men who were too terrified to cross the threshold; the proximity of the pub to the bus station could provide a good excuse as to why they might be going in there. But so overwhelming was the guilt about the nature of their sexual desires that they couldn't even lie convincingly about their reasons for visiting the Glass Bucket. A lot of ashamed, isolated men tramped up and down St Andrews Street, again and again, night after night. Torn between desire and terror.

THE GLASS BUCKET ON ST ANDREWS STREET IN 1977.

Later on in the seventies, a pub called the Gauger opened on the Seagate, about the same distance away from the bus station as the Glass Bucket. Another world! The music was deafening – you could probably hear it on the Perth Road. It let itself be known as a pub that welcomed both gay men and lesbians. In fact, the pub was divided into two areas, so that there was a kind of sexual segregation. The area with the pool tables seemed to be entirely occupied by short, eh'm-no'-takin'-nae-shite-frae-naebody lesbians; the area nearer the bar was the preferred area of the gay men, many of whom were drinking at a speed that suggested they were in a competition; Neddy Scrymgeour's heart would have been broken. The Gauger seemed to represent the future of gay venues. Shouting and limited physical contact became the norm. And, like it or not, more people went in there than ever went into the Glass Bucket; so, that was a bit of a setback for the prevailing climate of shame.

It was easy to have quiet conversations in the Glass Bucket and easy for your neighbours to overhear them. I recall hearing a conversation one night between two Dundonian men about the same age as myself. They had clearly known each other well in the past. One of them was explaining that they wouldn't be able to spend time with each other, now that he had a wife and bairn. No identifying words like 'gay' or even 'homosexual' were used but this was clearly a conversation between two men who had once been close; they might even have been lovers. There was no anger; no tears; no recriminations; just an air of sadness. The unmarried one appeared to accept the situation; they continued sitting quietly with each other and they were still doing so when I left to catch the bus to Kirkbuddo.

The Glass Bucket pub is no more; there is now a café on the site. I went to look for a photographic image of the pub as it had been back in the seventies but image there was none. Back in the seventies the Glass Bucket had succeeded in being invisible, except for those who needed to know about its inner life, and the invisibility continues today. I hope that some of the former customers are able to share their memories of the times when they put shame behind them and walked into a pub to meet people like themselves.

Bob Cant is the co-editor of Radical Records: Thirty Years of Lesbian and Gay History (1957-1987) *and the editor of three anthologies of oral history. He was a founding member of the Millthorpe Project, which records the life stories of LGBTIQ+ trade unionists. His novel* Something Chronic *was published by Word Power Books in 2013.*

In 2023 a new pub opened on the site of the Glass Bucket and revived its former name. Announcing the launch, a picture of the original was discovered.

CLUB NIGHTS

CHEW DISCO was a Liverpool DIY art and clubbing project founded by Khalil West and Emma Obong. Heavily influenced by Black queer feminism and early post-punk, hip hop, queercore and rave scenes, its flagship mixed-sexuality party featured live performances from famed and underground artists (guests included Vaginal Davis, Mykki Blanco, Trash Kit, Cakes Da Killa, Shopping and Golden Teacher) and raised money for non-Western sexual minority and women-centred initiatives.

Khalil West holds a PhD in History from the European University Institute.

Multidisciplinary artist Vaginal Davis performing for Chew Disco at the Kazimier, Liverpool, November 2013.

Justin writes...

Club Kali was set up in 1995 by collaborators DJ Ritu and Rita in order to create a diverse club space from a South Asian perspective. Safe and celebratory, the club night at the Dome in London's Tufnell Park mixes Bhangra, Bollywood, Arabic music and Western pop. It is now the world's largest and longest running LGBTIQ+ club celebrating South Asian heritage. Looking back on Club Kali's significance, Rita reflects: 'We set up Club Kali, and we intended it to just be a club night. And it became a community, a global queer community.'

Club Kali's longest serving Chutney Queen on stage celebrating the club's birthday in 2022.

Justin writes...

Transfabulous was founded by Serge Nicholson and Jason Barker in response to the Gender Recognition Act 2004, which allowed Britons to define their gender, but *only* as either 'male' or 'female'. By limiting recognition to neat transgender clinical transitions from male to female or female to male, the legislation did not fit the reality of gender expansive communities or lived histories, and it left non-binary people entirely outside of legal gender recognition. But 'it felt a more hopeful euphoric time', remembers Nicholson, 'and we sought each other out, marching together at Prides, in community organising and in expressing our gender diversity in our arts activism'.

Between 2006 and 2012, Transfabulous events were curated to challenge the gender binary and included nightclub parties, fundraising performance evenings and picnics, as well as three International Festivals of Transgender Arts. Their radical brand of performance activism opened up to audiences different ways of thinking about bodies and offered the support of a community they might not have known was already there. Nicholson recalls, for example, that the 'FtM Full Monty was a riotous tongue in cheek moment in trans performance history'. Writer and filmmaker Juliet Jacques recalls a performance of 'Barker's Menstrual Cycle, in which he came onstage riding a bike and dressed as a giant uterus, talking about wanting to have children as a trans man and so stopping his testosterone intake, and the social and physical complexities that ensued'. Jacques immediately knew that 'I was in a space where no discussion of our bodies and the struggles that came with them was off-limits'.

TRANSFABULOUS POSTER DESIGNED BY JASON BARKER, 2011.

A Night of Tall Women and Short Men

a party for all trans-people, families+friends, DJs, comedy, cakes, and the FTM FULL MONTY TROUPE!!! all proceeds to TRANSFABULOUS our forthcoming Trans Arts Festival

www.transfabulous.co.uk

Saturday 2nd of July - Pride Night!
The Pleasure Unit, 359 Bethnal Green Rd
8 - 2am. £5 entry with flyer

JASON DONE THIS!

2: SOCIALISING AND SEX | 85

OUT ALL NIGHT IN...

KREMLIN NIGHTCLUB, BELFAST.

BELFAST

In March 1999, a year after the Good Friday Agreement signalled the end of the Troubles, Kremlin opened its doors. An extensive Soviet-themed nightclub in Upper Donegall Street, it has been at the centre of Belfast's burgeoning queer quarter and is still the city's most prominent LGBTIQ+ venue to this day.

Andy Malone is a TV and documentary producer.

BRIGHTON

'My experience was that there was usually one place that you could go where you could mix with other women. And occasionally, that would shut down and you might be without somewhere for a while. But after the Longbranch, there was Caves, which was in Sillwood Street. You actually had to go down the stairs into the basement, the archetypal gay club thing. But inside, it was all dark like a cave. It had these white stippled walls, and you felt like you were underwater. I remember the first time I went there, very young and naive. You had to sign in, and I signed in with my real name. And I was in teaching at the time, and somebody said: 'you know the police will get to see those books'. And I thought: 'Oh, God! I'll be outed at work' ... this was '84, '85, that sort of time.'

Jill, Brighton Group interview for Queer Beyond London (2017)

MANCHESTER

'There were a few other venues we could go to as trans people [in the 1970s]. One, surprisingly, was the Millionaire's Club. You could get a membership card, and they seemed very laid-back. And another one I joined, which happened a little bit later, was the casino. And not because I wanted to gamble, but because you could go along in your car, and they'd park your car for you and look after it. And you could buy a reasonably priced meal and watch everybody gambling and then go into the city, go clubbing or round the pubs. And when you came back, they got your car for you, and you went off home. And it cost nothing for the membership. That was a wonderful way to feel safe. wish they had that now.'

Jenny-Anne, Manchester Group interview for Queer Beyond London (2017)

SHEFFIELD

'Sheffield, which I didn't know terribly well, but certainly in the mid-seventies, the gay scene, lesbian scene, was much more integrated. The men had their own, the girls had their own pubs. But every month, at Sheffield City Hall, there was a gay disco. And the integration between the women and the men, it was fantastic. There was the odd scuffle. Usually, a well-oiled dyke could take exception to what some femme queen had said. But it was fantastic interaction.'

Roy, Leeds Group interview for Queer Beyond London (2017)

PLYMOUTH

'There used to be sort of special nights, women's disco nights, I can remember them being held in various places. One was the Crown out at Devonport. It used to be right at the very top. It was always kind of felt you were way out of the way. [*laughs*] But that at least happened on Fridays and possibly Saturdays. It was good for the weekend. But above Burton's used to be Speakeasy, on a Monday. A Monday was for lesbians … They didn't always last for a long time. The Crown did. It lasted for quite a while. But they kept closing down. Sometimes it was once a month, sometimes it was weekly. As I said, there was the Swallow. For women, there was the Penrose pub, which was actually run by parents of a lesbian, which was great actually. The reason I say this is it just gave a place for lesbians.'

Joanna, Plymouth Group interview for Queer Beyond London (2017)

BIRMINGHAM

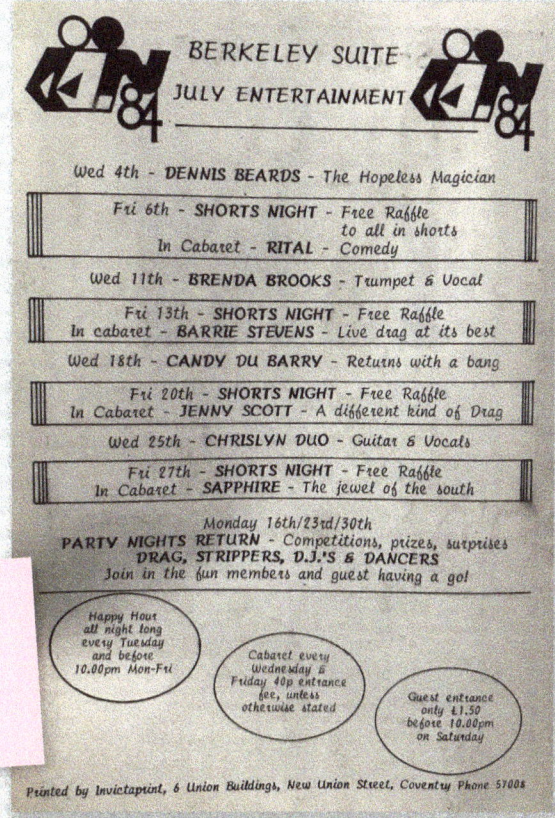

Birmingham Gay Festival programme in *Voice Magazine*, August 1984.

SAFARI NIGHTS AND BARN DELIGHTS

By Alf Le Flohic

SAFARI BAR

THE SAFARI BAR only existed for about nine months, perhaps a year, but it must be one of the most unlikely places for a gay venue. In 1983 a bunch of gay mates, who DJed in their spare time, approached the manager of Zootopia about running the café as a gay bar three nights a week. Zootopia was actually a small zoo in the corner of Hotham Park in Bognor Regis. Amazingly he agreed, and the Safari Bar was born.

Barrie Appleyard was one of the DJs and was responsible for the safari theme. He covered the bar, the stools and even the till in faux fur fabric, lined the walls in bamboo and draped flower leis around the bar area. To continue the jungle theme the ceiling of the function room was covered in bits of artificial Christmas trees. As Barrie recalls, 'During the daytime it was a cafeteria. The bar was gay on Wednesday, Friday and Saturday nights. We'd have the disco and we'd be playing all the latest Hi-NRG stuff.'

Wednesdays were 'Movie Nite', which Barrie confessed was often gay men's porn. Also on site were a couple of empty caravans that were used by the male patrons of the bar for a little sexy time. According to Barrie, 'In the dark you could walk into the zoo. Right underneath, dug into the ground, you had little animatronics like the Dwarves' Diamond Mine. You'd go down there for a bit of how's ya father as well.' Despite the porn and play, the Safari Bar proved to be popular with the local lesbians too, so the first Saturday of the month was a Girls-Only Nite.

↑ Safari Bar flyer, designed by Barrie Appleyard and Ian Harding, 1983.

The second Saturday was Cabaret Nite, and the drag performers Rebel Rebel still remember their appearance: 'The venue stuck in my mind - how could it not? It was weird as fuck, so tacky and camp. Jesus, I remember the smell of the place. That bloody parrot we had to walk by, having to say "Hello Captain" each time. If we didn't, it would proper go off.'

It may not have lasted long, but for that one summer Bognor was offering something entirely unique thanks to Barrie and his pals!

HAZELPITS, THE MAGIC FARM

Hazelpits was not your average farm, and Tim Day was definitely not your average farmer.

Tim began having private parties at his fruit farm in the village of Headcorn in Kent in the mid-1970s. He was also a regular at discos organised by the Medway Area Gay Independent Community, aka MAGIC, and he agreed to host a bigger event for them at his farm. The group's logo was designed by Chris Taylor, who said it once got them thrown out of a hotel when the owners realised that they weren't a real magic group!

MAGIC LOGO, DESIGNED BY CHRIS TAYLOR, 1977.

The MAGIC discos at Hazelpits began around 1978 with an empty barn for dancing, music from local DJs and alcohol supplied by the City Arms in Rochester. Peter, an early attendee, remembers them well: 'It was a Jacobean farmhouse. It had an RHS [Royal Horticultural Society] garden. Quite amazing to think down on the Weald of Kent you had hundreds of queens dancing and roaming about.'

There were limited places for a gay crowd to party at that time, especially in the countryside, so everyone turned up for some fun. Its popularity grew over the years, partly due to the Dutch barn stacked with hay, and the fields around the farm, as these became discreet locations in which amorous gentlemen could rendezvous undisturbed.

As the early 1980s progressed the music changed to Hi-NRG, and the numbers attending went higher too. When *Gay News* visited in 1984, it estimated around four hundred people were present. The villagers must have been aware of the parties but possibly not their nature, until one year a coach broke down and about thirty scantily clad leather queens had to push it through the village to the farm.

The parties stopped a year or so later, undoubtedly affected by the impact of HIV/AIDS on gay life. Sadly, Tim was no exception and died in his boyfriend's arms in 1991, aged forty-six. Maybe it was the dark times that ensued in the 1980s and 1990s that caused the queer joy of Hazelpits to slip from consciousness, until now.

⬇ Tim Day and John Bruce at Hazelpits Farm, *c*.1978.

Alf Le Flohic is a Brighton activist and queer community historian. These stories and others can be found in his book The Magic Farm and Other Queer Tales *(Colossive Press, 2014).*

MEN OF VICE ... IN AN A4 LAYBY

IN JULY 1983, the *Bristol Evening Post* reported that a Shirehampton picnic spot had been turned into a 'den of vice'. The report alleged that the wood was the site of organised male prostitution. Councillor George Moore, quoted in the article, had taken it upon himself to investigate the scene of the alleged crime, and had found several couples kissing and holding hands. 'There seemed to be more serious sexual activity going on in the woods, but quite honestly I did not like to go there', he said.

In an oral history extract, Charlie Beaton describes the story from the point of view of the local gay community, for whom this was a convenient and popular cruising spot. A group of friends organised a 'men of vice' picnic in protest, but the layby was closed to the public shortly afterwards.

A FLYER FOR THE PORTWAY PICNIC, HELD ON 7 AUGUST 1983.

'The local councillor in Shirehampton was concerned that men were having sex in the bushes in a layby on I think it's the A4. It's now closed, but then it was a little site run by the National Trust between the main road and the railway and the river. And it was quite a nice little woodland, and a very convenient place to go and have sex, 'cos there was always plenty of men there [*laughs*]. But the *Evening Post* decided, as a response to this councillor, to do an exposé. So, they published this thing in the *Evening Post* about 'men of vice', was their headline, saying how awful it was, all these men hanging out there. So, the following weekend, we went and had a picnic there, with a banner with 'men of vice' ... But it was, that was quite good fun. So then, I can't remember, I wasn't doing the publicity stuff, but some-

90 | A QUEER SCRAPBOOK

body must have then sent stuff to the *Evening Post*, saying that we'd had our men of vice picnic.

Interviewer: And how did the picnic go?

[laughs] Well, the photograph, most people have, have taken their shirts off, so it must have been a warm day. [laughs]

Interviewer: And did that deter, did that put an end to the use of that site, or?

I don't think... we'd have to go and look at the council's records to find out. It was actually then closed – they closed the lay-by, and I'm not sure that that was the reason. There was a public toilet there as well. It was very convenient, actually, for anybody travelling, to stop there, stretch your legs, use the toilet. But the concern was that there would be family groups stopping there, and then if they wandered into the bushes, they'd find actually that there were [laughs], that there was things they weren't expecting going on in the bushes. So, the authorities decided to close it completely, they closed the lay-by completely. It was a shame! I mean all they needed to do was to put a sign up saying 'Men only beyond this point' or something like that.

Interviewer: [laughs] That's true.'

Charlie Beaton interviewed by OutStories Bristol (2012): www.outstoriesbristol.org.uk

EVENING POST

No. 15,505—14p Saturday, July 9, 1983

The paper all Bristol asked for and helped to create

OUTCRY OVER MEN OF VICE

Picnic site sex scandal

A FAMILY picnic spot by the Avon is being turned into a den of vice, it was said today.

Male prostitutes have been seen operating in Crabtree Slip Wood, just off the Portway.

Avon councillor Mr George Moore has demanded tough police action to stamp out the problem.

When Councillor Moore investigated the area, he found several homosexual couples kissing and holding hands.

'There seemed to be more serious sexual activity going on in the woods, but quite honestly I did not like to go there,' he said.

'They had two or three men who seemed to be lookouts posted by the lay-by on Portway. It was well organised male prostitution.'

Councillor Moore took the numbers of nine cars which arrived at the lay-by within ten minutes. Men from the cars went into the woods. He passed the numbers on to the police.

ACTION

Bristol city councillor Mr Peter Abraham, who has also received complaints, said: 'One woman was walking with her daughter when they were confronted by two men in a full sex act.'

Local resident Mrs Sarah Prosser said: 'It's supposed to be a family picnic area, but no one goes there because of these men.'

Superintendent Ian Tweedie, of Southmead police, said today: 'We are aware of the problem and the social hazard it creates. Regular attention is being paid and positive action has been taken.

'We will continue to take this action until the problem is resolved.'

Some men have already been arrested for alleged sex offences in the area of the picnic site and toilets.

Barbara Webb, 'Picnic site sex scandal', **Evening Post,** *9 July 1983*

SEX AND THE CITY

MY GOOD FRIENDS from Gay Left, Nigel Young and Derek Cohen, were into leather, S&M and bikes much more than I was, but I was happy for them to take me to the Motorbike Show at the Earl's Court Exhibition Centre in August 1980. Beforehand, we stopped off at this fetish/leather shop at 267 Old Brompton Road. It was just a few doors from the infamous Coleherne pub, where we all had spent many an evening and late-night drinking and carousing until closing time. Then afterwards we'd head for a little cruise around the block or into Brompton Cemetery to see what was up. Risky and thrilling at the same time. [See photo on p. 53]

Gregg Blachford has collected and archived more than fifty years of gay life across the UK, Canada and beyond at www.greggblachford.com.

Chain Reaction was the UK's first lesbian SM club, self-described as a space 'For proud perverts of female sex. Made in the name of arts, porn and S-M'. Founded in 1987, Chain Reaction marked the beginnings of explicitly sexualised lesbian spaces appearing on London's lesbian scene. Taking over the Market Tavern (a gay male club in Vauxhall) on Tuesday nights, Chain Reaction provided a space for LGBTIQ+ women to explore their sexual desires, fantasies and fetishes. The proud SM dykes who patronised the club made up one side of the infamous lesbian sex wars, coming under attack by the lesbian feminists of the opposition who objected to a range of lesbian sexuality and sexual practice that they deemed 'patriarchal'. Chain Reaction bore witness to the 'battles' of the sex wars, with the club being picketed, and on one occasion invaded and vandalised, by a group of lesbian feminists.

Beth Charlton holds a PhD from UCL on London's lesbian spaces.

Justin writes...

Between 1996 and 2000, the private sex parties of the Black Perverts Network responded to the exclusion and marginalisation of queer Black and Asian men and their desires from overwhelmingly white mainstream gay spaces. The Black Perverts Network's invitation-only parties at the Brixton home of photographer and archivist Ajamu X were safe and affirming places to explore desires, kink and fetish.

The Tumulus is a place in one of the meadows on Hampstead Heath enclosed by a circular fence. Its history much debated - burial ground of Boadicea or a rubbish dump. To enter you have to jump the wrought iron fence (there is no gate) and on top of the mound is a small clearing circled by trees hidden from public view. This is a future historical LGBTQ place as I will, in the not too distant future on a warm summer's evening when the Heath is becoming quiet and dusk is looming, jump the fence with my partner and spend an hour or two exploring each other's bodies as the day moves into night.

TUMULUS, HAMPSTEAD HEATH, LONDON.

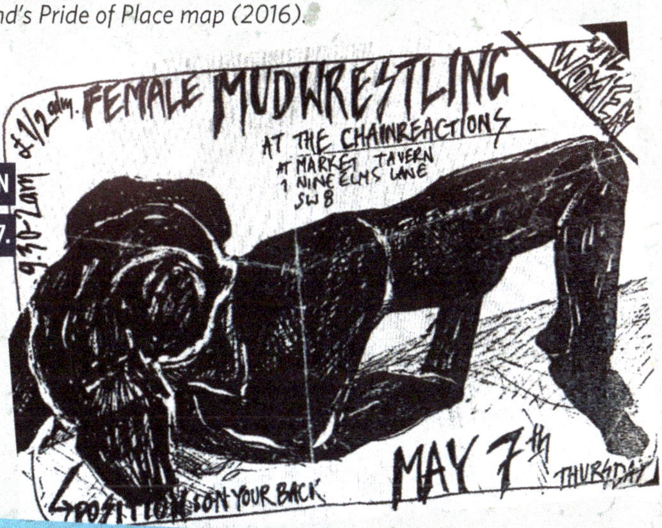

Submission to Historic England's Pride of Place map (2016).

A POSTER FOR A CHAIN REACTION EVENT, 1987.

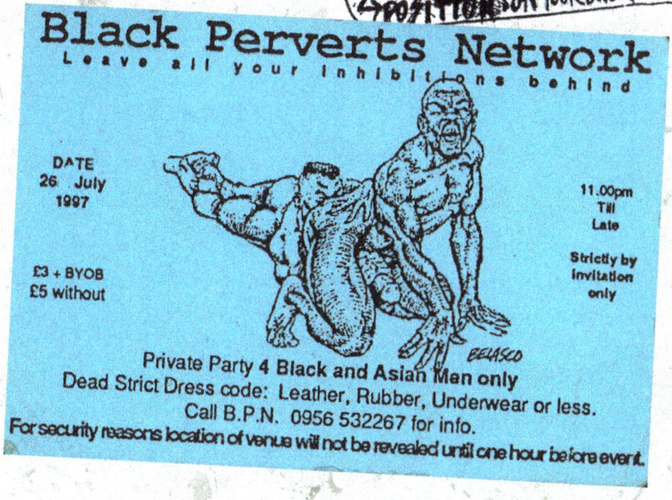

← An invitation to a Black Perverts Network gathering in 1997, featuring an illustration by James Belasco.

THRILLING BITS:
ADVENTURES IN LESBIAN SEX

IN THE LATE 1980s, Lisa Power and her girlfriend began the UK's first lesbian mail-order sex toy company, Thrilling Bits. Based in London, they sent merchandise around the country, bringing their products to places where they wouldn't otherwise be available. The folded pages of pink A3 that comprised the catalogue illuminate a network of consumers, lesbian entrepreneurs and readers who sought the products in the catalogue as well as the opportunity to meet each other through its contact ads. The second catalogue (1988/89) and its 'stone faces' Russian-style logo played with the imagery of Soviet kitsch, popular at the time, while also poking fun at Russian homophobia. The text roughly translates to 'Lesbians are cool'. But despite the playfulness throughout the catalogue, there was a serious side as well. The 'Lesbian S/M Safety Manual' was a staple product in Thrilling Bits, and the second catalogue likewise featured a lesbian dental dam for sale during the height of concern and fear around HIV/AIDS, discussed further by Power below:

'[Thrilling Bits] was part of the rumbling end of the S&M debates and the lesbian sex wars and stuff and we were pro-sex but we weren't S&M or anything like that. But there were no decent sex toys ... we started to do this mail order business which was hilarious because we kept very anonymous who was doing it to start with and we had enough contacts in the lesbian and gay press to be able to get stuff out without it being obviously us. ... But we just felt that it should not be silenced, and women shouldn't be shamed for anything they wanted to do sexually that didn't hurt someone else. ...

I remember going up to the main place in England that sold wholesale sex toys, this giant warehouse in Coleshill which sold to Ann Summers and everybody else, going up there and trying to explain to them that some of the stuff that they were selling just didn't fit women's anatomy – it fitted what men thought women's anatomy was. And also the quality of the goods wasn't very good ... they had quite poor motors in them and if you had strong vaginal muscles when you orgasmed you gripped this thing and the motor couldn't work. And it would rev furiously and then break and then smoke would issue from your vagina and we had a number of complaints of this. We had to stop selling them because it was kind of scary. ...

I remember when we had our first batch of dental dams and the other people who were helping to start Stonewall would talk about it occasionally ... and we were having a meeting in my living room about something. And we brought these dental dams out to show these guys. Dental dams were a load of old rubbish frankly. ... Latex, and the idea was that you held it over a woman's vulva and licked. It was basically supposed to be condoms for lesbians except they were thicker than a condom and frankly if sex was any good at all you forget which side was which within five minutes. So, they didn't actually bear the slightest use at all. But they sold terribly well. But I remember bringing these things out and lifting one and it sort of went round the group of people who sat on the sofas and chairs and holding it by one corner and handing it to another man who'd hold it by one corner who'd hand it to someone else who'd hold it by one corner. It got to Ian McKellen and Ian seized it by both hands and went, 'What are you meant to do with it? Is it this?', and shoved it over his face and stuck his tongue through ... 'Is that what it was meant do?' Love you, Ian.

Interview with Lisa Power by Evelyn Pitman, 31 July 2019, From a Whisper to a Roar project, Bishopsgate Institute Archives

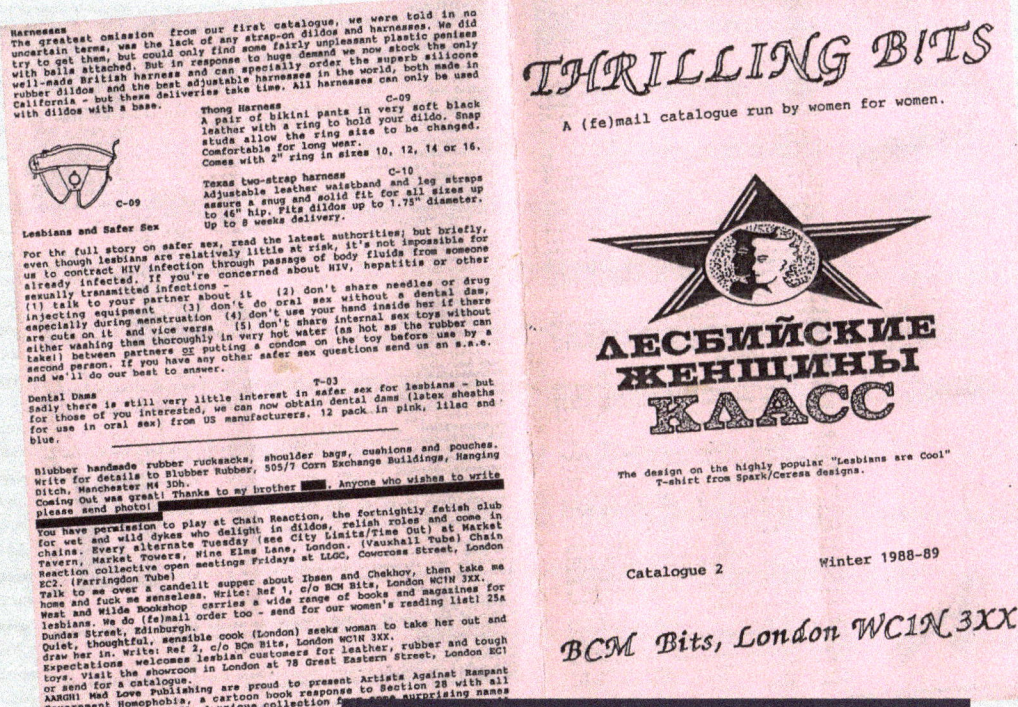

THE SECOND *THRILLING BITS* CATALOGUE, WINTER 1988/89.

AGAINST THE LAW: SEX AND ACTIVISM

IN 1998, A GROUP of men in Bolton who came to be known as the 'Bolton 7' were convicted for acts of buggery and gross indecency after a videotape of their private sexual activities came to the attention of police. Even though the Sexual Offences Act 1967 had partially decriminalised sex between men, the act's definition of 'private' limited sex to two people. Further, while the heterosexual age of consent had long been set at sixteen, consent for sex between men had only been reduced from twenty-one to eighteen in 1994, and one of the Bolton 7 was seventeen years old when the video was made. Campaigns in their defence highlighted the homophobia embedded in the law, and the case was eventually taken to the European Court of Human Rights. In 2001 the Home Office settled out of court.

While laws that specifically target homosexual offences have largely been removed, and the age of consent was equalised at sixteen in 2003 in England and Wales, many men who were convicted in the past continue to hold criminal records for offences that are no longer considered crimes in the UK. Since 2012, anyone convicted of homosexual offences that have been abolished has been able to apply to the Home Office for a disregard, effectively erasing all record of the crime having ever happened. But the low application rate and the fact that some consensual adult offences remain outside the scheme mean many victims of the UK's homophobic laws remain criminalised.

Defend the Bolton 7, Bolton 7 Defence Campaign flyer, Manchester, 1998.

SEXUAL HEALTH

'WRAP IT UP' STICKERS CREATED BY ALF LE FLOHIC, EARLY 1990S.

SEXUAL HEALTH initiatives from national and local organisations, community initiatives, activists and artists have all used art and creative expression in their work. In the early 1990s, for example, Alf Le Flohic created 'Wrap it up' stickers that he and Harry Hillery stuck to cash machines around Brighton to promote safer sex. More recently, the charity NAZ, which delivers culturally specific sexual health services to Black, Asian and minority ethnic communities in London, partnered up with the Leeds-based MESMAC sexual health organisation on the Sholay Love campaign. Evocative and powerful art posters and other outreach materials sought to raise awareness around HIV testing and to improve knowledge around sexual health among South Asian men who have sex with men. And across the Pennines in Manchester, the Young Lesbian and Bisexual Women's Peer Education Health Project used playful imagery for its campaign LIK:T, directed at lesbian and bisexual youth.

↑ Guide to Wellness poster produced for the LIK:T campaign, Manchester, 2004.

SHOLAY LOVE CAMPAIGN POSTER.

STAYING IN:
TESTIMONY FROM THE QUEER PANDEMIC

BETWEEN 2021 AND 2023 Justin Bengry and Molly Merryman led the Queer Pandemic Project, which undertook fifty interviews with LGBTIQ+ people across the UK about their unique experiences of the COVID-19 pandemic. These are some of their stories.

'I worked in a printer and there wasn't any printing to do. I just needed to be there, essentially, and then that prompted me to think, "I don't really want to do this job. It's not fulfilling, I'm not helping anyone." And seeing how the NHS and care workers and support workers were working through the whole virus to help people, I thought, "I kind of want to go into that as like a daytime job." So that prompted a big career change, so a month ago I started a job as a support worker, and it's been really fulfilling to support the people but I'm also, in a way, there to be their friend.'

Jason, Banbury

'So, we're a household of two. And as we don't have any children ... the lockdown meant that we were locked down together as a couple, so we had different experiences to those people who have families, not necessarily worse, but just different. ... I know people who've said that when the lockdown happened, they had to really go back in the closet because then they were living at home, working at home, and if their parents weren't aware of their sexuality or gender identity, then they were kind of trapped in their home environment all the time. But luckily for us, because we're both out and living comfortably in that way, it didn't really have an impact through that.'

Kuljit, Southampton

'Basically, the problem was I was not touched at the beginning of the pandemic for three months. ... I love to be by myself, but I do also have a need to be touched ... I started getting almost like cold turkey, like, drug withdrawal. And I started having night sweats, I started having the shakes, I started having kind of, like, slurred speech and brain fog and – and, you know, part of me was thinking, is this the stress of the pandemic? But this seems much more like – it was more like a physiological need. ... I was looking at all these reports about skin hunger and basically that's what I was suffering from. I was suffering from skin hunger and – and this is something that I am sure many people of the LGBTQ community who live alone were also suffering from.'

Lalith, London

'What [the pandemic] highlighted for me was the whole thing about living alone. My previous relationship ended ... so in some ways, I was still adjusting to the fact that I was going to be living alone ... But I do think the actual pandemic meant for me personally, I'm sure for lots of other people, that I really had to reflect on my life, particularly as a single person, but in terms of my relationships with other people, who was important to me ... I do feel I've maintained those relationships. Interestingly, I also started to walk with a wider group of people. I don't mean altogether, but you know, a wider range of people. ... So in actual fact, in some ways I spent more time with people than I probably did before pandemic.'

Alison, Leicester

BRIGHTON SCENE AND CLUB ADVERTS.

CONCLUSION

THE WAYS IN WHICH LGBTIQ+ people build community and find others have been central to our history and the record we create to show we were, and are, here. Our strategies in doing so might be tentative, cautious and discreet, like the small ads or pen club that started this section. Or they might be assertive and blunt, as in the proudly defiant invitations created for the Black Perverts Network. Building and supporting our community can be overtly political, as in Belfast where some of Cara-Friend's founders and early volunteers still faced the dangers of state criminalisation. So often, our strategies to come together are also creative and, well, queer, like the gay nightclub in the Bognor Regis zoo! Over and over again, however, from the Sholay Love sexual health posters to event flyers, like those of the Chain Reaction lesbian club or Brixton Fairies Halloween Dance, we see that socialising and sex cannot be disentangled from arts and culture, the focus of the *Queer Scrapbook*'s next section.

⬇ A ticket to the Brixton Fairies' Halloween Dance, London, ?1982.

SECTION 3:
ARTS AND CULTURE
Curated by Matt Cook and Jaya Rathbone

THERE WASN'T much to anchor me, growing up gay in a Staffordshire village in the 1970s and 1980s. What there was came through film. I watched the adaptation of E. M. Forster's novel *Maurice* and the biopic of playwright Joe Orton, *Prick Up My Ears*, months apart in 1987. For the first I was with my mum and dad in our local cinema in Burton-on-Trent, covered with embarrassment. I went on my own to the second when I was staying with my brother in London. Emerging onto the Holloway Road afterwards, There was a thrill in realising how close I was to some of the scenes of Orton's sexual adventuring, but, as a nervy and nerdy eighteen-year-old, I swerved back to the surety of my brother's flat.

Orton's 1960s offered a glut of urban sex; Maurice and Scudder's more rural affair and escape was just about watchable with my parents. I was drawn by the irreverence of the one and the earnestness and safety of the other. These first viewings sparked a sense of possibility for me, partly because their rendition of the past suggested a deeper cultural and historical anchorage to the identity I was beginning to own. A year later, studying English and drama at university in Sheffield, I didn't manage to join Gaysoc, but I did daringly (for me) write an essay on two gay plays I'd just seen: Martin Sherman's *Bent*, which unfolded the horrors of the Holocaust for men badged with a pink triangle, and Gay Sweatshop's production of Noël Greig's *The Dear Love of Comrades* (1979), which explored the intersecting desires and politics of romantic socialist – and friend of Forster – Edward Carpenter (1844-1929).

I saw the latter at the Leadmill, a then partially council-funded venue in Sheffield, and was compelled by the sense of coming together with other men (mostly) to consume 'our' history and 'our' culture – in this instance a play by a Sheffield-based playwright about a man who had lived just outside the city with his lover. There was something groundbreaking about seeing *Bent* that same year: a West End production of a 'gay' play by an early Gay Sweatshop playwright and with soap star Michael Cashman in the lead opposite theatre legend Ian McKellen. Together they reminded the mixed audience of the horror of Nazi erasure and more tacitly of contemporary moves to silence gay men and lesbians in the context of the AIDS crisis and Section 28, which had just landed on the statute books and banned the 'promotion' of homosexuality by local authorities – including in council-funded libraries, museums and arts spaces.

Arts and culture, in short, mattered to my evolving sense of self: here was a way of envisaging identities, communities, desire, sex, comradeship and politics, of conjuring pasts overlooked in most history books, and of imagining a future. As I moved from Staffordshire to Sheffield and on to London, and visited other places across the British and Irish Isles, I was always drawn to the arts and their confirmation of a world often beyond my experience. They provided me and countless others with some precious validation and a way of communicating. No wonder that the arts became a way, in the 1960s, of pressing for reform, in the 1970s of becoming visible, and in the febrile 1980s and 1990s of fighting back. No wonder, too, that there was pushback from the confused, sceptical and outraged – as we'll see!

Matt Cook

This section has spreads on 'Art, Craft and Design', 'Music and Dance', 'Theatre and Performance', 'Film', 'Literature, Books and Bookshops' and 'History and Heritage'.

Matt Cook, *c.*1976.

ARTS, CRAFTS AND DESIGN

ART AND QUEER COMMUNITY IN KENT

By Clare Barlow

THE ARTIST Tony Atwood died in 1961, the last member of a ménage à trois that began in 1916 when Tony was invited to be a part of Edy Craig's household in Smallhythe Place, Kent. Here, Tony joined Edy and her partner, Chris St John, in what was known as the Priest's House, a few hundred metres away from the main house, occupied by Edy's mother, the actress Ellen Terry. Edy's invitation to Tony came with the caveat that 'if Chris does not like your being here, and feels you are interfering with our friendship, out you go!' But Tony fitted in well and gained a reputation as the peacemaker, despite having a nickname among the trio as 'the Brat'.

Their relationship and identities, like that of their friends and distant neighbours Una Troubridge and Radclyffe Hall, blurred the boundaries of gender and sexuality. Unlike Hall, none of them predominantly wore masculine dress, preferring loose smocks, and it is hard to know what pronouns each would have preferred, if more options had been commonly available. Chris had renamed themself Christopher Marie St John and described themself as being 'very glad I am one of those who easily forget what manner of man and woman I am', suggesting a non-binary identity. Atwood went by both Tony and Clare but was referred to as Tony by friends, while Edy's identity appears to have been seen as more feminine, causing Una Troubridge to refer to the trio as Edy Craig and 'the Boys'.

As with most historical queer couples – and most historical straight couples – there is no surviving document proving beyond any doubt that their relationships were sexual, but the evidence of their love is overwhelming. When Chris first met Edy, Edy was mending a mitten and inadvertently pricked Chris's finger with the needle. Chris later described this as 'Cupid's dart, for I loved Edy from that moment'.* Vita Sackville-West, with whom Chris had a brief affair, described Edy to a friend as 'the most tearing old Lesbian – not unlike your friend Radclyffe Hall – but without any charms for me, I hasten to add'.**

Smallhythe, then, was the setting for a radical experiment in queer love and community that is commemorated in Tony's intimate depictions. Tony trained in London at the Slade and exhibited at the

* Christopher St John, 'Close-up', in Edy: Reflections of Edith Craig, ed. Eleanor Adlard (Frederick Muller, 1949), p. 19.

** Victoria Glendinning, Vita: The life of Vita Sackville-West (Penguin, 1984), pp. 250-1.

New English Art Club and later the Royal Academy. In contrast to these public paintings, the Smallhythe works are deeply personal, capturing the daily life of the trio.

One image depicts the theatre they created in a converted barn: Edy sewing costumes, accompanied by friends Irene Cooper Willis and Charles Straite. Edy, Chris and Tony started this theatre after Ellen Terry's death as a memorial and staged dramas and pageants there, many of which promoted women's rights. This was a lifelong passion of Edy and Chris, whose house in Bedford Square had been a safe-house for suffragettes on the run from the police. Another image shows Edy reading in bed, covered in papers and holding a cat: a matter-of-fact image of an ageing partner and beloved pet.

These small domestic works provide intimate testimony of the fabric of lives lived lovingly together. And testimony of this kind is

← Interior of the Barn Theatre, Smallhythe Place, Kent, with Edith Craig (sitting), by Tony Atwood, 1939.

EDITH CRAIG, BY TONY ATWOOD, 1943.

important, for without it, it is easy for the queer past to seem like a history of nothing but grim persecution. Edy, Chris and Tony lived in a time when there was little positive public representation of people who might now identify as LGBT or Q. Sex between men was illegal until 1967, and their friend Radclyffe Hall's novel *The Well of Loneliness* had been prosecuted in 1928 for obscenity. Yet in Tony's unselfconscious depictions of their lives, Smallhythe becomes a kind of queer utopia: a place where queer people could come together, share their activism and love one another. Such art is quietly radical and deeply sustaining.

Clare Barlow is Director of People's History Museum, Manchester. Her previous projects include curating the major exhibition Queer British Art, 1861–1967 *at Tate Britain and* Being Human *at Wellcome Collection.*

106 | A QUEER SCRAPBOOK

ST IVES, CORNWALL: 16 AUGUST 1976

By Ian Massey

THE PHOTO BELOW is of me aged twenty, in the garden of the Barbara Hepworth Museum, St Ives, Cornwall. There for a short family holiday, it was my first visit to St Ives and, magnetised by the place, I've been returning ever since. In fact, as my sister (who took the photograph) has always said, that introduction to St Ives had a transformative effect on my life. It was certainly the reason I ended up studying art in the south-west and went on to research many of the St Ives artists, whose work continues to fascinate me.

For me at the age of twenty, the idea of sexuality was akin to a foreign country. It was only when I got to art college, two years or so after this photograph was taken, that I began tentatively to explore physical intimacy. While art college was liberating in many ways, it did not preclude being subjected to homophobia. This, notwithstanding the fact that some of the key artists of the period – Hockney and Warhol, for instance – were themselves outwardly queer.

IAN MASSEY AT THE BARBARA HEPWORTH MUSEUM, ST IVES, 1976.

To return to St Ives: it was through my great interest in Hepworth that I discovered the sculptor John Milne (1931–78), who was, like me, a gay working-class lad from the north-west of England. Milne worked as Hepworth's assistant in the early 1950s and from 1956 lived at Trewyn, a large house surrounded by high granite walls, situated immediately behind her garden. And in researching him and his circle I began to discover a previously undocumented queer history of St Ives, one that is integral to the story of twentieth-century modernism. This history is central to my book *Queer St Ives and Other Stories* (2022).

Dr Ian Massey is an independent art historian and curator. His publications include a monograph biography of the artist Patrick Procktor and a co-authored catalogue raisonné of paintings by Keith Vaughan. He is now writing a book about the artist Mark Lancaster while also working on a major show at Tate St Ives.

The cover of Ian's book features this image from 1959 of sculptor John Milne and his friend Julian Nixon, looking over St Ives from the garden at Trewyn. Nixon had earlier spent a year in a psychiatric hospital, a condition of his sentence for committing 'acts gross indecency' with other men in 1954.

Knitting pattern sold in aid of Leeds Lesbian Line, c.1988. See over for the finished product!

STOLEN GLANCES – THE EXHIBITION

Stolen Glances listed in this issue will take the form of an exhibition of the work by ten women photographers from Britain and North America, to challenge the heterosexual orientation of conventional romantic and erotic imagery. 'Stolen Glances' will open at the Stills Gallery during the Edinburgh International Festival from 10 August to 14 September, and will then show at Cambridge Darkroom before touring the UK and North America. A conference is to be organised for Sunday 1 September which will explore the issues raised by the exhibition.

The Lesbian Lavender List, issue 33 (1991)

Few people would think it wise that gay activities should be deliberately drawn to the attention of immature youngsters. That is why it is so worrying that schools in the Lothian Region are being invited to let pupils attend an exhibition of explicit lesbian photographs. Few parents would want their children exposed to this material at such a young and impressionable age.

'The Voice of Scotland', **Sunday Mail** *(11 August 1991)*

LESBIAN KNITS, c.1988.

FINE ART SHOCKER

I was utterly amazed at the comments of a Swindon lady about what she saw on the front page of a 'Gay' newspaper. The picture in question was of two nude females embracing and was painted in 1886 by Gustav Courbet and entitled 'Le Sommeil'. At the time it was aimed at heterosexual males rather than homosexual females. Many paintings of this nature are held in art galleries throughout the world and are considered masterpieces: so I would suggest that the unnamed lady with puritanical ideas should not set foot in an art gallery lest she suffer a coronary. Most other newsagents in town stock magazines of a similar nature on full display to the public. I haven't noticed them making front page news.

*David C. Fletcher,
Galsworthy Close, Linden*

Letter to Swindon Evening Advertiser (30 November 1979)

'*Jackie Clayton:* The idea for [Intentional Promotions] really started when I was in the Lesbian and Gay Society – it was December [1987] actually, as we first found out about Clause 28 [see page 103 for more on the Clause], and everybody, like, we just felt really shitty … we were just really isolated and lonely. And a few of us had found each other and were finally starting to feel okay, and then the clause was proposed and it just felt like the biggest blow in the world. And I remember standing up in the Gay and Lesbian Society, because we were discussing if we should do something and we didn't know what to do. And I stood up, and I remember saying, 'I want to intentionally promote homosexuality'.

I shocked myself, I shocked everybody else, I remember doing that, because it was like, 'we can't do that, that's just wrong'. But I just thought if they're accusing us of that anyway, we might as well just do it. And then the plan was to try and work out how to do it … So we all piled down [from Leeds] to London really early on a march … and we got to see some of the old GLF badges, the Gay Liberation Front stuff, and thought, 'we wanna do something'. And we knew there was a badge machine at the university, so we decided to start making big badges [for] the march against Section 28 and … [for] the university Awareness Week the week before.'

Jackie Clayton interviewed by Ray Larman for West Yorkshire Queer Stories (2019). For more: https://wyqs.co.uk

INTENTIONAL PROMOTION BADGE AND CASE.

MUSIC AND DANCE

BADGES... AND MUSIC
By Paul Furness

IN 1978 I WAS working as a medical records clerk at Leeds General Infirmary. Part of my job was to compile information on patients who had died or been discharged. I did this by reading through a patient's notes - everything was on paper back then! - and once I found the medical diagnosis, I had to tick a series of boxes on a form which 'went to Harrogate'. In order to enter the diagnosis, I had to convert it into a code that I would find in two massive books called *The International Classification of Diseases*, which was issued by the World Health Organization. One day I was going through a pile of notes when I became engrossed in those of a man in his late twenties who had died from a series of psychosomatic illnesses. The doctors had suggested to the patient that he might be gay, but he wasn't having any of it and continued to attract the illnesses which eventually took his life. His cause of death was diagnosed as 'homosexuality'. When I looked it up in the books, there it was - 302.0.

I was a twenty-year-old kid from Seacroft who had just come out - in the Fforde Grene pub [in the Harehills area of Leeds] of all places! - and I couldn't believe that being gay was considered a medical illness. I was also involved in Rock Against Racism at this time, through which I became friends with the singer Tom Robinson. I had access to an odd little machine, a bit like one of those old credit card machines, which made name badges for NHS staff. It was a plastic badge with room for an embossed strip of plastic with your name on it, so I made two of these which said '302.0'. I kept one and the other I gave to Tom. Tom was incensed by what I told him. He wore the badge on stage, signed his autographs as 302.0 and, when he introduced the song 'Glad to be Gay', he always told his audience that it was about people medically classified as 302.0 and pointed at the badge he was wearing. This must have been about the start of 1978, because when his 'Rising Free' EP came out later that year, it had 'Glad to be Gay' on it and, around the edges of the record sleeve, it had the Gay Switchboard phone number - and 302.0.

Sometime later, the Tom Robinson Band were playing a gig in Chicago when a fan threw six or seven T-shirts on the stage that had

302.0 in big numbers across the front. Tom then sent a postcard to my home in Seacroft telling me about this and saying 'What in the world have you started, Paul?' Then I got on with my life and forgot all about it. Always kept the badge, though, and I always remember the story of the man who died from 'homosexuality'. Years later discovered that a big campaign was waged against it internationally in 1990, and the World Health Organization eventually removed being gay from its *International Classification of Diseases*. Thanks to this campaign, the 'illness' and the code 302.0 no longer exists, and this story has a link to Leeds!

Paul Furness is a Yorkshireman and lifelong socialist.

302	Sexual deviation
302.0	Homosexuality
302.1	Fetishism
302.2	Paedophilia
302.3	Transvestitism
302.4	Exhibitionism
302.5	Voyeurism
302.6	Sadism
302.7	Masochism
302.8	Other
302.9	Unspecified

302.0 Diagnostic coding as reproduced on Tom Robinson's 'Rising Free' record sleeve

JAZZ IN CARDIFF'S TIGER BAY

By Idroma Montgomery

LILIAN JEMMOTT, who died in 1976 in Cardiff, was a Black Welsh jazz musician from the city's Tiger Bay area. Born in 1909 to a white Welsh mother and Black Barbadian father, she was raised above the family restaurant on Bute Street, in a lodging house that also provided temporary accommodation to Black seafarers. In the surrounding streets were sailors, labourers and families from British colonies across Africa, Asia and the Caribbean, as well as European immigrants, and it was in this multicultural entertainment district that she learned music and began performing.

While she likely only played church and school dances as a teenager, she would have been aware of the more raucous Tiger Bay venues, including brothels and bars frequented by sailors and sex workers, where other Black Welsh musicians performed. These musicians, with Lilian, were subsequently part of the transformation of the London jazz scene in the 1930s. She moved to the English capital in 1929 and from there toured Britain and the Netherlands with all-Black bands. She was now using the racially charged name Spadie Lee and claimed New York's Harlem as her place of origin – signalling its already mythologised cultural status. When in London, she played under the restrictions of the city's 'colour bar', which informally banned non-white people from certain pubs, clubs

Idroma Montgomery's illustration of Lilian Jemmott, based on a surviving 1930s photograph from the Netherlands.

114 | A QUEER SCRAPBOOK

← St Mary's Church on Bute Street, where Lilian likely performed as a child and where she later married.

and restaurants – except as entertainers. In Soho's more ephemeral Black clubs, she played for mixed and often partially queer audiences – sometimes in male 'drag'. She befriended queer figures such as the interior and stage designer Oliver Messel, and by the early 1950s was often at the piano in the infamous Chelsea lesbian club, the Gateways.

Lilian continued to return to Tiger Bay on tour and to visit relatives, and her short-lived marriage of 1938 was solemnised in her childhood church on Bute Street. She moved back permanently in 1961, by which time her career was in decline because of the changing post-war music scene and her own alcoholism. She spent her later years playing piano in the hotels of Tiger Bay, though by this time the area was a shadow of the bustling port and entertainment district she had known in her youth.

Idroma Montgomery holds a PhD on the lives and migrations of Black queer women in inter-war Britain and America from Birkbeck, University of London.

WOMEN'S LIBERATION ROCK IN MANCHESTER

Luchia Fitzgerald (b.1947) and Angela Cooper (b.1950) were both born in Catholic mother and baby homes – in Cork and Salford, respectively. They met in a Manchester queer pub in 1969 and together opened the city's first women's refuge, established a radical printing press and formed the Northern Women's Liberation Rock Band. They saw a real connection between music, activism and community – as is clear in these extracts from their interview with Sarah Feinstein in 2016.

The New Union was one of a small cluster of queer venues in and around Manchester's Canal Street in the 1960s. The Rembrandt Hotel (pictured here, c.1965) had a more respectable reputation than its near neighbour.

'*Luchia*: Friday, Saturday and Sunday [the New Union in Manchester's Canal Street would] had a good old cabaret. And it would be all different queens and little acts that would come on and do things. They'd ask people to get up from the floor. Very talented people that were held back in

life because they were gay. They showed off their stuff in the Union [in the early 1960s]. It was great, we saw a lot of raw talent in there. Oh, we'd dance the night away there on the floor the minute the queens got up to sing their songs, and various other things. We'd be all be up there, like you'd see in a disco today. ... You went into the Union every night and everyone was there that cared about you. [In the later 1960s] fashion changed, which was a relief for everybody ... music changed as well.

Angela: [In the 1970s] you're getting 2,000 women at a women's conference, a lot of whom would be lesbians. We were making our own networks that were away from the gay scene [in Manchester], and we started to organise our own discos, women's discos. Booking rooms above pubs, playing our own music. That's where the women's band idea came out of, we didn't want to be dancing to Brown Sugar and all of that. ... I remember we were trying to have discos where we only played women's records, which could be challenging. So we'd look and think, we're not having Marvin Gaye, but we'll have the Supremes.

In our band [the Northern Women's Liberation Rock Band] we had Maoists, we had radical feminists, which is what we'd be, Libertarians, Socialist Feminists or whatever. We had a transgender person – we were ahead of our time with that. And so we tried to represent everybody, our views. Some of the political ones were involved in strikes. So we would go and do benefits. We'd do benefits for lesbian groups, we did a benefit for *Spare Rib*, we went down to London and played down there. We played at the Styal [women's] Prison. We got in touch with them and said, would they like us to come and play? And of course they said yes. And it was quite a solitary experience in a way. We all went in in our van, yeah. It was a good atmosphere. But then, of course, we came out, and they didn't. And you sort of realised they were in there.

Luchia: My friends [at Styal] ended up waving to me from the floor, I wanted to run up when we walked in, I could hear them. I turned around and there's all the old buddies [from the Union]. The thing that really ticked me off ... when I was on that stage and I was looking at some of those women, I was thinking, they're in here because their crimes are society-driven, as one would say, you know. And that really upset me.'

Luchia Fitzgerald and Angela Cooper, interviewed by Sarah Feinstein, Manchester Digital Music Archive (2016)

THE GAY BOGIES
By Kai Bossom

THE LEGEND OF THE Gay Bogies is a tale of four gay men finding acceptance and community in a British seaside town, at a time when there was not so much of either for queer people. Hastings' Traditional Jack in the Green (JITG) is best described as a fantastical, viridescent and energetic spectacle that celebrates the release of the spirit of summer. The main procession, led by the leafy, tree-like figure of the Jack, marches through the narrow streets of Hastings Old Town every May Day. The bogies, dressed in green rags and painted faces, accompany Jack – they dance, drum and rub green paint onto the noses of onlookers. They are renowned for their fierce protectiveness of their leafy giant and their absolute willingness to accept people for who they are.

The story begins in the early 1990s, when two friends travelled from London to Hastings to lend their creative expertise to the event's preparations. Marti Dean and Simon Costin had never been to Hastings before – they were invited by a mutual friend from the town. She offered a great day out, in return for the pair's support. The two friends got more than they bargained for. Marti recalls being 'completely blown away by the friendliness, magic and the vibe' after his first JITG encounter. Back then, crowds were smaller and locals would look on with curiosity at the eccentric procession. The event's magical energy captivated Simon and Marti and ensured that they would continue to return. Joined by friends Craig Sheppard and Spencer Horne, Marti and Simon came back to Hastings year after year. The friends would perfect their extravagant bogie costumes in the early hours after long nights at the pub. According to event founder Keith Leech, when this new group appeared in their fantastic and flamboyant get-ups, someone had quipped that the group 'look so smart, they must be gay'. So the friends were dubbed 'the Gay Bogies'.

It was not long before the group learned of this and were happy to confirm that they were actually gay. The response was to be immediately embraced by the community, who chatted with them like they were old mates. According to Keith, it was 'from that point on they became and remain great friends and

GAY BOGIES SIMON COSTIN, JANE WILDGOOSE AND CRAIG SHEPPARD.

← Simon Costin and Marti Dean of the Gay Bogies, who have celebrated 'the release of the spirit of summer' in Hastings since the early 1990s.

an integral part of things'. Marti, Simon, Spencer and Craig became part of what is now 'traditional' at this annual folk festival, 'the Gay Bogies on Acid'. JITG incorporated the group into the official proceedings, and by doing so they created space for the four friends, and any other nominated Gay Bogie, to be their true selves. Decades later and you can still find the Gay Bogies among the proceedings, alongside 'Jackie and the Queens' – the first troupe representing Hastings Pride. The Gay Bogies reconfigured the LGBTIQ+ community locally and made it notably more inclusive.

Kai is a volunteer at the Hastings Queer History Collective. Their research continues to uncover hidden LGBTIQ+ histories in the seaside town and to celebrate the stories of those that came before.

WINGING IT AND SINGING IT IN YORKSHIRE

'When I left London and moved back to Yorkshire I thought the way that the trans choir [I previously attended] did it still kind of enforced a binary, because we were still using the soprano, alto, bass, tenor structure, and I was ending up still singing the more woman's parts, which I didn't want to be ... And I was talking to my friends and I was like, 'I really want there to be a trans choir [here] but I've never run choirs before [*laughs*] and I don't really know what I'm doing', and my friend was like 'just do it, no one really knows what they're doing', [*laughs*] 'just wing it'. And so I put it out there and some other people seemed to have the same idea at the same time.'

Claye interviewed by Ray Larman, West Yorkshire Queer Stories (2019)

THEATRE AND PERFORMANCE

GAY SWEATSHOP

ON TOUR/WINTER 1976

ANY WOMAN CAN by Jill Posener

Oct 15 Reading University
Oct 20-23 Derby Playhouse
Oct 25-30 Haymarket Theatre, Leicester
Nov 6 Nuffield Studio, Southampton
Nov 10 & 11 Plymouth Arts Centre
Nov 12 Bath Arts Workshop
Nov 15-27 Project Arts Centre, Dublin
Nov 29-Dec 4 Scottish Tour
Dec 5 Gateway Theatre, Chester
Dec 6-8 Lancaster University
Dec 15 Dovecot Arts Centre, Stockton

INDISCREET (The Revenge of Mr X)

by Drew Griffiths & Roger Baker
NB New re-written version of the show seen at Southampton and the ICA
Oct 11-Nov 7 Mickery Theatre, Amsterdam and on tour in Holland
Nov 15-27 Project Arts Centre Dublin
Dec 5 Gateway Theatre, Chester
Dec 6-8 Lancaster University
Dec 16 & 17 Maris Club, Newcastle

IN LONDON

Dec 7-18 ICA Tuesday Saturday
A new lunchtime play at 1.15 pm
Dec 21-24 A Gay Panto!
Late night entertainment for the festive season.

Gay Sweatshop was a theatre company that ran from 1974 to 1997. Initially based in Balham, south London, the troupe spent a lot of time on the road — including for this 1976 tour. They faced controversy at each stop, even receiving bomb threats in Dublin. A year later Gay Sweatshop split into separate men's and women's groups.

It's difficult to rebut the criticism of 'Metrocentrism', but Gay Sweatshop did their bit against the London bias by performing their wonderful show 'The Dear Love of Comrades' in Aberdeen and Edinburgh. This was particularly fortunate for Edinburgh gays who were unable to get to the carnival as their coach had broken down on route.

Peace News, 6 July 1979

Noël Greig's *The Dear Love of Comrades* (1979) explored the conjunction of sexuality and radical politics in the lives of middle-class romantic socialist Edward Carpenter (1844–1929) and his working-class lover, George Merrill (1867–1928), who lived together in a cottage at Millthorpe in rural north Derbyshire.

← The futuristic *Blood Green* explored 'transexualism' and violence against women. It was well received, though the critic at the *Cork Examiner* was unimpressed: 'Blood Green was, as far as I am concerned, an enigma that was totally forgettable' (20 October 1980).

Theatres have long been sites of queer community and connection — for the people working there and for theatre-goers, like this 'man from a small market town' interviewed for the 'Consenting Adults' BBC TV documentary screened in 1967 (see also pp. 58–61).

'*Do you find it very difficult to find and meet other homosexuals?*

Yes I do, very much. Where can one meet homosexuals in a small town where everybody knows you? Plus the fact that there's not many homosexuals in the town where I live. The only other place that you go is to go around the toilets and I don't wish that.

Where did you used to go to meet other homosexuals?

Well I used to try a lot of things actually. I know that they sound perhaps very stupid but I like the theatre, I like the cinema. I used to book two seats, quite expensive ones because I like the good things. And, hoping I would sell the other ticket just before the performance started. That way I would make sure that there would be somebody that was single sitting next to me at the cinema or the theatre.'

Although it may be considered fashionable to be gay, or at least to tolerate homosexual men and women, in 1977, being gay still has much stigma. This was the message to come out of 'Not in Norwich'. A one act play performed by members of the Royal Court's Theatre Scheme, and given its second showing at Jackson's Lane Community Centre, Highgate, on Saturday, as part of Gay Pride Week.

Hornsey Journal, *8 July 1977*

← The once-vilified playwright Oscar Wilde (1854–1900) is celebrated for his Irish roots and queer cultural theatrical credentials in this 1997 sculpture. Situated opposite the playwright's childhood home in Merrion Square, Dublin, it was the work of sculptor Danny Osborne.

Peter Holdsworth, Bradford Telegraph and Argus, 10 February 1988

▪ Review
A lukewarm kiss

Kiss of the Spiderwoman at Bradford Playhouse.

HAD the Bradford Playhouse and Film Theatre been transported to Nazi Germany last night, the cast, producer and possibly the management might have found themselves hauled out by brownshirts to be beaten, kicked and not unlikely shot.

For Hitler's thugs were paranoiac not only about homosexuality but about anyone or anything having any compassion for those affected.

Kiss Of The Spider Woman, which opened at the Playhouse last night, DID try to throw light on and seek sympathy for a developing homosexual relationship between two prisoners sharing a cell in an Argentina jail. And John Waller's far from sensational production WAS partly backed by the local authority because of the financial assistance given to the Playhouse by Bradford's council.

Danger

So what would have happened had the already notorious Clause 28 of the Local Government Bill started operating? That clause states that a local authority shall not "promote homosexuality or publish material for the promotion of homosexuality ... or ... give financial or other assistance to any person for that purpose."

Those behind the bill insist, of course, that it is not intended to affect the Arts. Yet there would be nothing to stop the more restrictive arguing in court that a play like Kiss Of The Spider Woman "is published material which promotes homosexuality while having local authority support."

I am not suggesting there are brownshirts on the horizon — yet. But I am suggesting there are many plays now in danger of being battered and banished victims of those who would have even a hint of homosexuality drummed off the stage.

Such a throwing-out clouds what should be the real issue. That is whether any particular play is a good or a poor one. Ironically in the circumstances, I have to say that Kiss Of The Spiderwoman by Manuel Puig proved not very memorable. It had neither the labyrinthine power of Puig's original novel, nor an iota of the impact made by the superb film based on that book.

The two-strong cast too lacked the nuances of complex emotions in seeming to avoid deliberately any histrionic fireworks.

Peter Holdsworth

FRINGE FIFTH FOR CLYDE UNITY THEATRE

Fresh from their sell-out success at the 1991 Glasgow Mayfest, Clyde Unity Theatre will make their fifth visit to the Edinburgh Festival Fringe this August. The company will perform two shows by John Binnie at Theatre Workshop. THE PLAYS: the world premiere of LOVE AMONG THE JUVENILES deals with the lives of and loves of Finn and Ailsa. While Ailsa pines for her African lover, Finn embarks upon his first gay love affair, and it's sweet, sexy and scary. A warm and tender Glaswegian play about the traumas of first love.

1991 press release

Tony Kushner's Pulitzer Prize winning *Angels in America: a Gay Fantasia on National Themes* had its UK premiere at the National Theatre on London's South Bank in 1992.

PRESS RELEASE

BRITISH PREMIERE OF TONY KUSHNER'S

ANGELS IN AMERICA

Tony Kushner's play 'Angels in America' is to have its British premiere at the Cottesloe Theatre on Thursday 23 January (previews from 17 January).

ALTERNATIVE MISS IRELAND

By Fintan Walsh

IRELAND'S ALTERNATIVE Miss Ireland (AMI) queer beauty pageant first took place on April Fool's Day 1987, at Sides club on Dublin's Dame Lane, to raise funds for the Rape Crisis Centre. After an extended hiatus, the event resumed in 1996, three years after homosexuality was decriminalised in the Republic of Ireland, to raise money for HIV and AIDS charities desperately in need of resources at the height of the crisis. Referred to locally as Gay Christmas, the pageant was modelled on Andrew Logan's Alternative Miss World, which began in London in 1972. Organised initially by Ross Elliot Tallon, Frank Stanley and Niall Sweeney, AMI's team expanded over its eighteen-year run to include some of the country's leading activists, artists and producers. Following its final production at Dublin's Olympia Theatre in 2012, AMI had generated over of €250,000 for HIV/AIDS charities.

AMI contestants were selected from a combination of direct entry and regional heats. Entrants were eventually also drawn from Alternative Miss Philippines, a competition which developed from within Ireland's Filipino nursing community, which had grown rapidly in the 2000s as a result of targeted recruitment by the Irish health service. Those who made it through to the main event performed in daywear, eveningwear and swimwear segments, ultimately judged by a celebrity panel and audience reaction. While open, in principle,

Tonie Walsh participating in the first Alternative Miss Ireland, 1 April 1987.

to any person, thing or animal (one year, cabaret performer Agnes Bernelle's dog took part), and with no strict dress code, contestants typically challenged norms around gender, sexuality and ethnicity, including those enshrined by the Church and State in twentieth-century Ireland, and the sanitised standards promoted by traditional beauty pageants. Routinely taking place on the Sunday closest to St Patrick's Day, the pageant positioned itself in a stridently subversive relationship to hackneyed notions of Irish national identity.

Winners were awarded for 'transgressing beauty and inventing new desires', and conferred with the title 'Queen of Ireland'. This was bestowed with the placing of the Medusa Crown of Shamrocks on the winner's head, in a move that perverted deep-rooted traditions serving different idolised 'queens', including the Virgin Mary and the mythological national emblem of Ireland, Cathleen Ní Houlihan. In addition to its critical fund- and consciousness-raising activities, AMI also succeeded in bridging links between Ireland's queer activist circles, social scenes and arts sectors, in particular its theatre and performance culture. The riotous aesthetics, ribald comedy and bold political statements that characterised the event nurtured a burgeoning generation of queer performance artists, in particular Ireland's leading queer performance and events company THISISPOPBABY, which was formed in 2007 and continues to collaborate with AMI artists and producers. Its long-standing emcee was drag performer Panti Bliss (Rory O'Neill), who made international headlines in 2014 when she gave an impassioned speech about homophobia on the main stage the Abbey Theatre (Ireland's national theatre). It was a move that was deemed to play a pivotal part in Ireland's same-sex marriage referendum in 2015, harnessing national support and bolstering political commitment.

↑ Poster for the final Alternative Miss Ireland in 2012, featuring a fragmented image of Panti Bliss. Designed by Pony.

POSTER FOR THE FIRST ALTERNATIVE MISS IRELAND IN 1987.

The history of AMI demonstrates the vital imbrication of activism, sociality and artistic production to the growth and sustenance of queer life and culture, and the power of collective activism to produce cultural and political change. AMI's archive, including production notes, minutes, photographs and publicity materials, is preserved in the Irish Queer Archive collection at the National Library of Ireland.

Fintan Walsh is Professor of Performing Arts and Humanities at Birkbeck, University of London. Recent books include Performing Grief in Pandemic Theatres *(Cambridge University Press, 2024) and* Performing the Queer Past: Public Possessions *(Methuen Drama, 2023). For more on AMI, see Fintan's book* Queer Performance and Contemporary Ireland *(2016).*

DUCKIE
By Ben Walters (aka Dr Duckie)

THE LONDON-BASED queer performance collective Duckie has been running nights, shows and creative projects since 1995. The gang who started it were producer Simon Strange, host Amy Lamé, DJs Chelsea Kelsey and Kim Phaggs (aka the London Readers Wifes [sic]) and 'door whores' Jay Cloth and Father Cloth. Producer Dicky Eton and host Azara Meghie came on board later. Hundreds if not thousands of other artists and collaborators make up the collective's extended family.

Duckie are best known for putting on small and large piss-ups with good tunes and quick, dirty, arty live turns. As well as lengthy residencies at the Royal Vauxhall Tavern and Eagle London, they've produced tongue-in-cheek 'Gay Shame' parties at Pride weekend and a cycle of 'vintage events' animating queer nightlife scenes from London's past. But they've also developed a nifty line in long-running community-based projects, such as the Posh Club (an afternoon cabaret for older people without many friends or family), Duckie Homosexualist Summer School (a training camp for young LGBTIQ+ performers) and the Slaughterhouse Club (an art project working with people living with homelessness and addiction).

Somehow, taking such different shapes and engaging such different people, these various things all feel utterly 'Duckie'. Perhaps that's because they can all be thought of as 'homemade mutant hope machines': forms and processes that emerge from lived experience, operate relatively autonomously, adapt to changing conditions and routinely generate belief in the possibility of better worlds. More than that, they start to bring those worlds into being, one event at a time.

This links to what the researcher José Esteban Muñoz called 'queer futurity': the importance of marginalised people thinking, feeling and acting together toward imagined better worlds that glimmer on the horizon. Muñoz mostly framed this queer hope as fleeting and ephemeral. But Duckie's projects make it quite concrete and routine, through 'holding forms' (to use a favourite term of Simon Strange) that can be reproduced across multiple events and in multiple locations. Call it 'reproductive queer futurity'.

So reproductive queer futurity is the theory, homemade mutant hope machines the practice. Homemade mutant hope machines come in many different forms, from a private journal or sketchbook to legal reform and social justice movements – from the art you make

ROYAL VAUXHALL TAVERN.

in your bedroom to the ballroom community to ACT UP. But whatever the scale, certain things make hope machines more powerful and effective. Participating in creativity, for instance, can strengthen community and a sense of agency. Embracing queer family structures of belonging and care meanwhile enables material support and the transmission across generations of hard-won forms of understanding and effective action.

It's also worth taking fun seriously. Fun is usually trivialised: if something is fun, it can't be important; and if something is important, it can't be fun. But this normative assumption opens up some interesting wiggle room. It means people having fun give themselves permission to try new things – new ways of feeling, relating, acting – that can point the way to new worlds. And it means that people observing fun don't pay much attention ('Oh, they're just having a bit of fun'). So, in queer contexts, fun can be a powerful technology for both intervening in existing civic structures and creating new ones, all under conditions of reduced scrutiny. Queer fun is an underground training facility for utopia.

Duckie are in the business of helping queers have the kind of fun they want to have. This is a big deal. Queer fun offers relief from the drudgery and oppression of the normative world. It also helps develop forms of critical and practical resistance to that world. And, most importantly, it rehearses the better worlds we want, need and deserve. It makes them start to happen. Duckie do all this by conceiving and creating their own homemade mutant hope machine. What's yours?

Ben Walters (aka 'Dr Duckie') completed his doctoral research on Duckie and homemade mutant hope machines in 2019. Find more on Duckie at duckie.co.uk and on Ben's research at duckie.co.uk/dr-duckie.

Matt Cook adds...

Think Duckie and people often think Vauxhall in south London, but they have got about - with jaunts to Blackpool, Hebden Bridge, various towns along England's south coast, and Hull when it was UK City of Culture in 2017. That year also marked the fiftieth anniversary of the partial decriminalisation of sex between men, and so for their residency in the city Duckie brought together artists and local LGBTIQ+ groups to create '50 Queers for 50 Years', featuring a myriad of stately homos of England, from Dusty Springfield to Freddie Mercury, Clare Balding to Quentin Crisp.

Getting out of London is part of a shift in queer creative subcultures, writes Duckie producer Simon Strange:

'Unlike my generation, the cool queer kids don't move to London anymore. Late capitalism has made the cost of housing in London untenable for most ordinary young people. Most of the gay bars and clubs in the capital closed down and the creative, ambitious benders and transgenders fled to the funky seaside towns of Margate, Ramsgate, Hastings, Eastbourne. And whilst we have seen a nasty conservative backlash to the trans revolution, systemic homophobia has largely been dismantled, resulting in the vibrant clandestine queer scenes of smaller towns going overground.

There is a healthy queer arts and culture scene in many regional towns and cities these days. The fleshpots of Blackpool and Hebden Bridge have always had a queer DNA and a commercial gay scene, but check out other hotbeds of radical queer action like Curious in Newcastle, Club Urania in Cambridge, Eat Me in Liverpool and Fierce in Birmingham.'

Duckie on the road: Mods and Rockers night in Brighton, 2014.

FILM

VICTIM, 1961.

↑ The ABC cinema, Plymouth, where Michael first saw *Victim*. The city's cinemas were, he said, good places to meet other men.

'*Michael:* Then in 19[61], I was sixteen, this film came out called *Victim*, with Dirk Bogarde. I went and saw that, and I shouldn't have done, because it was an X so you had to be eighteen to get into an X, and I was sixteen. Got into this X film. Thinking oh, there'll be all these gay men around. There wasn't, it was me sat in the cinema watching this film.

You were just alone in the cinema?

Michael: Yeah. It was like, for God's sake, where is everyone? Obviously people didn't want to go and watch it. And I watched it and thought: wow, that's so powerful. I watch it now and think, God, dated. But for its time it really was totally, totally ground breaking. I always remember the speech that Dirk Bogarde came out with talking to his wife, and literally screaming out: 'I wanted him'! And I just thought, yeah, I can identify with that. Without thinking it too deeply... I knew I was queer, there was no such thing as gay then. That I was, you know, I liked men.'

Michael O'Callaghan interviewed by Justin Bengry (2016)

130 | A QUEER SCRAPBOOK

Splish Splash

The Irish Gay Rights Movement are showing the much-praised documentary film on David Hockney and his milieu, 'A Bigger Splash', in 46 Parnell Sq. West on Monday, April 10. This opens a season of films about homosexuality. Others will be Robert Aldrich's 'The Killing of Sister George' (May 8), Mike Sarne's 'Myra Breckinridge' (June 6) and Fassbinder's 'Fox and His Friends' (July 3).

Hibernia (Dublin), 6 April 1978

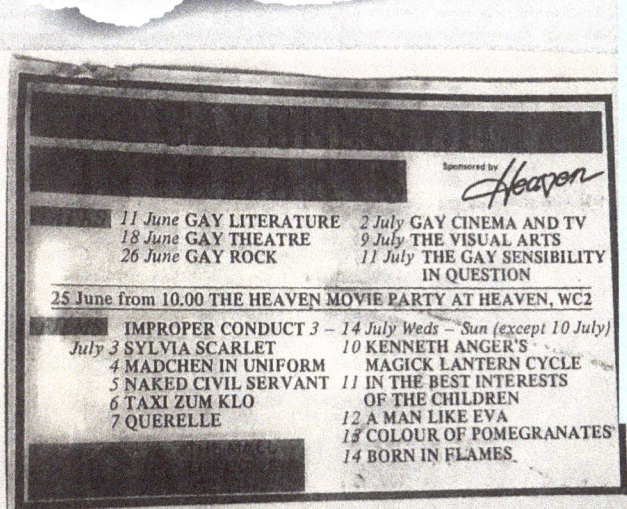

Film seasons and arts festivals became regular features of the LGBTIQ+ calendar in cities across Britain and Ireland from the late 1970s. LGBTIQ+ conferences often included film screenings, performances and creative workshops.

↑ In 1985 the Institute of Contemporary Arts ICA in London organised a festival exploring 'the gay sensibility in the arts', including talks on gay literature, theatre, rock and the visual arts, and a 'movie party' at the nearby gay nightclub, Heaven. (*City Limits*, June 1985). For the following two years the Tyneside Cinema in Newcastle curated 'Gays Own Pictures'. These seasons ran concurrently in London venues – including the ICA and National Film Theatre – and from 1988 became the London Lesbian and Gay Film Festival (renamed BFI Flare in 2014).

RISKY, ADVENTUROUS AND RECKLESS

BRADFORD playhouse and Film Theatre is hosting the Lesbian and Gay Festival for the second year running – and organisers say viewers can expect films which are risky, adventurous and reckless.

Bradford Star, 4 January 1990

↑ Poster for the Second Irish Lesbian and Gay Film Festival, 1992.

↑ The Glasgay arts festival ran in Glasgow from 1993 to 2014. The Glasgow Film Theatre was one of many venues across the city.

This 2021 documentary, one of several outputs of the Rebel Dykes History project, tells the story of a loose grouping of young lesbians in the 1980s London, linked by their shared activism and sex and SM positivity.

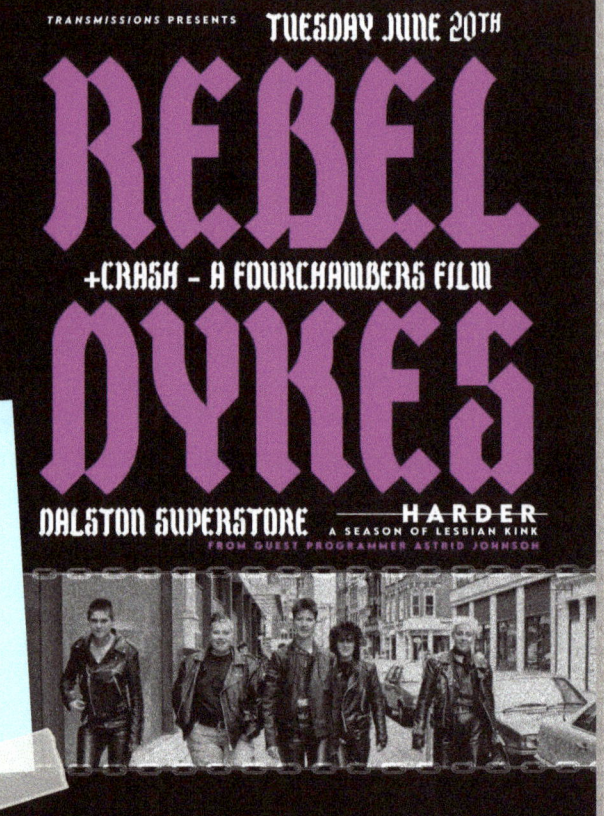

132 | A QUEER SCRAPBOOK

GAY DAYS

We all need cheering up ... but I am not so sure Bristol's Arnolfini Cinema have the answer when they advertise 'a season of gay films'.

Bristol Evening Post, *6 June 1979*

On a Gay Day You Can See Forever

Tax payers' money is being used to subsidise a gay film festival at Derby cinema. The event, entitled On a Queer Day You Can See for Ever is being staged at the Metro Cinema until May 21. But director Laurie Haywood defended the festival saying lesbians and gays are part of the community.

Derby Express, 23 April 1992

> There was pushback against these various celebrations of LGBTIQ+ film – especially when 'public money' was involved.

NOWT SO QUEER AS SOME FOLK

WHY IS IT, do you reckon, that there is widespread distaste about the nation's, indeed the world's, homosexual population? Simple: nothing to do with Aids, homophobia or anything like that. It's the image some of them present to the media, which suggests they are complete weirdos ... Take the films made by and about homosexuals in the Sixth London Lesbian and Gay Film Festival, a selection of which will be shown at Cornerhouse in Manchester from Saturday until mid-June. Foremost is 'Cream Soda', and I quote: 'A lesbian road movie about two women travelling around the coast of Britain in search of dolphins, but who end up discovering more about themselves.' Dolphins? Dolphins? And what about another film, 'Times Square'? 'Two women meet in a mental hospital, run away, steal an ambulance and buck the system in one of those rare and exciting buddy movies.' It isn't supposed to be a joke? And the title of this mini-festival is enough to make you doubt whether the organisers have lost their marbles: it is 'On a Queer Day, You Can See Forever'.

Oldham Evening Chronical, *4 January 1992*

Unionist picket

Northern Ireland's first ever Lesbian and Gay Festival, to be held in Belfast this month, will be picketed by unionist councillors from the city. Films with titles like LESBIAN LOVE STORIES and TOGETHER ALONE will be screened from June 21, but Councillor Frank Miller wants them scrapped.

The Evening Chronicle, *1992*

HOMECOMING IN BRIXTON AND HUDDERSFIELD

By Jaya Rathbone

TOPHER CAMPBELL'S 1995 film *The Homecoming* follows photographer Ajamu X's journey from his adult home in Brixton, south London, to his first solo exhibition, *Black Bodyscapes* at the art gallery in Huddersfield, the West Yorkshire town where he was born and brought up. The film maps Ajamu's queer creative and political coordinates in Brixton. It takes in bisexual artist Pearl Alcock's 1970s Black queer shebeen on Railton Road and the gay squats that provided a base for the Brixton Faeries theatre troupe around the same time. It flags the old home of C. L. R James, the Trinidadian historian and journalist, where *Race Today* was first produced and where James – and Ajamu – met gay Nigerian photographer Rotimi Fani-Kayode.

Fani-Kayode lived on Railton Road in one of the Brixton Housing Co-op flats formed out of the gay squats in the early 1980s. He was part of the Brixton Artists Collective on Atlantic Road, which was key to the queer and especially Black queer art scene – particularly after the pioneering 1983 exhibition *Work by Gay Women and Men*. These sites and more in *The Homecoming* bring Brixton's Black queer creative scene into view – a scene inflected by other places and experiences including, for Ajamu, formative years in Huddersfield, the film's ultimate destination.

Topher and Ajamu went on to trace this and wider Black queer networks in London and well beyond in the process of collecting for the 'rukus! Black LGBT Archive', now held at the London Archives but originally in Ajamu's Brixton flat – a multipurpose space of archive,

STILL FROM THE HOMECOMING.

The Homecoming: A Short Film about Ajamu

Queer activist and artist Ajamu prepares to leave Brixton for an exhibition of his work in his hometown, Huddersfield

art-making and parties, including for the Black Perverts Network. These activities are interconnected for Ajamu, and part of an archival impulse to create and sustain a sense of Black queer history, selfhood, home and family. We see this with rukus! and also with Ajamu's own photographic work, which forms into an *Archival Sensoria* – the title of his 2021 solo show at London's Cubitt Gallery. The Black Perverts Network meanwhile provided space to explore bodies and pleasures away from white racism, gay male body fascism and the legacies of bodily trauma and pain. It is through our bodies, Ajamu writes, that we 'bring our archives with us'.

C. L. R. JAMES PLAQUE, RAILTON ROAD, LONDON.

For more on Brixton's Black queer history and Ajamu see Jason Okundaye's Revolutionary Acts (2024).

Jaya Rathbone is a postgraduate student working on racism and racialisation in post-WWII social services in England. She is also co-curator of this section of the scrapbook.

'I grew up in Huddersfield. And basically, my parents arrived in '61 from Jamaica, and my grandparents actually came to Bradford in about '57 or '58. I have three brothers and two sisters who were born and raised in Jamaica, and they're what you call the 'sent-for kids', and they were brought over in the seventies. And so it had been kind of very ... fixed ideas around masculinity and religion and that kind of stuff. And then basically me, around sixteen I kind of liked being post-punk or rock or goth or whatever, y'know. I was that odd Black child walking around, into this weird music, and I was into wearing soccer boots and mascara and frilly shirts ... The person I blame for all this, interestingly enough, is Marc Almond from Soft Cell. Seeing Soft Cell on *Top of the Pops* that year, it triggered that idea that there is something else somewhere else, and then of course he was singing about Soho and London and whatever. It just opened up this window for me.'

In this interview extract, Ajamu describes his childhood in Huddersfield ... and the impact of 1980s music and fashion.

Ajamu X, *West Yorkshire Queer Stories*

3: ARTS AND CULTURE | 135

LITERATURE, BOOKS AND BOOKSHOPS

UNICORN BOOKSHOP, BRIGHTON

UNICORN BOOKSHOP, BRIGHTON.

Alternative bookshops were important community and activist hubs in British cities in the 1970s and 1980s. Unicorn Bookshop was one of the first, opened by American beat poet Bill Butler in 1967. Police soon raided the store and prosecuted Butler for selling 'obscene publications' – including the hippie *International Times*, which celebrated a 'new attitude' of permissiveness and carried queer contact ads. Patrick, who discovered the psychedelically painted store as a teenager and worked there for a while, remembers it 'being a bit upmarket' in its stock – unlike a 'dirty bookshop' on nearby North Road that stocked 'lurid gay books' amid the straight.

GAY'S THE WORD, LONDON

Gay's the Word on London's Marchmont Street opened its doors in 1979. It rapidly became an important cultural hub and a meeting place for a range of groups. Among them were Lesbians and Gays Support the Miners (LGSM), which formed and met at the bookshop during the strikes of 1984–85 and forged a link between queer Londoners and striking miners in the Dulais Valley in South Wales. The bookshop itself came under attack during this period, from random passers-by and Customs and Excise, which seized thousands of pounds of stock in a raid in 1984, including work by Jean Genet, Tennessee Williams, Christopher Isherwood and Gore Vidal. The bookshop directors were charged with conspiracy to import indecent material, and a defence fund was launched to pay legal costs. Upwards of £55,000 was raised from donations, benefit gigs and badges. Charges were dropped in 1986.

IN OTHER WORDS, PLYMOUTH

Prudence and Gay met and worked together at Manchester's Grass Roots bookshop in the 1970s before moving to Plymouth to open In Other Words in 1982 (the same year that thousands lined the streets of the city to watch the Falklands War victory parade). In Other Words evolved into something of a community hub in the absence of sustained non-commercial community spaces elsewhere in the city. Hannah, a bisexual woman, indicates the personal and political significance of the store to her:

> 'You could pick a book up on feminism and you could pick a book up on bisexuality. It was brilliant. And then they had that coffee shop for a little bit downstairs. I say coffee shop ... it was literally just a coffee machine. But it was lovely. It wasn't just a place with feminist books; it was LGBT, it was a place to feel at home really. ... I was always going to In Other Words, even before I came out, so these places were part of my life.'

Hannah, speaking at the Queer Beyond London workshop, Plymouth, 2017

↑ Prudence and Gay at In Other Words bookshop on Mutley Plain, Plymouth, c.1982.

COMPENDIUM, CAMDEN

Compendium books in Camden opened in 1968 and ran for 32 years. After it closed, it was remembered as 'Britain's pre-eminent radical bookstore'* with increasingly well-stocked lesbian and gay shelves.

* *The Guardian*, 9 Dec. 2002).

LAVENDER MENACE, EDINBURGH

Lavender Menace opened its doors in 1982 on Edinburgh's Forth Street, a year after the partial decriminalisation of homosexuality in Scotland (twelve years after England and Wales). In 1987 it moved to Dundas Street and reopened as West & Wilde, where it hosted events with the likes of Armistead Maupin, Sarah Schulman, David Leavitt and Edmund White for the next ten years.

Manchester booksellers conference

A two-day conference will be held in Manchester on Sunday 11th and Monday 12th April on lesbians and gay men in the book trade. It will be jointly sponsored by **Lavender Books in Edinburgh** and Gay's the Word Bookshop in London. Speakers and workshops will cover such areas as advertising, distribution, and communications between publishers and booksellers.

The Bookseller, March 1982

LAVENDER MENACE SIGNS.

→ A clipping from West & Wilde's newsletter, with a clear nod to their previous incarnation, Lavender Menace, 1991.

BOOKS ON DISPLAY IN LAVENDER MENACE.

WOMEN'S PLACE, CORK

By Orla Egan

Women's Place (1982–90) was an inclusive social and arts initiative established as part of the Quay Co-op on Sulivan's Quay, Cork. The Quay Co-op brought together gay men and lesbians, women's groups, left-wing organisations, environmental and anti-nuclear groups. It housed a cafe, bookshop, women's place and meeting spaces that were used by various 'alternative' groups in the city. A number of rooms were set aside for the development of the women's place, allowing it to host a number of groups and projects. It was an important base for the Cork Lesbian Discussion Group, the Cork Lesbian Collective and Lesbian Line. Other groups included the Cork Rape Crisis service and the Woman's Health Group. A women's library provided valuable resources. The Women's Place, Cork, participated in a number of exchanges with women in Belfast in the 1980s, funded by the Co-operative North programme.

Orla Egan is a queer archival activist. She has been actively involved in the Cork LGBT community since the 1980s.

↑ The Women's Place (1982–90) was an inclusive social and arts initiative in Cork.

3: ARTS AND CULTURE | 139

PLACING QUEER MID-CENTURY FICTION

By Christopher Adams

THE PAGES of mid-century queer fiction offer diverse settings for stories of queer love, discovery, sadness and triumph – from the bisexual women living on a Thames houseboat in Mary Renault's *The Friendly Young Ladies* (1944) or a young trans woman making a life for herself around Cottingham and Hull in Geoff Brown's *I Want What I Want* (1966), to London's queer streets in dozens of novels.

BOARDING SCHOOLS FROM BRIGHTON TO EDINBURGH

With their same-sex environments, boarding schools have long provided settings for the exploration of queer affections in such novels as H. A. Vachell's *The Hill* ('A Romance of Friendship') (1905), E. F. Benson's *David Blaize* (1916), Arthur Waugh's *The Loom of Youth* (1917) and Beverley Nichols's *Prelude* (1920). Mid-century writers continued to use these idyllic – though heavily class-bound – institutions and the communities that surround them to create stories of queer adolescent yearning and – occasionally – fulfilment. Nancy Spain's crime romp *Poison for Teacher* (1949) is set in the fictional Radcliff Hall, a stand-in for Roedean School on the outskirts of Brighton, and is full of tongue-in-cheek references to queer goings-on. In his memoir *Broken Images* (1949), John Guest recalls an intense relationship with another school pupil at Fettes (Edinburgh). Later in the period, titles such as William Cooper's *The Ever-Interesting Topic* (1953) and Michael Campbell's *Lord Dismiss Us* (1967) use boarding schools scattered throughout Britain to similar effect.

THE HILL BY H. A VACHELL, 1905.

A CHINESE GARDEN IN DEVON

One of the most evocative uses of setting is Rosemary Manning's *The Chinese Garden* (1962). Written in the mid-1950s but shelved until the author felt the time was better able to handle a lesbian storyline, *The Chinese Garden* is set in 'Bampfield', a stately home turned girls' boarding school in the Devon countryside (a thinly veiled description of the historic Poltimore House). The central character, Rachel, is being groomed by her Latin teacher while in an on-again, off-again relationship with another girl at the school, Margaret. She discovers a derelict Chinese garden on the school grounds and returns to it frequently, but as her self-awareness of her own desires grows, the garden itself begins to change, becoming 'very lush, and overgrown with new shoots'. Rachel senses something 'of the corruption of Bampfield itself' in the 'vapours which wrapped the shrubbery in the early morning and evening ... as though veiling it from the world's eyes for some secret and appalling rite'.

One day, Rachel finds Margaret in the garden, reading a book:

A CHINESE GARDEN BY ROSEMARY MANNING, 1962.

'Have you read this yet?' asked Margaret suddenly, and held out a book. Rachel looked at the title. It was Radclyffe Hall's *The Well of Loneliness*.

'No,' she said. 'I haven't.'

'I've nearly finished it. I bought it in the holidays. I keep it in the pagoda, in a box.' ...

'Will you read it if I leave it here?' ...

'I can't promise,' said Rachel uncomfortably. 'I've got such a hell of a lot to do.'

She rose, anxious to prevent Margaret from saying anything further. When she looked back from the edge of the pool, Margaret was walking slowly over towards the boathouse, reading as she went.

A LONDON PUB

London's urban anonymity proves a powerful draw for characters seeking queer encounters in its bars, clubs, parks, bookshops, concert halls, guest houses and areas of Kensington, Piccadilly, Pimlico and Soho. London features critically in such works as Angus Wilson's *Hemlock and After* (1952), Compton Mackenzie's popular *Thin Ice* (1956), Brigid Brophy's *The King of a Rainy Country* (1956),

THE HEART IN EXILE BY RODNET GARLAND, 1953.

James Courage's *A Way of Love* (1959), Martyn Goff's *The Plaster Fabric* (1957) and *The Youngest Director* (1961), Maureen Duffy's *The Microcosm* (1966) and Mariana Villa-Gilbert's *A Jingle-Jangle Song* (1968) - to name but a few. But negotiating the queer urban environment comes with challenges - from understanding social codes to avoiding police entrapment.

In one of the best-selling queer novels of the period, *The Heart in Exile* (1953), Rodney Garland (the Hungarian émigré Adam de Hegedus) writes of the complexities of one such vital queer space - the queer pub:

'Inexperienced people, outsiders, usually became puzzled when by chance they enter a pub taken up by the underground. If the sudden gaze of uneasy or expectant eyes did not disturb them too much they could not help becoming conscious that the atmosphere verged between strain and exaggerated hilarity. Comparatively few people come alone, except if they happen to be regulars. The usual custom is to come in pairs, then ignore each other for most of the evening, except when the strain becomes too great. If one talks to an unattached person there is usually tension. The man is ill at ease, it takes time to sum you up and the process occupies most of his mind and renders him tongue-tied. He doesn't know whether you are a plain-clothes man or not. This, of course, is usually easy to decide; your age, your clothes, your appearance give the information in a few seconds. But there are other considerations: he doesn't know what you demand; he can guess, but only trial and error can supply the answer.'

A FLING IN BANGOR

With the notable exceptions of Forrest Reid's Tom Barber trilogy - *Uncle Stephen* (1931), *The Retreat* (1936) and *Young Tom* (1944) - and Maurice Leitch's *The Liberty Lad* (1965), Northern Ireland rarely featured in queer fiction of the era. However, one of the most remarkable queer novels of the mid-century has a Northern Irish setting. Written when the author was only sixteen, Kenneth Martin's *Aubade* (1957) tells the story of teenager Paul, who lives in a seaside town on the Northern Irish coast – identifiable as an idealised version of Bangor. From across the water he can see 'another coast on the horizon', but 'when he was very young Paul did not know what it was'. At church one Sunday, Paul spies handsome medical student Gary, and the two spend a romantic, sun-soaked summer together, riding around in Gary's sleek, white car.

Expeditions along the coastal landscape foster their mutual attraction, and the beach is also the place where the two young lovers spend their final day before parting. Upending assumptions of novels from the time period, *Aubade* ends not because either protagonist commits suicide or fails to come to terms with his homosexuality, but rather because Gary secures a job abroad:

> 'On the last Sunday, they drove to a beach miles round the coast. Gary parked the car on the road above, and they had to scramble down a bank and through woods before they came to the beach. The sea was blue and the day was cloudless, but when they undressed and lay on the sand, Gary said, 'It's colder to-day. That's the first time I've noticed it.'
>
> 'The summer's ending,' said Paul. 'When you've gone, I shall often come to this beach, and all the other places we went to together. Only then it will be winter, and the sea will be rough, and the seaweed will be tossed high up on the beach ... Someday, when you're famous, and you will be, never doubt that, I shall write to you and ask you if you remember a boy called Paul Anderson. And you'll say, "Oh, yes, he used to have a schoolboy crush on me".'
>
> 'No,' said Gary violently. 'You must never think that. You're too mature to have a schoolboy's crush on anyone, and I'm certainly too old.'
>
> 'I know, I know,' said Paul, 'but I was only making that up to hear what you would say. Let's go for a swim.' ...
>
> They stayed out in the car all night ...'

AUBADE BY KENNETH MARTIN, 1957.

HISTORY AND HERITAGE

EXHIBITS FROM THE MUSEUM OF TRANSOLOGY.

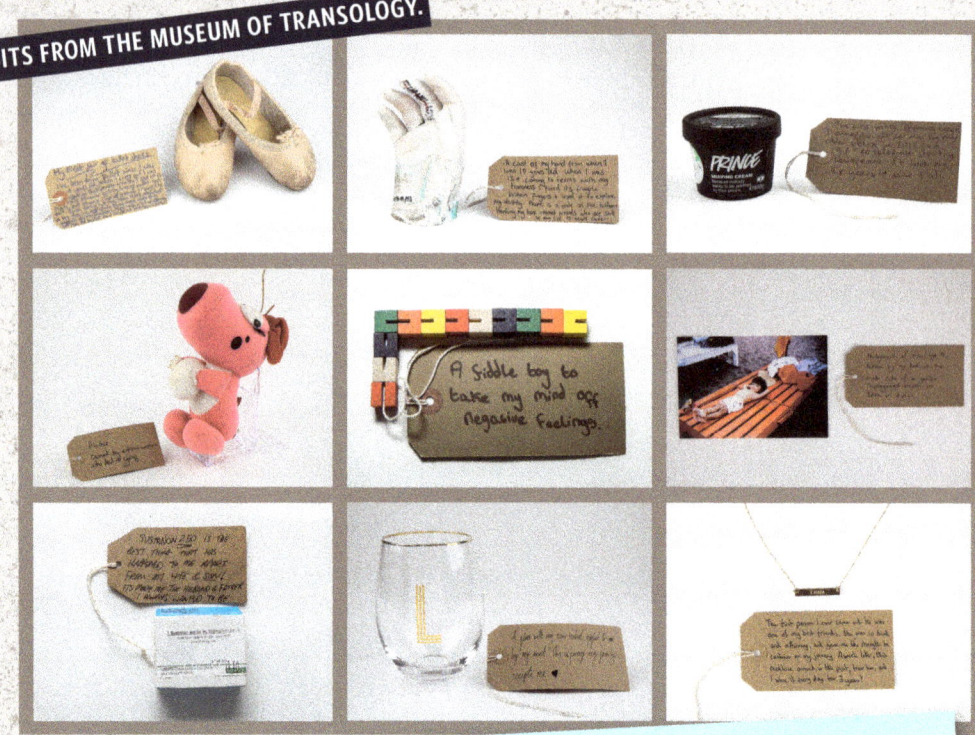

Founded in Brighton in 2014, The Museum of Transology now has 16 local collections in museums across the UK and Ireland. The crowd-sourced objects each have handwritten tags explaining their significance. The label on the hand mannequin, for example, reads: 'A cast of my hand from when I was ten years old. When I was 13+ coming to terms with my transness, I fixed its fragile broken fingers and used it to explore my identity. There is a note on the bottom thanking my trans internet friends who are still in my life 10 years later'. Attached to the pill packet is the note: 'Sustanon 250 is the best thing that has happened to me apart from my wife and son! It's made me the husband and father I always wanted to be'. The tag on the shaving cream says: 'The first pot of shaving cream I owned, brought for me by my older sibling in 2017 as a gift to celebrate starting testosterone. It took me six years to use it all.' And attached to the soft toy, the poignant note: 'Plushie. Owned by a transwoman who died too young'. See museumoftransology.com

The West Yorkshire Queer Stories oral history project (2018–20) was one of a large number of community history projects across the country supported by the National Lottery Heritage Fund from 2003. For more on the HLF see page 151.

↑ Poster for the Cork LGBT Archive, set up in 2013 by Orla Egan. It includes material on the McCurtain Street Gay Centre in the 1970s, on the national gay conference in the city in 1981 and on activism and the local scene.

Nineteenth-century prints and figurines, like this one held by the National Museum of Wales, celebrated the 'Ladies of Llangollen', Eleanor Butler (1739–1829) and Sarah Ponsonby (1755–1831). The upper-class pair left Ireland to set up home at Plas Newydd in north Wales and gained local and national celebrity.

SERVANTS, CONVICTS AND KWEENS
By E-J Scott

DRAWING FROM history to inspire public arts events that bring us together to reimagine, relive and respond to this history is a collective act of remembering, which in turn creates new shared memories. Heritage events are an ode to the past that create the queer folklores of the future. Indeed, it's sometimes a challenge for producers of these performative gatherings to know whether to apply to the National Lottery or the Arts Council for funding. Often, the tactical answer is both.

Duckie's *Lady Malcolm's Servants' Ball: 1932* (2014-16) began with a two-year volunteer research project into historic collections at museums including the V&A and the British Museum. It culminated in an unforgettable night (twice, actually, because tickets flew out so quickly that it had to be restaged), with twenty-one performers enacting their interpretation of the volunteers' findings at the Bishopsgate Institute (home to dozens and dozens of LGBTIQ+ community collections). They included the perspicacious playwright Neil Bartlett, who queerily conjured up communications with straight-acting servants of the past. Inside the dimly lit, spooky Victorian library, Neil gathered an intimate audience round a table (bless him – he delivered the performance half a dozen times or more, to give as many people as possible the chance to participate) and asked a London butler from the inter-war period about his active, early twentieth-century homo-sex life, while a punter hidden underneath the table knocked out coded answers. It was as witty as it was insightful, an immersive theatrical exploration of class, gender and sexuality between the wars. The tipsy audience, wearing their fancy dress and whispering questions of their own, stepped into the mise-en-scène with their own lived experience, providing them with a personal script that crossed centuries.

Bird la Bird's *Travelling Queer History People's Show* – 'a revolutionary exploration of the deep queer past' – traced the lives of queer convicts from the early nineteenth century, from Millbank prison across the British Empire. Her evening performance at Leeds City Museum (09 February 2019) as part of the West Yorkshire Queer Stories events programme was packed to the rafters. English Heritage's national youth engagement programme, Shout Out Loud, provided access to the Wernher Collection at Ranger's House for queer young people. They created a new LGBTIQ+ tour spanning from the ancient world to the present day, using objects from the collection.

In York, a young Fran Mahon sits in their bedroom collaging a zine they've called *The Kweens Haus: Kings Manor's Queer Heritages*. Fran explains: 'I am not ... interested in scouring the annals of philosophical societies and museums to find evidence ... Annihilation is a hard process to reverse ... What I am concerned with is queering our past, present, and futures. Transforming historic, archival and memory loss into a presence and future that is remembered now.'*

When young people are turning up to historic houses as a hobby on a Saturday and going home to make zines about it, it's fair to say something is afoot. That 'something', of course, is us finding our collective footing. *The Kweens Haus*, *Travelling Queer History People's Show*, *Lady Malcolm's Servants' Ball*, and many, many other queer happenings and DIY publications are testament to the innovative lengths we will go to in order to enjoy the process of fighting persecution while rejecting victimisation. After all, even if our memories are getting richer and longer, we're here for a gay time, not a long time.

* See https://www.hgc.hosted.york.ac.uk/the-kweens-haus-queer-heritage-and-camp-at-kings-manor

↑ **From the zine *The Kweens Haus: Kings Manor's Queer Heritages* by Fran Mahon.**

'OUT ON AN ISLAND: PRIDE IN SELF, PRIDE IN PLACE' PROJECT

By Franko Figueiredo-Stow and Caroline Diamond

'OUT ON AN ISLAND' is a celebration of the Isle of Wight's LGBTIQ+ heritage and history in a pioneering community project, funded by the National Lottery Heritage Fund and run by StoneCrabs Theatre together with a dedicated team of volunteers.

The project was conceived from a need to connect. We wanted to meet other Isle of Wight LGBTIQ+ people and to find out if a local LGBTIQ+ community existed. It was at one of the rare LGBTIQ+ nights on the island in 2016 that the discussion began. We wanted to form connections with other LGBTIQ+ people using a project, perhaps through theatre, oral histories or the written word. On hearing many unexpected stories that night – about a thriving gay scene in the 1990s or local newspapers naming and shaming gay men, for example – it felt imperative that the island's queer history be unveiled and shared.

The Isle of Wight has castles, monuments, manor houses, royal residences and rich landscapes. It is known worldwide for its music festivals and nationally as a destination for school trips and for its high percentage of second-home owners and retirement properties. Journalists paint the island as a place stuck in the 1950s. There are thirty-eight heritage societies here, and until a few years ago these seemed to be concerned only with preserving the stories of its land, its buildings and its aristocracy; they had little to say about the diverse local community.

There were people who refused to recognise LGBTIQ+ oral histories as an important tool to fill the historical gaps. When we advertised for stories and memorabilia, some people told us that our research had only 'a tenuous link to heritage' and that their Heritage Society was not 'the place to debate about homosexuality'. News of our activities received comments online such as 'Why do gay people have to march and shout it from the rooftops, straight people don't', 'What is happening to the world?', 'God Save Us...'. The dissenting voices were, though, outnumbered by others supporting and encouraging us.

When we approached LGBTIQ+ people to ask if they would let us record their histories, responses ranged from suspicious and reluctant to enthusiastic. One said: 'trust me, you don't want to hear my story, or those of the gay people I knew. Unless you want to know about police harassment, the *County Press* outing thirty-nine gay and

3: ARTS AND CULTURE | 149

bisexual men and homophobic treatment from islanders ranging from verbal to full on intimidation and violence until I got away in 1995.' But people did share their stories and we found others that showed a rich queer artistic lineage on the island.

Our research found more than ten notably creative people who lived on – and were inspired by – the island, and who became important in our LGBTIQ+ history. These figures and their work helped us to map the island in new queer ways. Collaborating with designer Spike Spondike, the project produced the 'Isle of Wight LGBTQ+ Heritage Trail Map', which is now included on the local tourist board website. The map takes you on an arty, queer tour of the island.

Pride is held in Ryde, the gateway to the island and home to eclectic independent shops like the Velvet Pig for vintage fashion. Victorian photographers Hughes and Mullins worked nearby and photographed Oscar Wilde when he visited in 1884 to give his talk 'On Dress'. Take a trip from East to West Wight and you will find Farringford House, the home of poet Alfred, Lord Tennyson from 1853. Tennyson had a close relationship with Arthur Henry Hallam. In Freshwater, author Virginia Woolf spent many summers in her great aunt's home – inspiring her 1923 play 'Freshwater'. Poet Algernon Swinburne spent his childhood on the island and is buried at St Boneface Parish Church. War poet Robert Nichols and author Patrick Gale were both born here (at East Shanklin and Newport, respectively).

Mapping the Isle of Wight's historic creative queer credentials has allowed us to connect – with each other as an LGBTIQ+ community, with our island allies and with the past. It also made us realise that we had a connection to wider queer histories and histories of creativity stretching across the British and Irish Isles and beyond.

Caroline Diamond is project manager of StoneCrabs' Out On An Island LGBTQ+ project. A northerner who has lived on the Isle of Wight for twenty-five years, she has worked with her local LGBTIQ+ community since 2015. After coming out as a lesbian later in life, she became dedicated to finding creative ways of supporting others with issues from loneliness and isolation to poor mental health.

Franko Figueiredo is a Latinx theatre writer, director, facilitator. They are co-founder and artistic director of StoneCrabs Theatre Company. Trained in Brazil and the UK, Figueiredo has collaborated with various theatre companies, conducted international workshops and co-edited Out On An Island, while also serving as a trustee for local cultural organisations.

CONCLUSION: QUEER ISLAND STORIES

By Matt Cook

OUT ON AN ISLAND was one of many LGBTIQ+ arts and community history projects that won funding from the National Lottery Heritage Fund (HLF) from 2003. rukus! (pp. 134-135), Duckie (pp. 127-129), the Museum of Transology (p. 144), and West Yorkshire Queer Stories (p. 145) were others. The HLF changed the landscape for queer creative, history and heritage work – with projects running across the UK and in a different mode from the more hand-to-mouth community initiatives of earlier decades, which sometimes gained small grants from the Arts Council or left-wing local authorities, but more often ran on less than a shoestring. Any council funding was met with newspaper letter page outrage and, from 1988, arguably contravened Section 28 of the Local Government Act – as detractors were keen to point out.

The act certainly didn't put a stop to this work from the community grassroots – in fact, there was an outraged upsurge of creative energy. Once Section 28 was repealed in 2003, there was nevertheless more scope for LGBTIQ+ community artistic and historical work; LGBT History Month (from 2005) soon provided a platform to showcase it. Some have noted a change in tenor in this later work – it is often more professionalised, visible and somewhat (only somewhat) less contentious in a changed cultural climate. The excitement in working at a creative and historical cutting edge remained, however, and there has not only been a growth and diversification in the work itself but a much wider geographical spread. The queer arts across these islands have been on a journey that tells its own story of shifting cultural mores, norms and styles.

@ OXFORD'S BODLEIAN LIBRARY, 2025

SECTION 4:
ACTIVISM AND COMMUNITY

Curated by E-J Scott

FOR MANY OF US who came out in the 1970s, 1980s and 1990s, our first ever Pride march was a rite-of-passage: both into the queer community and into a lifetime of activism. Whether you were holding up a banner or holding the hand of a lover, those tentative steps towards freedom intersected personal struggle, societal belonging and a taste for social justice. It wasn't just the brave act of coming out in public, or simply the overwhelming sense of empowerment felt from speaking out with confidence. Above all, it was the fact that we were all there *doing it together* that marked our entry into the community and secured our place within it, strengthening our conviction to defend our collective rights.

For many of us, there was no turning back. The smiles shared across one's shoulder with a complete stranger, the passing of a water bottle (back in the day it was more often a light for a fag), the voicing of a chant in unison (for the lucky ones, a cheeky snog with a stranger)... All of these moments became unforgettable memories that would serve to remind us that we are not alone, 'we are family', and collectively we count. Arguably now more of a party than a protest, Gay Pride has grown and significantly changed direction, as have our struggles and the context within which we take them on (including the way the state has redefined our right to protest and its right to police us when we do). But remarkably, in 2025, Trans Pride marches, picnics, parties and fetes were held in twenty-one locations (and counting) across the UK. These public actions – many expressions of trans joy, as much as they were expressions of anger – are a historic continuation of the role that activism plays in uplifting LGBTIQ+ community solidarity despite the populist fanfare stoking cultural divisions.

The first Gay Pride march took place in London on 1 July 1972. In a remarkable demonstration of queer solidarity, in 1981 it upped sticks to Huddersfield, with

↓ No Pride in War is a coalition of LGBTIQ+ and anti-war activists who were formed in response to the involvement of military presence and a flyover by the Red Arrows at London Pride in 2016 (see p. 180).

152 | A QUEER SCRAPBOOK

thousands travelling north to protest the sustained harassment of the local community by the West Yorkshire police force. (This was the same force that ignored serial killer Peter Sutcliffe's murder of thirteen women – most of them sex workers – from 1975 to 1980, despite having interviewed him nine times.) In 2023, trans activists organised a grand total of 194 vigils across the UK in memory of Brianna Ghey, murdered at just sixteen years of age (DCS Mike Evans of Cheshire police declared it not to be a hate crime). Just as the Gay Liberation Front (1970–73) and ACT UP (1987–) crossed the Atlantic to start branches in London, so branches of the Gay Liberation Front soon spread beyond the capital and across the UK (the annual national Gay Liberation Front conference was held in Birmingham in 1972). From the struggle for equal rights, including same-sex marriage and adoption, to the sustained challenges to hetero- and gender-normative models by radical queer activists, the collective queer willingness to act has become so commonplace that placard-making workshops are now held in community bookshops, bars and clubs prior to protests. Paint, pint, protest, party... It's a familiar recipe, with a long history.

BISEXUAL ACTION, MANCHESTER.

It's not only LGBTIQ+ rights that we rally behind. In 2024, the LGBTIQ+ community used Instagram to organise meeting spots to form 'queer blocs' at mass pro-Palestinian rallies. From 1981 to 2000, lesbians camped out on Greenham Common, protesting against nuclear armament. In 2023, thousands marched in face masks (despite being gripped by the fear of COVID-19) to stand up against racism at the Black Trans Lives Matter rally in London. And despite the 2018 London Gay Pride march being stopped by a small group of anti-trans protestors, the Museum of Transology has since collected over two hundred 'L with the T' protest signs from across the UK and Ireland: material markers that bear witness to lesbian and trans solidarity, despite the political and media rhetoric overamplifying accounts of disunity.

United we stand, because divided we fall. This section's collection of examples of queer activism serves to demonstrate the queer community values that tie us together. In our struggle for justice, freedom and equality for all, we forge stronger bonds than identity politics could ever rally. Actions speak louder than words – holding our heads up high, holds our community together.

E-J Scott

↑ 'Free Sarah Jane Baker' protesters outside HM Prison Isle of Wight, 5 December 2023.

BTLM London 20

BTLM London 20

BTLM London 20

BTLM London 20

BTLM London 20

BTLM London 20

BTLM London 20

BTLM London 20

BTLM London 20

Museum of Transology polaroids of trans activists at the Black Trans Lives Matter protest, 27 June 2020.

4: ACTIVISM AND COMMUNITY | 155

UK BLACK PRIDE

LADY PHYLL, UK BLACK PRIDE

'Founded in 2005, UK Black Pride is the world's largest celebration for LGBTIQ+ people of African, Asian, Caribbean, Middle Eastern and Latin American descent, and is a safe space to celebrate diverse sexualities, gender identities, gender expressions and cultures.'

Lady Phyll, UK Black Pride

↓ RAINBOW NOIR was established in Manchester in February 2013, founded by four black queer women who were inspired to create a space in the city led by and for our community.

Chloe, Rainbow Noir Lead Organiser

BLACK TRANS LIVES MATTER PROTEST, LONDON, 27 JUNE 2020

Protest placard saved by the Museum of Transology at the Black Trans Lives Matter protest, 27 June 2020.

E-J recalls...

THE BLACK TRANS LIVES MATTER march was held in the middle of the two lockdowns, and I can remember how scared we all were that if the cops didn't turn on us and the TERFs and the far right didn't have a go at us, then we'd probably all just die of COVID anyway! We didn't use to collect objects like this for the Museum of Transology, but I knew instinctively that our curatorial process had to play second fiddle to the importance of saving such a significant moment in trans history. So a couple of us went down to the march with masks on and black plastic bin bags and we stood there with cardboard signs we'd written on with Sharpie pens saying 'Give us your signs, Museum of Transology', and in the end when I got them back to the Bishopsgate Institute in a black cab – it took me hours and hours to hail one, as no driver wanted to stop at the rally or to pick up this little trans dude with a mountain of placards – we'd saved ninety-five signs. We've now got more than two thousand placards from years of collecting at rallies ever since. Black trans history has changed the way we save all trans history forever more.

RAINBOW REFUGEES CAST
A COMMUNITY LIFELINE

THE UK IS NOT a popular place for LGBTIQ+ people to seek asylum (there were only 1,377 applications in 2023, 2 per cent of overall claims). The process of applying can be harrowing and invasive because proving your sexuality and gender identity is an almost impossible feat when you come from a country where it is unsafe to express yourself freely. Across the UK and Ireland, queer refugee activist collectives offer personal support and professional expertise to those in desperate need. Their extraordinary, highly organised efforts are rarely given the recognition they deserve. This is queer activism on the frontline.

Lesbian Immigration Support is a local grassroots project in Manchester that's been run by volunteers since 2007. The women offer lesbian asylum seekers emotional and practical help, like buddying up on trips to the Home Office, helping applicants prepare for their asylum interviews, acting as witnesses and writing letters of support. Micro Rainbow run safe houses for LGBTIQ+ asylum seekers and refugees, providing over thirty thousand bed nights a year. African Rainbow Family (working out of Manchester, Birmingham, Leeds and London) advocate for legal support for the 60 per cent of LGBTIQ+ asylum seekers who have no solicitor or caseworker. Is Rainbow Muid, We Are Rainbow offer peer support for people seeking international protection in Ireland.

There are many more volunteer organisations across the UK and Ireland dedicated to helping some of the most vulnerable members of our community survive the navigation of an almost impossible system.

'LISG [Lesbian Immigration Support] are more than just a support group to its members – 'It's emotional, it's social, it's everything. But also you have to help yourself,' said one asylum-seeking member. 'I've found my place in Manchester,' said another, comparing the safe space of the group and people's individual and complex identities within it to the ludicrous asylum process, during which you are meant to explain who you are 'in a few sentences, in a few pages'.'

↑ The Gays Against Nazis badge featured the anti-fascist arrow of the Anti-Nazi League (ANL).

Right to Remain, 10 July 2015. For more: https://righttoremain.org.uk/

CHALLENGING THE IDEA THAT 'HOMOSEXUALITY IS UNAFRICAN'

IN THIS INTERVIEW for West Yorkshire Queer Stories, Samra talks about challenging the idea 'that homosexuality is un-African' and emphasises the importance of activism coming from a place of love.

'A friend of ours is an asylum seeker here from Uganda. When they were detained, we organised this action to shame Qatar Airways and make them not fly the plane. There's a real difference for me personally with activism where it comes from a place of love: like where it comes from a place of 'I love you deeply' or 'I love the planet deeply' or 'I love this area deeply', and it's not coming from a place of 'I hate this'. Theresa May is not even in my mind. I just love this person so much that I am not going to allow this to happen. I feel like, once you have that energy, you're able to utilise that, and that spreads and that moves.

My housemate initiated the whole thing and was key to pushing it, along with someone else from Leeds No Borders. But I suppose I would really like to support more – think about ways to support queer asylum seekers and refugees. Because it's one of those things where, here, being queer for me is, like, I can just get on with things and I can do my day-to-day. It's not that big a deal for me. And I was speaking to my friend about this yesterday, like ... to what extent is being queer like a massive part of who I am? I think it is but it's not something that can be observed. It cannot be observed in the same way that people see me as being a woman or being Black and so – not to make a hierarchy of things – but it's not at the forefront of who I am, whereas for those coming from places like Uganda – and I think that personal connection to the country makes me feel like I should really be doing something – makes me feel like I want to be doing these things and do more.'

Samra Mayanja interviewed by Lydia Valentine for West Yorkshire Queer Stories (2018). For more: https://wyqs.co.uk

GLITTER CYMRU was founded in 2016 and is a social and support group for LGBTIQ+ global majority people. The Glitter banner was made by the group in 2018 and has been used at various Pride events, including the first Welsh BAME Pride, held on 10 August 2019 at Cathays Community Centre, Cardiff. It is now saved in the Amgueddfa Cymru collection.

With thanks to Mark Etheridge, Principal Curator of Collection Development: LGBTQ+, Amgueddfa Cymru – Museum Wales.

GLITTER CYMRU BANNER.

WORKERS' PRIDE

RELEASED IN 2014, the movie *Pride* turned the efforts of LGSM (Lesbians and Gays Support the Miners) thirty years earlier into the stuff of legend. It's a star-studded example of a broader, longer, far-reaching history of workers' rights and queer rights coming together as a united union struggle. Trade unions have been active in the fight for LGBTIQA+ rights since the 1970s, with the National and Local Government Officers' Association (NALGO) establishing gay and lesbian workers branches in 1972. By 1976, it had passed a lesbian and gay inclusion policy and adopted the sub-group name of NALGAY. It soon went on strike to defend one of its members who'd been subjected to homophobia by their employer. The unionists won.

From opposing Section 28, to campaigning for HIV access to healthcare, to the Trades Union Congress's call for same-sex marriage (and the rights this bestowed upon those workers), union activists have made a critical contribution to securing protections both in the workplace and beyond. The work of lifelong activist Bob Cant is worthy of a special mention, as the five boxes of his archival material at the Bishopsgate Institute – which span thirty years and as far and wide as Scotland, Ireland and back to Haringey – reveal.

Among reems of documents covering his work as an educator and trade unionist and his anti-racist activism are sixty cassette tapes of oral history interviews, multiple audio CDs, including one labelled 'BBC Radio Scotland Sense of Place, Programme 2, "Dumbledykes"', plus his interview with Seth Atkin on his life as a gay trade unionist, recorded in 2008 as part of the Millthorpe Project: Interviews with Lesbian, Gay, Bisexual and Trans Trade Unionists (deposited at the British Library's Sound and Moving Image Archive). His dissertation, written for his Diploma in Industrial Relations and Trade Union Studies at Middlesex Polytechnic, has the serious title 'Gays and Trade Unions: An Exploration of the Way Gay People Are Oppressed at Work and of the Strategies Used and Required to Resist' (1981). But perhaps even more intriguing is his typed memoir, entitled *Belonging/Not Belonging: Tales of Times I Spent with Friends and Comrades and Fuckbuddies between 1967 and 1981*.

↑ **Lesbians and Gays Support the Miners 30th anniversary badge.**

THE BLACK LGBT+ UNION MOVEMENT

UNISON IS the largest trade union in the UK, with more than 1.3 million members from the health, education and public services sectors. In 2023 it celebrated the Year of Black Workers, recognising the key contributions these members had made to the movement.

Unison's General Secretary, Christina McAnea, wrote publicly to give special credit to the way in which Black, queer activists had shaped the union and its work. Her commendations included Rizwan Sheikh, who campaigned tirelessly for both lesbian and gay and Black issues, who was said to have been 'immensely proud of being the first Black co-chair of UNISON's national lesbian and gay committee' as it was known at the time, before changing its name to the LGBT+ national committee. Sheikh also campaigned for supporting migrant workers in the North. His work, among others – including Eastern Regional Secretary Tim Roberts (who secured Unison's place in the annual UK Black Pride celebrations) – highlights the union's role in recognising the way in which class, race and queer struggles intersect.

Equally active and influential was Bev Miller, the first lesbian chair of the national Black members' committee. And then there's the first ever trans man to co-chair the national LGBT+ committee, Dave Merchant, a pioneer who propelled the fight for trans equality forwards, both inside Unison and in the workplace. The 1990s saw national lesbian and gay committee members Ted Brown and Dirg Aaab-Richards successfully campaign against homophobia in the media at a critical moment at the height of anti-AIDS hysteria. Their campaigning triggered an advertising boycott of the *The Voice*. The terms of resolution included issuing an apology for the coverage of the death of Black gay footballer Justin Fashanu and the cessation of homophobic editorial in the future.

The list goes on… Claire Andrews was renowned for her policy-driven vision for the future of the Black lesbian and gay movement. Paul Amann was a member of the standing committee for more than twenty years, frequently focussing on the rights of refugees. Far from exhaustive, this list of vibrant, committed and vocal campaigners represents a wider group who understood – and continue to understand – how the fight against homophobia, transphobia and racism is inseparable from the union's core mission.

Homosexuality – a dirty word?

…butch, femme, fairy, queen, homosexual, gay – ad infinitum. A multitude of different names for a person who is exploring one aspect of human behaviour. Almost all these names have become or were originated as terms of abuse and denigration. To admit to oneself let alone to another any homosexual feelings is to accept the attitudes value judgements and myths implicit in the names above. Naturally, many people will deny to others recognition of their own homosexual feelings. They fear justifiably hostility, abuse, ridicule, or at best patronizing tolerance. These fears are just one of the reasons for the Homophile Society (Gaysoc) insofar that it enables the individual to talk freely to others experiencing the same difficulties without fears and with access to knowledge and information ordinarily inaccessible.

Guild Gazette *(Liverpool)*, 20 March 1973

NALGAY

GAY RECRUITS

Homosexual council workers are being recruited by an organization set up to fight sexual discrimination in local authorities. 'Nalgay' is the latest special interest group of the National and Local Government Officers' Association.

Birmingham Post, 22 July 78

OutRage! flyer: 'Homosexuality and Human Rights on the Isle of Man'.

Union ban on isles meetings

BRITAIN'S biggest white-collar union NALGO, has voted at its annual conference in Douglas Isle of Man not to hold any more conferences there or in the Channel Isles, 'until such time as the laws on homosexuality are reformed.'

A motion passed by the conference noted that the 1967 Sexual Offences Act – legalising homosexual acts between consenting adults in private – did not apply in the Isle of Man or the Channel Isles.

Lancashire Evening Telegraph, 17 June 1983

Homosexuality and Human Rights on the Isle of Man

In April of this year the Isle of Man Legislature decided to maintain the illegality of consenting homosexual acts in private.

In doing so the island has isolated itself as the last remaining place in Europe where homosexuality is still a prosecutable offence and can be punished by a life sentence.

In addition this legislation against homosexuals is in direct contravention of the European Convention of Human Rights which the Isle of Man signed through London in 1953.

The UK government has stated that it will force the Tynwald to change the legislation if it does not do so of its own accord. This could set a dangerous precedent of intervention in the island's affairs by Westminster.

The Isle of Man must show the World and Europe that it is prepared to assume its rightful place as a modern and civilised society. It must demonstrate that it will not prosecute its citizens for a victimless consenting activity.

The Isle of Man has a population of 70,000. As statistically one in ten people are gay, this means that 7,000 people are living under the fear of prosecution and abuse. A modern society should be practising tolerance and understanding not repression. If it is one thing that has driven the Eastern European countries to break their shackles it is right to have freedom of choice.

There are things that we all do not like about other people, their politics, their views, their lifestyle, but we must always strive to allow freedom of expression and choice.

The spread of AIDS has shown us the dangers of intolerance and repression. Only through education has the incidence of AIDS been controlled until now new cases of AIDS are lower amongst homosexuals than heterosexuals. There are many gay men who may be married with children who are afraid of asking for advice for fear of being persecuted. This can only increase the spread of AIDS and inhibit promoting the 'safe sex' message.

THE ISLE OF MAN MUST ASSUME ITS PLACE IN EUROPE! SUPPORT US AND WRITE TO KENNETH BAKER

Write to Kenneth Baker, Home Office, Queen Anne's Gate, London SW1H 9AT and show your support for the decriminalisation of homosexuality

Produced by OutRage!, LLGC, 69 Cowcross Street, London EC1M 6BP, tel:071 490 7153

TUC NEWS

A delicate problem for NALGO'S National Executive. Having arranged the annual union conference in the pleasant atmosphere of the Isle of Man they found their metropolitan district representative violently opposed to the venue.

The reason? The Isle of Man still considers homosexuality an offence and this, it is feared, might cramp the style of some of the members – not to say land them in the local nick.

A worried NALGAY Executive decided it was too late to change anything but appointed its general purposes committee to look into the Island's 'future suitability' for local government officers in the light of this anti-homosexualist legislation.

Private Eye, 18 September 1982

Isle of Man Weekly Times

'Gay rights' protest march and conference decision under fire

N.A.L.G.O. LOCALS CALL FOR UNION APOLOGY

ANGRY members of the Isle of Man branch of N.A.L.G.O. led by the new Douglas Town Clerk, have disassociated themselves from the N.A.L.G.O. conference delegates who paraded through Douglas last Thursday as a protest against Manx laws prohibiting homosexual activity here. And in doing so they have: CONDEMNED conference delegates who voted in favour of a resolution to boycott the Island as a conference centre as 'bad mannered'; ACCUSED the entire conference of being 'misguided'; and CALLED for an apology to the island from what they described as 'the more responsible members of N.A.L.G.O.'

Isle of Man Weekly Times, 21 June 1983

Manx Catty

THERE is only one place in Europe where homosexuality between consenting adult males is still considered a criminal offence – and that is the Isle of Man. Not the Isle of New Man, evidently.

But with the double standard which British law applied in the dark ages before its enlightenment, lesbianism is legal. This anomaly rests at the door of the homophobic male lawmakers: They do not find the idea of gay women offensive, probably because it feeds their fantasies.

Western Daily Press, 2 March 1991

Chanting N.A.L.G.O. crowds block road
'GAY' RIGHTS MARCH ON TYNWALD

DELEGATES at the 1983 N.A.L.G.O. conference in Douglas agreed by a majority vote yesterday afternoon to a motion calling for the boycott of the Isle of Man as a venue for future trade union conferences. It happened after 300 chanting Gay Rights supporters from the union marched on Tynwald to hand in a petition declaring that they were disgusted to learn that the conference is being held on an island where homosexuality is still totally illegal.

Lunchtime traffic was halted for about 20 minutes as the protestors stood in the road outside government offices chanting gay slogans.

They had proceeded from the Palace Lido and through the crowded Strand Street at lunchtime, chanting and waving banners. And outside Government Office they blocked the road with some women activists leading bursts of chanting. Most traffic was diverted through Hill Street, but a bus driver pressed on and his determination eventually got him through.

Manx Star, 17 June 1983

LIVERPOOL LESBIAN AND GAY ACTION

By Kay Jones

'We welcome any lesbians or gay men who wish to actively fight heterosexism and sexism and are opposed to all forms of racism and ableism.'

Liverpool Lesbian and Gay Action, 1990

Liverpool Lesbian and Gay Action was a political group made up of lesbians and gay men. The group challenged and fought heterosexism through campaigning, being out, direct action and 'generally having a good time'. They were based at the Mutual Aid Centre, Seel Street. The organisation came out of Liverpool Stop the Clause, which was formed in 1988 to fight the introduction of Clause 28 of the Local Government Bill. Liverpool Lesbian and Gay Action did many things, including:

- Lobbying local union branches about their lack of equal opportunities policies
- Raising money for ambulance workers on strike
- Lobbying Liverpool City Council to request a Lesbian and Gay Sub-committee
- Helping to organise Liverpool Lesbian and Gay Pride

A banner colourfully displaying the name of the group, made by Dawn Brayford and Pura Ariza, was used at London Pride and many other demonstrations in Manchester and Liverpool.

Kay Jones is Lead Curator of Urban and Community History, National Museums Liverpool.

LIVERPOOL LESBIAN AND GAY ACTION BANNER.

MARY WINTER: SACKED FOR WEARING A LESBIAN LIBERATION BADGE

By Paul Fairweather

WHEN I ARRIVED in Burnley, I kept asking people: do you remember the case of Mary Winter, who was sacked by Burnley Bus Company in 1978 for wearing a Lesbian Liberation badge? But no one had heard of her. And we couldn't find anything in the local archives at Burnley Library or in the local press either. Yet, I remembered that the first time I had been to Burnley had been to speak to Burnley Trades Council about the Mary Winter case. Her local trade union was not supporting her but, following our meeting, the Trades Council had agreed to.

LESBIAN LIBERATION BADGE.

In 1978 LGBTIQ+ people had no protection at work. You could lose your job because of your sexuality or gender identity, and often your trade union would refuse to support you. Badge-wearing was also popular at the time. It was often used as a visible sign of your politics and sometimes even of your sexuality. I remember wearing a huge white badge that said 'Yes, I'm Homosexual Too'.

Mary refused to take off her Lesbian Liberation badge and was sacked for it. This inspired her to start a campaign that culminated in a demonstration outside the bus station in Burnley, which featured on the front page of the *Burnley Express*. Mary's campaign was also supported by the actress Vanessa Redgrave, who was a member of the Workers Revolutionary Party at the time and standing in a by-election in Moss Side in Manchester. Redgrave was a well-known supporter of gay rights at a time when few celebrities were, and her support gave the campaign a boost.

Mary Winter's struggle to be herself at work and the lessons that her campaign can teach us are no longer forgotten.

Paul Fairweather has been active in a wide range of LGBTIQ+ community and campaigning groups since the early 1970s. He has worked in the field of equality and diversity for many years and now works as a trainer/consultant on LGBTIQ+ issues. He is the project coordinator of Hidden Histories, which celebrates the LGBTIQ+ history of Burnley and East Lancashire and was funded by the National Lottery Heritage Fund.

'YES, I'M HOMOSEXUAL TOO' BADGE, LATE 1970S.

AIDS MEMORIAL QUILT, DEVON

By Daniel Fountain

THE UK AIDS Memorial Quilt tells the stories of many of those lost in the early days of the HIV/AIDS epidemic in the 1980s and 1990s. The quilt consists of forty-eight panels measuring 12x12 ft, each comprising up to eight smaller panels that usually measure 6x4 ft, the average size of a human grave. For the majority, each panel commemorates a specific person who died of AIDS and has been lovingly made by their friends, lovers or family. Others were created by charities and groups who sought to remember a wider collective of people. At the time of writing, the quilt represents approximately 384 people from all around the United Kingdom. As an ongoing project, this figure is ever-increasing. The quilt is usually housed in storage, but its stories and histories continue to be told by the six charities that make up the UK AIDS Memorial Quilt Conservation Partnership: George House Trust, Terrence Higgins Trust, the Food Chain, Sahir House, Positively UK and Positively East.

The panel pictured here was created by two charities – Body Positive Devon and Body Positive Somerset. As an independent and autonomous initiative started by

A panel on the UK AIDS Memorial Quilt, created by Body Positive Devon and Body Positive Somerset, 1993.

HIV-positive people, Body Positive Inc. was set up in the early 1980s and was distinctly different from other organisations. Body Positive had, and maintains, the unique perspective of 'knowing first hand' what it is like to live with the virus and the issues surrounding being HIV positive, enabling them to tailor their services accordingly. Groups were established both in the UK and internationally. This panel was made by coordinators and members of the two South West UK-based Body Positive groups and was submitted to the Conservation Partnership in September 1993. Accompanying the panel was a letter explaining some of its iconography and the difficulty the group faced when trying to decide how to effectively represent the varied personalities of loved ones and friends from the region. Its background is a vibrant blue silk taffeta which, the group note, 'is the symbol of the clear blue skies we shared through the summers and the dove of peace acknowledges their resting place ... [it] is the sea that we paddled in, dunk wheelchairs in, and swam in as free as the representative dolphin'.

The majority of the panel is taken up by a map of the coast of south-west England in dark-green felt, where the names of various locations – Barnstable, Taunton, Exeter, Torbay, Plymouth and Penzance – are stitched in yellow thread. Each town is marked by a red ribbon. The green felt 'symbolises the moors of Cornwall, Devon and Somerset that we have trekked over and some now have as their final resting place'. In yellow lettering are the names of both groups accompanied by the phrase 'we will always remember'. The vibrancy of the yellow text reflects the 'copious amount of sunshine that has helped heal us and restore us. It is also a symbol of the beaches we have walked with our friends whose footprints have now been washed away'.

UK AIDS MEMORIAL QUILT ON DISPLAY AT TATE MODERN, LONDON, 12 JUNE 2025.

Dr Daniel Fountain is a curator and researcher exploring the intersections of queerness and craft. They are Senior Lecturer in Art History and Visual Culture at the University of Exeter. Daniel's books include Crafted with Pride (Intellect Books and University of Chicago Press, 2023) and Queer Crafts (Bloomsbury Academic, 2026). Further details can be found at www.danielfountain.com.

Following a spate of police entrapments (with one resulting in a suicide) and a refusal to decriminalise homosexuality in line with the UK, activists on the Isle of Man staged radical protests until the law was changed in 1992 — 25 years after England and Wales. In 2020, the government issued an apology and in 2022 it granted automatic pardons to the men who had been arrested.

Suicide after gay arrest

MANX civil liberties campaigners wrote to the chief constable yesterday expressing their concern at the suicide of a man who had been arrested under the island's draconian anti-gay laws.

The shock case came after a spate of recent arrests for gross indecency on the island which still outlaws homosexuality.

Members of the Manx Council for Civil Liberties are concerned that the apparent police crackdown which trapped the man, who later committed suicide, may have been a reaction to recent gay protest against the laws.

Morning Star, 15 February 1992

UGLY SCENES AT 'GAY' TYNWALD

GAY RIGHTS demonstrators wearing 'proud to be Queer' T-shirts were kicked and punched in a scuffle with elderly spectators during the annual Tynwald Day ceremony at Saint Johns on Friday.

The incident happened as Alan Shea, dressed as a concentration camp victim, presented a petition for re-dress of grievance on behalf of the Ellan Vannin Gay Group, protesting at Tynwald's refusal to reform Manx homosexuality law.

Abuse

Gay protesters at the side of Tynwald Hill briefly became the target of crowd hostility. Their banners were pulled down and blows and abuse were directed at them from surrounding spectators. One gay said he had been kicked in the leg and punched in the face.

Apart from Mr Shea, who lives in Douglas, the demonstrators had all travel to the island for the occasion as members of 'OutRage!', the London-based Gay and Lesbian 'direct action' group.

[...] There was some abusive barracking from the onlookers, one of whom observed, 'You'll notice there's no Manxmen among them'. Another remarked, 'They should be rolled down Slieau Whillian in a spiked barrel!'.

Manx Independent, 9 July 1991

Manx gay sex ban lifted

THE ISLE OF MAN's MPs have bowed to international pressure and decided to scrap the island's laws banning homosexual sex. The Manx parliament's House of Keys voted after a heated all-day debate yesterday to fall in line with demands from Europe to allow sex in private between consenting adult males. The reform was pushed through by only two votes in a 13–11 split at the house amid claims that the island had been blackmailed into change by the UK. The UK government had told the Islanders their laws on homosexuality were in breach of the European Convention on Human Rights.

Kent Today, *1 April 1992*

Gays kissed and fondled each other

SIR – I would like to put the record straight concerning your reporter's account of what took place at the Tynwald ceremony, concerning the homosexuals.

I and another lady on another stall watched as they plotted with their imported camera crew to cause more of a scene than the one at the foot of Tynwald Hill.

They laughed and giggled like a group of tarts, then made a beeline for the stall who were the only opposition to their filthy habits there that day – a Christian stall who were not too afraid to bring their light from under a bushel and say that it is unholy, unnatural, and unthinkable.

They climbed the Millennium stone, a national monument, so they could shout, flaunt and provoke these God fearing people into some sort of retaliation. The mothers and children who had gathered at the stone to eat their lunch had to leave because of the display these gays put on.

A crowd had soon gathered, and one man grabbed my walking stick so he could use it on them. I quickly grabbed it back. They kissed and fondled each other to cause as much trouble and distress to the Manx people until the police moved in.

Isle of Man Examiner, *16 July 1991*

HUNGER STRIKE OVER GAYS LAW

A 27-year-old man has gone on hunger strike in the UK in protest at the treatment of homosexuals in the Isle of Man, according to a Gay newspaper in London.

'Capital Gay' says Michael Cole began the hunger strike in London, after writing to Prime Minister John Major, 'over the Government's failure to change the law in the Isle of Man'.

The publication quotes Mr Cole as commenting, 'I come from Jersey. It's not as harsh there but I know the pressures of a small island community. What really upset me was the suicides'.

'I understand the pressures. I can relate to them. There was a time when I felt like that. I've been trying to think what individuals can do. By keeping silent we're condoning what's going on. In London we can forget what other people are having to fight'.

Manx Independent, *10 March 1992*

Isle gay activist made 'an outcast'

A man who helped overturn the homosexuality ban in the Isle of Man says his campaign has made him an outcast. Gay activist, Merseysider Alan Shea, said: 'I have lost my freedom because I am recognized everywhere I go. It is almost impossible for me to get a job on the island and the doctor has warned me that the campaign has put me under a lot of stress. I started off a young man on this campaign. I feel like an old one now but having said that I think it was well worth what I have lost. Even if I knew when I started out on the cause what lay ahead I still wouldn't have changed thing.' Mr Shea, formerly of Kirkby, Merseyside, has lived on the island for the last nine years, and took up the cause after hearing about a gay man who committed suicide while awaiting trial on an indecency charge.

Daily Post, *9 April 1992*

YORK, 1988
By Kythé Beaumont and Sally Weston

THERE WAS A history of activism in York – this was around feminism and left politics and not particularly around lesbian and gay issues. There was a radical bookshop and campaigns against pornography and sex shops, against violence against women and promoting reproductive rights.

Before Clause 28, there hadn't been a history of lesbians and gay men working together on a campaign. Once we decided that a march was a good way of protesting and raising awareness, we needed to find some gay men to see if they would be interested in joining us. Nobody really knew any gay men, so the first action was to print some leaflets inviting men to join us in planning and organising the march. We leafletted the York Arms, then a 'known' gay-friendly pub. Gay men joined us and we began to plan a march, a press campaign and activities for after the march. Friendships struck up and York Lesbian and Gay Solidarity (YLAGS) began!

We had arrived in York from London in 1985. I remember marching in 1988 against Clause 28 from the river through the streets of York to a rally in St Sampson's Square. This was one of the first Lesbian and Gay marches to be held in York. Although there were two hundred of us, there seemed to be a relatively small number of people, with a strong likelihood of being spotted by neighbours or colleagues. Even though we were out and proud, it still felt a bit risky and very different to the huge numbers and festive (if increasingly commercial) atmosphere of Gay Pride in London.

A large group of us from Lesbian Line and the Women's Centre travelled to a march in Manchester – we hired and filled a coach; again, this was all very new. It felt great to be part of a much larger movement in the UK.

I remember talking to our next-door neighbour, who was a secondary school Eng-

A poster for the Lancashire Lesbian and Gay Coalition's 'Never Going Underground' rally held in Preston on 30 November 1991. The adapted London Underground logo and the chant were both widely adopted by queer protestors right across the UK in their collective struggle against Section 28.

lish teacher who routinely used authors such as E. M. Forster as a way of discussing sexuality and offering support to pupils who were questioning their sexuality (mostly secretly) or those who were suffering from bullying because of their sexuality. She didn't think she could continue doing this. It would only take one pupil to talk to their perhaps fundamentalist parents for a complaint to go to the head, and she would be at risk of losing her job.

Kythé Beaumont and Sally Weston are local organisers in York and co-founders of YLAGS.

↑ York Lesbian and Gay Solidarity (YLAGS) at the 'Stop the Clause' march in York, 1988.

SOME PEOPLE ARE BI
By Jen Yockney

In 2007 STONEWALL launched its 'Some People Are Gay, Get Over It' campaign with bus ads, billboards and more. It was a brilliant and high-impact initiative. But by that point bis and bi groups had spent nearly two decades critiquing Stonewall's work for erasing bisexuality and biphobia.

Manchester group Bisexual Action held a quick fundraising appeal and printed thousands of postcards on purple instead of the red of Stonewall's campaign, using a near-identical font to offer a bi version of the slogan. The reverse of the card was pre-addressed to Stonewall HQ, challenging them over three of their recent instances of bi erasure and calling on them to do better. They appeared at a variety of Pride stalls and LGBTIQ+ conferences nationwide. After a few years and personnel changes, Stonewall also took up the bi version of the slogan.

Jen Yockney is the editor of Bi Community News.

↓ A flyer addressed to Ben Summerskill of Stonewall, challenging the organisation to do more to lobby for bisexual people.

JIMMY SOMERVILLE: THE ACT UP TOUR

By George J. Severs

OF THE MANY groups to respond to the HIV/AIDS epidemic, perhaps the most famous was the AIDS Coalition to Unleash Power, known to most as ACT UP. American chapters of the group were started by high-profile literary and artistic figures, the playwright Larry Kramer and the writer Sarah Schulman being among New York's most notable examples.

While most British ACT UP members did not enjoy such a level of celebrity, there were some prominent individuals. Best known was the singer Jimmy Somerville. Born in Glasgow in 1961, Somerville was living in London at the end of the 1980s following a successful career with the bands Bronski Beat and the Communards. He was already a noted gay rights campaigner before his time with ACT UP: Bronski Beat's album *The Age of Consent* (1984) lambasted the injustices faced by lesbians and gay men. Somerville was not a fair-weather celebrity supporter of ACT UP London. Instead, he threw himself into agitating with the group. In 1989, he was one of ten people arrested outside the Australian Embassy in London as ACT UP staged a protest against the introduction of HIV testing for new entries to Australia.

Somerville also used his musical talents to raise money for ACT UP London. In May 1989 a benefit was held at the Fridge nightclub in Brixton to raise funds for the newly formed chapter. Somerville was not the only celebrity to perform in front of the nine-hundred-strong crowd assembled for what *Capital Gay* described as 'a successful fusion of politics and pop': DJ Mark Moore 'pumped out the music' for much of the night

'Jimmy's on the road', an article in *Capital Gay*, 9 March 1990, previewing Jimmy Somerville's ACT UP Tour.

Jimmy at the recent Fridge benefit *(Photo: Gordon Rainsford)*

WHATEVER the rumours about Jimmy Somerville leaving the country for warmer climes, he's still going ahead with his tour next month, *The ACT-UP Review*, with all money raised going to help British ACT-UP groups.

Jimmy, famous as much for his Aids activism as his singing ability, will be performing at five venues in April, all of them clubs or small, friendlier halls.

Unlike recent guest appearances he'll be playing full sets, with numbers from his Bronski Beat and Communards days as well as from his recent *Read My Lips* album. And for anyone going to the Heaven set, Jimmy is promising some pleasant surprises

- **Manchester** Hacienda Tuesday April 10th
- **Nottingham** Rock City Wednesday April 11th
- **Liverpool** University Thursday April 12th
- **Glasgow** Barrowlands Saturday April 14th
- **London** Heaven Wednesday April 18th

(Tickets are available in advance or on the door at all venues except Heaven, which is door entrance only)

while images from ACT UP protests in the UK and USA were projected onto three large screens around the venue. According to reports in the gay press following the event, the climax of the evening came when Somerville and Erasure frontman Andy Bell performed as the 'ACT-UP All Star Revue'. In a powerful nod to the mortal urgency of the epidemic, the pair sang Gloria Gaynor's 'I Will Survive', a song already appropriated by lesbians and gay men as a 'gay anthem' and which the HIV/AIDS crisis had added yet more meaning to. Somerville continued to use his artistic energies to raise funds for ACT UP. In the early 1990s, he toured clubs across the country with 'Jimmy Somerville: The ACT UP Tour'. The singer told an interviewer that

↑ Jimmy Somerville pictured for the 'What's on' column in *Capital Gay*, 18 April 1990.

> 'This tour is to raise money for ACT UP in the UK. It's not just a London-based organisation anymore – there's an ACT UP in Edinburgh, Leeds, Manchester and Brighton. And money raised from this will go to each group. ACT UP is an organisation based on AIDS activism which is something I strongly believe in. We're trying to raise consciousness, to make people realise that this is a human issue. For too long it's been seen as a sordid story you read about in newspapers, but AIDS is affecting real people's lives.'

'Jimmy Somerville: The ACT UP Tour', Bishopsgate Institute Library: LGBTM/7/3

This was the message that Somerville took to venues across the UK in April 1990, starting with Manchester's Haçienda club and ending at London's flagship gay club Heaven. The tour raised some £6,000 for ACT UP chapters in the UK.

George J. Severs is a historian of modern Britain, activism, sexuality and religion at the Geneva Graduate Institute.

Gay men were targeted aggressively by Cornwall police throughout the 1970s. Newspaper reports twenty years later reflect lingering attitudes of homophobia embedded in the late tackling of the AIDS crisis in the region.

Homosexuals pledge courtroom protest

HOMOSEXUAL rights campaigners are threatening to stage a demonstration when 16 men from Cornwall appear in court to answer charges relating to alleged homosexual activities. Supporters from London and other parts of the country have already offered to send protesters.

And Cornwall's convener for the Campaign for Homosexual equality, Mr. Noel Thomas, said yesterday that a list of those charged issued by police last week showed there was a 'witch hunt' against alleged homosexuals in the county. Five of those charged are members of the Cornwall branch of CHE.

'There is now obviously a justified case for public protest. The prosecution can't be stopped now,' Mr. Thomas said. 'We must bring to the notice of the public the disgusting fact that alleged homosexuals are being hunted by the authorities.

If it means waving banners and demonstrating outside a court, then we shall have to do it.'

THE ACCUSED

Roger Edwin Thomas, Maynes Caravan Site, Redruth; Stephen Trevor Tossell, 22 Beacon Parc, Helston; Thomas John Sowell, 3 Falmouth Road, Redruth; Joseph Henry Wearne Clemo, 6 Fernhill Road, Newquay; John Francis Jotcham, 20 Foundry Row, Redruth; David Knuckey, Richmond, Redruth; Herbert Charles John Hyde, 3 Higher Ninnis, St Day; Thomas Neil Cottrell, 31 Tresothick Park, Helston; William Mitchell, 8 Menjivey Place, St Ives; Roger David Hunt, 27 Laburnum Close, Falmouth; Joseph Bernard Beard, 25 Belle Vue, Redruth; Geoffrey David Michael Parkin, 54 Murdoch Close, Redruth; Jeremy Harvey Ball, 25 Park Road, Redruth; James Brian Tremayne, Karenda, Trehayle Terrace, Redruth; Peter Brian Trevellan, 13 St Clements Close, Truro; Brian Francis Summers, 6 [illegible] Avenue, Falmouth.

Western Independent, Plymouth, 20 March 1977

Police accused of purge on Cornish homosexuals

The Campaign for Homosexual Equality and the National Council for Civil Liberties yesterday accused the Devon and Cornwall police force of mounting a witch-hunt against homosexuals. The accusation [follows] a series of arrests in recent weeks in which at least 28 men have been charged with a variety of homosexual offences in contravention of the 1967 Sexual Offences Act.

One of those involved is a 29-year-old Cornish social worker, whose name has been given to the Guardian. He has been charged with committing an act of gross indecency with another man. The act is alleged to have been committed two or three hours before the younger man celebrated his 21st birthday, after which the offence would no longer have been indictable.

Guardian, London, 7 March 1977

CORNWALL WITCH-HUNT

IN CORNWALL, 16 gay men have been charged with committing acts of 'gross indecency', following an intensive investigation by the police last February (see *PN* March 11). 11 of them pleaded guilty in court to a total of 34 offences and sentences ranged from six months imprisonment suspended for two years and £20 costs; to fines of up to £100.

Two men who pleaded not guilty were dismissed after the police offered no evidence. Four men charged with similar offences from the same investigation are waiting to appear in court.

Peace News, *29 July 1977*

Gays accuse Cornish police

CORNISH police were accused yesterday by the Campaign for Homosexual Equality of conducting a witch-hunt against gay people.

Morning Star, 18 March 1972

Gays strike back

A GAY activist has hit back after councillors criticized a decision by Cornwall Health Authorities to spend £50,000 on HIV/Aids prevention for gay men.

Malcolm Lidberry, from Cambourne, whose partner is dying from Aids, said the money was a 'late gesture in the face of a growing problem.'

Western Morning News, *12 February 1996*

WOLVERHAMPTON CHALLENGES CLAUSE 28
By George J. Severs

IN MAY 1988, the British government passed a law that forbade local councils from activity that could be seen to 'promote homosexuality'. Clause 28, the part of the bill that contained this infamous wording, cast a long shadow over LGBTIQ+ communities in the UK. London's queer newspaper *Capital Gay* described it as the 'challenge of the century'.

This challenge did not go unmet. LGBTIQ+ people and their allies came out to protest plans for the new law in their thousands. The most famous of these demonstrations happened in, or were linked to, London. Lesbian activists invaded the BBC's *Six O'Clock News* studios, shouting 'Stop Clause 28', shortly before abseiling into the House of Lords in protest at the vote that finally passed the new law. Huge demonstrations were staged at remarkably short notice in London and Manchester, and activists chartered trains between the two cities to ensure both were equally well attended.

Because of these demonstrations, London and Manchester dominate our understandings of what resistance to Clause 28 looked like. However, one of the final challenges to Clause 28 before it passed into law came from the small West Midlands city of Wolverhampton. There, the Wolverhampton Lesbian and Gay Rights Group had prepared a film titled *Get Your Clause Off Our Lives*, playing on the homonym of 'clause' as a section of a bill before it comes law (i.e. Clause 28) and the claws of a monster or enemy. According to the *Pink Paper*, the film 'includes footage of Nazi treatment of homosexuals and interviews with politicians and activists and makes links with the way we are currently being treated'.

The comparison to Nazi Germany did not come out of nowhere. In 1986, the leader of Wolverhampton's neighbouring South Staffordshire Council, Bill Brownhill, told a council meeting that 'I would put 90 per cent of queers in the ruddy gas chamber'. This outburst, which had been supported by the council's opposition Labour leader, had helped to put the Wolverhampton area on queer activists' agendas. A march to protest Brownhill's statement took place in the village of Wombourne, near Wolverhampton. Twelve protestors were arrested and detained for two weeks over Christmas 1986. They later received compensation for false imprisonment and wrongful arrest.

Therefore, when a senior Conservative councillor at Wolverhampton Council, Gordon Jones, banned the showing of *Get Your Clause Off Our Lives* in April 1988 (before Clause 28 had been enacted), activists were ready. Jones objected to the film's screening in the council-owned Lighthouse Media Centre, arguing that he could not 'permit public buildings or facilities to be used to promote homosexual activities'. Here he deliberately echoed the wording of Clause 28, anticipating its mandate that 'a local authority shall not intentionally promote homosexuality'.

A demonstration opposing this decision was immediately called. Activists flocked to the Civic Centre on Wolverhampton's St Peter's Square at 1.30 pm on 4 May, when Wolverhampton's councillors convened for a full council meeting, just twenty days before Clause 28 became law. This demonstration attracted people beyond Wolverhampton's burgeoning community of queer activists. Members of Brighton Plus Area Action Against the Clause travelled up from the south coast, while the Nottingham Dykes group held aloft a banner they had carried from the East Midlands.

Ultimately, the clause passed and became Section 28, enshrined in law until its repeal in 2000 in Scotland and 2003 elsewhere in the UK. London and Manchester may well have been the epicentres of opposition to Clause 28, but Wolverhampton shows the ways in which the growing network of activists responded quickly to mounting localised homophobia caused by Clause 28.

Gay Liberation Front and Teachers Against Section 28 badges.

4: ACTIVISM AND COMMUNITY

SECTION 28

From the private collection of Brightonian queer activist and broadcaster Melita Dennett

A FLYER FOR THE ACT UP MARCH ON BRIGHTON, PART OF THE 'NATIONAL TOUR' AGAINST SECTION 28.

A FLYER FOR 'A YEAR OF LESBIAN & GAY ACTION FIGHTING SECTION 28, EURO-TOUR'.

CYLCH BANNER.

28...25.....?
MAE'CH CYMALAU'N HALA CRYD ARNOM.

Legislated by the Conservative government in 1988, Clause 28, or Section 28, 'prohibited the promotion of homosexuality by local authorities'. Public and school library shelves were stripped of books mentioning queer sex, love or life, council-run public health services were not permitted to disseminate information pertaining to same-sex activity, LGBTIQ+ teachers were forced into the closet, and gay and straight students alike failed to receive any education around sexual diversity. This fostered social hostility towards the community, informed by widespread disinformation spun by the tabloids at the height of the AIDS crisis that could not be effectively countered with education.

CYLCH was founded in Aberystwyth in 1990. Members campaigned for lesbian and gay rights and against homophobia. In 1991 they published the first issue of *Y Ddraig Binc* (The Pink Dragon) – Wales's first dedicated gay and lesbian publication.

A banner made from a plain, cream-coloured woven cotton bedsheet was used by CYLCH in a demonstration (organised by NUS GaySoc) against Section 28 outside Aberystwyth Town Hall on 14 February 1991. It featured a painted slogan in Welsh, a play on words that roughly translates as 'your clauses make us sick'.

With thanks to Mark Etheridge, Principal Curator of Collection Development: LGBTQ+ at Amgueddfa Cymru – Museum Wales.

> 'Children who need to be taught to respect traditional moral values are being taught that they have an inalienable right to be gay. All of those children are being cheated of a sound start in life.'
> Margaret Thatcher, Conservative Prime Minister, 1988

4: ACTIVISM AND COMMUNITY

LGBTIQ+ PEACE ACTIVISM

Paula Smith interviewed by Gill Crawshaw for West Yorkshire Queer Stories (2019). For more: https://wyqs.co.uk

'I think my favourite type of activism is grassroots, it's about helping people directly. I get frustrated with fighting the government. I get frustrated with fighting overall and, you know, fascism as a whole, it's so difficult and hard, it is really hard. What I like to do is help an individual, help a person, one-on-one kind of human contact type activism. Because I think, selfishly, it's more rewarding for me. Whether it's the smaller things like giving somebody a lift, to actively going out and helping them with their benefit claim or, you know, whatever, like any kind of activism, it's all activism in the long run.'

Rachel Melly, campaigner. Courtesy of the Peace Museum, Shipley

'All the kind of different oppressions and stuff are all related ... It was announced that the Red Arrows were going to be flying over Pride and be part of the Pride parade ... And the Red Arrows are obviously RAF and they're used all around the world – flying over Saudi Arabia and that sort of thing – to promote arms sales to oppressive regimes and then they wanted to come and be part of London Pride, which made me really angry and yeah, made me realise that they were really closely linked. And lots of LGBTQ people had a big problem with that, so yeah, so I campaigned against the Red Arrows being involved with Pride.'

We want to make sure LGBTQ+ histories are represented in our collection all year round, which is why we've incorporated the objects we used in our Peace OUT exhibition in 2019 into our permanent collections. In Peace OUT, we looked at LGBTQ+ activism as peacemaking, focusing on how people working for equal rights are engaging in a form of peacemaking. There are also places, however, where LGBTQ+ activism and what we would traditionally consider as peace activism cross over, such as with the No Pride in War campaign. The No Pride in War network is a culmination of several different groups, and also has many individual non-associated members. This includes the Peace Pledge Union, LGBTQ+ groups such as Lesbians and Gays Support the Migrants, and anti-military groups such as Campaign Against Arms Trade.

The No Pride in War poster (see p. 152) was created to show the group's opposition to the presence of the Red Arrows at Pride in London in 2016, the event around which the network originally formed.

With thanks to Charlotte Hall, Curator, The Peace Museum, Shipley.

'In the early eighties I was involved in some of this women's activities at Greenham Common. By that time I was living in Yorkshire, and ... I can remember standing on the streets of Harrogate singing songs with a group of about six or eight women, bringing awareness to the people of Harrogate [laughs] but it was significant in Harrogate because of Menwith Hill and the nearby – you know there were also demonstrations going on at Menwith Hill and camp set up there for a while ... I used to attend demos there. And I spent Christmas at Greenham once, in a very small tent [laughs]. By that time, connecting it to the LGBT stuff – I didn't come out till I was thirty. So the, all the Quaker stuff really is part of my heterosexual life, and the ... peace activism sort of, from involvement with Menwith Hill and Greenham Common, is very much to do with my new life as a lesbian, and feminism and around women. So I spent, yes, a Christmas – I can't remember which year, probably about '82 or I should think, in a small tent, in the snow [laughs] at Greenham! For a couple of nights. Family thought I was mad, but completely understand, 'cos of the whole background, standing up for what you believe in – or in this case, lying in a cold tent, with your big woolly socks on.'

↑ 'We have a dream/Mae gennym freuddwyd'. Banner made for a march from Bath to Greenham in June 1983.

Susan was recorded by Lydia Valentine for West Yorkshire Queer Stories on 9 October 2018

4: ACTIVISM AND COMMUNITY | **181**

CAMPAIGN FOR HOMOSEXUAL EQUALITY

Group 'not accepted by society'

The Sexual Offences Act – Legalizing homosexual acts between adult males in private – had done nothing to enable the homosexual to become more accepted in society, a meeting of 50 social workers, doctors and homosexuals was told last night. The meeting was the first 'teach-in' on homosexuality called by the Liverpool group of the Campaign for Homosexual Equality held in the Liverpool Cathedral. The poor group convener, Mr. Robin Bloxsidge, told the predominantly male gathering that while the 1967 Act had been a milestone in some respects, it had left much unsaid. There was still substantial job discrimination against homosexuals and they were still open to blackmail. 'It is not fear of the law, but fear of the homosexual secret becoming known which gives the blackmailer his success,' Mr. Bloxsidge said.

Liverpool Echo, 21 September 1972

Friend, the telephone advisory service run by Liverpool's Campaign for Homosexual Equality group, receives up to 30 phone calls each three-hour evening session. 'Many are from women,' says one volunteer, 'the majority are married. If a husband is gay, he can make some pretext for an evening out. If a wife has kiddies, it is far more difficult.'

Newspaper cutting held in the Lesbian and Gay Newsmedia Archive

↑ The first Welsh branch of CHE was the Cardiff and Newport branch, founded in early 1972. It later merged with the Cardiff Gay Liberation Front. This badge was worn by the then group secretary of the CHE, who would go on to serve as convenor from about 1974 to 1977.

HOWARTH PENNY is 31. A year ago he gave up a well-paid civil servant's job to take on a breadline £1500 a year post fighting for the cause he believes in.

He's not ashamed to admit he is homosexual. He will be satisfied that his work has proved worthwhile if, within the foreseeable future, he can help to persuade tens of thousands of men and women throughout Britain fearlessly to claim the same.

He knows from personal experience the struggle they face. 'My family friends and office colleagues all knew I was gay and accepted the fact,' he recalls of his days living and working in London, 'but I still felt terribly isolated. At least the situation is far better now than it was five or six years ago.'

Now, as the Manchester-based full-time secretary of the Campaign for Homosexual Equality, he helps direct the aims and efforts of Britain's largest gay organization. There is a floating C.H.E. membership of some 15,000 and many thousands more who've belonged for a short time.

'The fight for equality', Liverpool Echo, 5 December 1974

CHE began in 1964, as the North-Western Homosexual Law Reform Committee (NWHLRC). At that time, all homosexual acts between men were illegal. The Wolfenden Report, published in 1957, had recommended that gay sex be decriminalised, but there was little sign of this becoming law. Allan Horsfall, a coal board employee and a Labour councillor in Lancashire, attempted to get the matter raised through his local Labour Party, but found the Party very resistant to change. He then joined the London-based Homosexual Law Reform Society (HLRS) and took part in its campaigns for law reform.

In 1963 the HLRS agreed to the setting up of local committees in different parts of the country. In practice only one such committee was created: the NWHLRC was facilitated by the Bishop of Middleton, and had its first public meeting in Church House, Manchester, on 7 October 1964. Allan Horsfall became its secretary.

Over the next three years the NWHLRC and the HLRS campaigned actively for law reform. This eventually bore fruit with the passing of the Sexual Offences Act 1967, which legalised gay sex, but only in England and Wales. Both parties had to be over twenty-one, no one else must be present, and the Armed Forces and Merchant Navy were excluded. At this point some of the supporters of the HLRS thought that their work had been done; for Allan Horsfall and the NWHLRC, however, it was only the beginning of a long process leading to full equality for gay people. In 1969 the NWHLRC was renamed the Committee for Homosexual Equality and in 1971, keeping the same initials, it became the Campaign for Homosexual Equality.

Following partial decriminalisation in 1967 it was clear that there was little prospect for the time being of further law reform; meanwhile there was a clear need for 'safe spaces' in which gay men and lesbians could be themselves. It was therefore decided to set up Esquire Clubs in towns around the country, on a model similar to northern working men's clubs. CHE organised a very memorable public meeting to discuss the issue in Burnley, chaired by the broadcaster Ray Gosling, but no Esquire Clubs were ever opened.

HOMOPHILE ORGANISATIONS

Gay Liberation Front (G.L.F.), Caledonian Road, London, N1. 01-837 7174. Mainly operates in London and a few other towns. Dash not Liverpool. Publishes 'Come Together' and Gay Manifesto.

Campaign for Homosexual Equality. (C. H. E.) 28 Kennedy St. Manchester. 2. 061-228 1985. 70 in England and Wales, groups in Liverpool and Wirral. Publishes 'Lunch', National bulletin and many relevant leaflets. Local group active politically and socially.

A Gay newspaper 'Gay News'. 10p available from Virgin Records, Bold St. and Probe, Clarence Street.

Any other information from the local situation available from Gay Sock on Inquiry via letter rack G or phone 709 4410 evenings.

'Homosexuality – a dirty word?',
Guild Gazette (Liverpool),
20 March 1973

CAMPAIGN FOR HOMOSEXUAL EQUALITY P.O. Box 427, 28 Kennedy Street, Manchester 60. Telephone 061-228 1986. In Liverpool 709 3586. Meetings held at the Gazebo, 23 Duke Street, Liverpool at 8:00 PM on 1st, 3rd and 4th Thursdays of each month. Also Gay societies at Liverpool University and Polytechnic. All meetings aimed at a greater understanding of homosexuality and its acceptance in the community.

Liverpool Echo, 7 September 1976

With thanks to the Campaign for Homosexual Equality. Find out more about CHE at www.c-h-e.org.uk/history.shtml

HERITAGE ACTIVISM

THE THIRST for queer history in the UK and Ireland has been well established for over half a century. Museum activists have campaigned loud and hard for a space on the walls of museums, for the chance to see themselves, their culture and their struggles represented with dignity and respect. This movement peaked with the dumping of pink filing cabinets across London on 18 November 2016. Demanding a museum to call 'home', the Queerseum campaigners danced around the cabinets to raise awareness of the queer history lying buried in archives across the UK and Ireland. 'I think it's really, really important to make our histories and collective memory accessible – especially for young people, because the fight is nowhere near over. And I think it's really important that young people recognise the fact that the privilege that we enjoy today didn't come from the government, it came from the grassroots and the activists,' said youth campaigner Nadia Asri, surrounded by pink cabinets in Picadilly Circus.

In the mid-2020s, the trans community has been placed front and centre in culture wars across the Global North. This is highlighted by the series of anti-trans protests that were staged outside libraries and museums right across Britain and Ireland, from Belfast to Bexleyheath to Bristol to Reading to Brighton to Lewisham. At the receiving end of the protests was Sab Samuel's (aka Aida H Dee) *Drag Story Time* act, a children's storybook event staged anywhere and everywhere from pubs to museums. Starting in 2017, far-right and conspiracy theorists calling themselves 'sovereign citizens' stormed the events, waving protest signs sporting slogans like 'Welcome Groomers'. These protests came to a head on 11 February 2023, outside the front of Tate Britian. With lines of riot officers dividing protestors on the left from those on the right, the performer had to be escorted by police through the gallery, and the families and young children attending the workshop had to be shut securely behind closed gallery doors. Lance O'Conner, aged fifty-nine, was found guilty of making comments moti-

Cover of *Trans-Inclusive Culture: Guidance on Advancing Trans Inclusion for Museums, Galleries, Archives and Heritage Organisations.*

Transcestry: 10 years of the Museum of Transology (2025).

vated by 'hostility towards sexual orientation and transgender identity'. His accusations of paedophilia were ruled by the court to have gone beyond freedom of expression into hate speech. It's an historic reminder of the inseparability of gay and trans struggles.

'Cultural organisations are rare spaces in the public realm where we can manifest and model inclusion and equity, where diverse citizens come together to explore and connect, to engage and understand, to express themselves and celebrate differences. Through the stories they choose to tell – and how they tell them – museums, galleries, archives and heritage organisations inform and enrich society's conversations about identity and belonging. As a result, groups engaged in struggles for rights, dignity and respect have long recognised the role that cultural organisations can play in upholding and affirming their lives and in fostering the conditions for mutual respect and understanding between different groups. For trans people – whose lives are so often written about by others and who frequently find themselves the subject of stories that are distorted, sensationalised and mobilised to prompt division and hate – cultural organisations can, at their best, operate as spaces where trans lives and experiences can be presented on their own terms. All of these characteristics of cultural organisations reveal their potential but also their complexity as sites where varied groups of staff, volunteers, visitors and partners, come together.'

Taken from Trans-Inclusive Culture: Guidance on Advancing Trans Inclusion for Museums, Galleries, Archives and Heritage Organisations, Research Centre for Museums and Galleries, University of Leicester, 2023. Free to download at https://le.ac.uk/rcmg/research-archive/trans-inclusive-culture

ANNE LISTER'S PLAQUE DEBACLE

IN 2018, YORK Civic Trust announced the unveiling of the UK's first rainbow plaque, honouring Anne Lister (1791-1840). Lister had significant relationships with women and is heralded as a lesbian icon. They are also hailed as a gender non-conforming legend by the trans community for breaking gender prescribed taboos like wearing masculine dress, having an aggressively entrepreneurial career and being married in a traditionally male role in a cis-heterosexually modelled ceremony. This led to divisions in the community over how to best honour Lister in twenty words! The first plaque favoured their career and gender defiance over their beloved status as a lesbian diarist. It was replaced by a newly worded plaque highlighting sexual identity. Whilst proving controversial, the Lister plaque goes down in queer history itself, because it provided us, as a wider community, with a tremendous learning – that history doesn't require us to cancel each other out. Indeed, it is impossible to consider Anne Lister as a whole person without looking at the way they lived life in all its fullness.

Above: Original rainbow plaque commemorating Anne Lister and Ann Walker's commitment at Holy Trinity Church, erected by York Civic Trust in July 2018.
Right: Replacement rainbow plaque erected at Holy in February 2019.

HUDDERSFIELD PRIDE, 1981

AT THE START of the 1980s, the Gemini Club in Huddersfield was repeatedly raided by police. Men were arrested for gross indecency. Their addresses were taken, and further harassment included officers turning up at their workplaces and outing them. *Gay News* reported the harassment, and in response, organisers decided to move the annual London Gay Pride march to the West Yorkshire market town. An estimated two thousand gay and lesbian rights campaigners assembled from around the country for what would go down in British gay and lesbian history as the first ever national Gay Pride protest. The march was led by the club's owner, John Addy, wearing green nail polish and driving his pink Rolls Royce. Locals recall that the attitude of the police was forever changed. Addy recalls his car being scratched up by activists who objected to his display of wealth.

GAY PRIDE IN HUDDERSFIELD, 1981.

THIS week is apparently 'Gay Pride' week. And not only do gay people have a week to themselves they also hold an association for deaf gays, disabled gays and for all I know, arthritic gay hay fever victims. What puzzles me is why a band of people who spend much of their time bemoaning the fact that they are not treated as normal consistently hive themselves off into totally unnecessary selective groups.

Liverpool Echo, 27 June 1979

PROTESTS NOT PRISONS

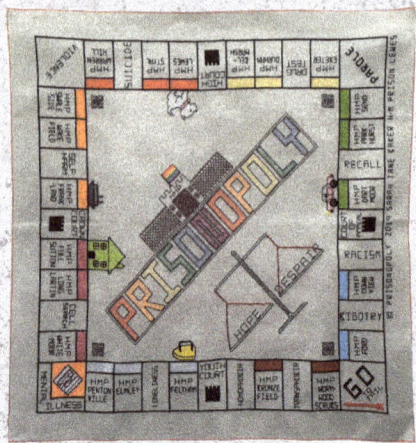

'On the 21st October [2023] we took a coach to protest outside H.M.P. Isle of Wight where Sarah is currently being held as a vulnerable prisoner. Not only is this moving her far away from friends and family but the healthcare provider has stopped her hormones! They are refusing to pre-scribe estrogen [sic] against specialist advice. This causing her physical and mental distress. It is yet another punitive and transphobic measure being taken again someone who was not even found guilty of the crime that has had her recalled!!'

@freesarahjanebakercampaign

↑ Prisonopoly cross-stitch by Sarah Jane Baker completed while incarcerated in the men's prison in Lewes.

Sarah Jane Baker (1969–) is a British transgender rights activist, author and prolific artist. She was a prison inmate in twenty-nine different male prisons over thirty years. She came out as trans in 2013 and was repeatedly denied healthcare in prison. Freed from prison, she has been a vocal activist, frequently taking direct action at protests. At the London Trans Pride protest on 8 July 2023, which met in Trafalgar Square, Baker scaled Nelson's Column carrying a loud hailer. Halfway up, she yelled out to the audience 'If you see a TERF [trans-exclusionary radical feminist], punch them in the fucking face'. Initially, the Metropolitan Police decided the incident was not worthy of investigation. But the intervention of Suella Braverman (appointed Home Secretary by Prime Minister Liz Truss), who called via Twitter for the police to reopen the investigation, led to the Met arresting Baker at her flat on suspicion of inciting violence. Four days after the event, she was taken into custody.

The Free Sarah Jane Baker protestors reported that Sarah was under probation for

'Imprisoned for Crime, Sentenced to Risk' direct-actions instigated by ACT-UP (Aids Coalition to Unleash Power) were held outside numerous UK prisons (this one is at Norwich prison, 15 January 1994). Protestors catapulted condoms over the walls.

Call for release of man given female hormones

The Mental Health Review Tribunal met in Liverpool yesterday to decide whether to advise the Home Secretary to release a prisoner who has been injected with female hormones to cure him of abnormal sexual urges. William Pate, 37, a homosexual, was sent to Broadmoor in 1966 under a Mental Health Act Restriction order after indecently assaulting a boy. In 1971 he was treated with anti-male oestrogen hormone pellets. This treatment, invented in 1963 for men with uncontrollable sexual urges, increases the number of female hormones in the body. It often causes the formation of breasts, although it cannot change a man's sex.

After treatment with female hormones, the subjects are sometimes shown pornographic films to ensure that they can no longer be sexually aroused.

Daily Telegraph, 29 November 1978

---

crimes she committed over thirty years ago, but in her recent court hearing, the court ruled her speech would not result in her recall to prison. Nonetheless, despite being found not guilty of 'commissioning an offence', she remained in custody at the all-male HMP Isle of Wight prison until 30 May 2024 (recalled on the grounds that she was out on licence). She was denied her oestrogen treatment throughout this period. In response to this, she has since founded the Trans Prisoner Alliance to help the estimated 295 trans people (2024) in the UK who are incarcerated in facilities according to the sex they were assigned at birth, rather than their gender identity.

TRANS PRIDE COLLECTIVE UK & IRELAND

TRANS PRIDE UK was founded by the Museum of Transology on 11 February 2023. With a grant from Art Fund, we invited activists from every Trans Pride organisation in the UK and Ireland to meet at Triangle LGBTQ+ Cultural Centre in Deptford. The groups brought objects to donate to the museum, listened to intergenerational talks, ate cake, sang tranny-oke and shared skills and strategies. They came from Birmingham, Brighton, Dublin, Hastings, Leeds, London, Manchester, Northern Ireland, Norwich, Plymouth, Scotland, Southampton and the South West. Since forming the collective, Trans Prides have joined from Portsmouth, Hull, Coventry and Winchester.

↓ Trans Pride Collective Logo designed by They Them Studio.

TRANSVESTISM AND TRANSSEXUALISM IN MODERN SOCIETY CONFERENCE

By Kit Heyam

THE UK'S FIRST national trans conference, 'Transvestism and Transsexualism in Modern Society', took place at the University of Leeds and Leeds Beckett University (then Leeds Polytechnic) from 15 to 17 March 1974. It was organised by the Beaumont Society, a peer support and activist group for those who were known at the time as transvestites and transsexuals. Initially, it was open only to those assigned male at birth. The conference was groundbreaking in being run by trans people, for trans people. It was an opportunity for networking, socialising, education, skill-sharing and community organising, with the aim of providing 'an interesting and rewarding experience, as well as an ideal opportunity to further the task of improving the understanding of this subject by the Medical profession, Social and Religious Workers, the Law, and the General Public'.

The conference organisation was spearheaded by North of England Beaumont Society representative June Willmott and a postgraduate student at the University of Leeds, named in documents of the time as both Colin and Caroline. The University of Leeds Gay Liberation Front also lent their support, organising the Saturday evening activities and cooking soup for the Sunday lunch. The organisers advertised widely, sending posters to universities across the north of England and press releases to local and national media, as well as targeted invitations to potentially interested parties: 'You, as a known Transvestite/Transsexual, are cordially invited to attend ...'. The programme included talks on the psychological, legal and medical aspects of trans experience, as well as discussions on topics crowd-sourced from the delegates themselves – ranging from 'Transvestites and the family' and 'The medical/psychiatric approach to transvestism and transsexualism' to 'Has bisexuality a future?' Alongside this, delegates had access to a book stall, a sale of 'ladies' footwear at bargain prices' in larger sizes, a film screening and a Saturday night 'disco-dance'. Ultimately, the conference attracted 102 delegates from across and beyond the UK, with 185 attendees at the disco.

June Willmott's opening speech expressed her 'most fervent' hope that the 'better understanding' brought about by the conference 'may ultimately mean that the transvestite and the transsexual can walk freely abroad in Society, offending no-one, better understood by some, and, we hope, tolerated by all'. The conference paved the way for all of this and more, nurturing the development of a trans community organised around self-understanding, informed consent, mutual aid and collective action. The Beaumont Society – now open to all trans people – still exists today as a 'national self help body run by and for the transgender community'.

Kit Heyam is a university lecturer, queer history activist and trans-awareness trainer who has worked with organisations across the UK. They are the author of Before We Were Trans: A New History of Gender *(Basic Books, 2022).*

Conference programme, 'Transvestism and Transsexualism in Modern Society', University of Leeds and Leeds Beckett University (then Leeds Polytechnic), 15–17 March 1974.

APPENDIX 'D'   Conference Programme (as sent to Delegates)

THE FIRST NATIONAL T.V./T.S. CONFERENCE AT LEEDS

On 15th, 16th and 17th March, 1974
"TRANSVESTISM AND TRANSSEXUALISM IN MODERN SOCIETY".
Organised by the Leeds University T.V./T.S. Group.

Principal Speakers

Dr. Elizabeth Ferris, MB., BS.,
(Gender Identity Research)

Miss M. E. Williams,
(Public Relations Officer, Beaumont Society.)

Mrs. C. F. Cordell,
(Social Worker, Founder of ACCESS)

Miss Julia Tonner,
(Transsexual Action Organisation U.K. Branch.)

Admission to the Conference is FREE, but any Donations towards the costs will be gratefully accepted.

Leeds T.V./T.S. Group,
153 Woodhouse Lane,   Tel 39071 Extn. 57
Leeds 2.

PROGRAMME

All times shown are approximate and may be subject to alteration.

Friday 15th March 7.30 – 10.30pm at the Guildford Hotel, Leeds. Reception and Coffee Evening for Delegates and Friends. Licensed Bar available.

Saturday 16th March At Leeds University Union Debating Chamber.

10.15 a.m. Opening address: J. B. Willmott (Conference Secretary)
10.30 a.m. Miss Margaret Williams (P.R.O. Beaumont Society)
"The Psychology of Transvestism and Transsexualism"
11.15 a.m. Miss Julia Tonner (T.A.O., UK Representative)
"Fit or Misfit?" The position of the Transsexual at work and leisure in modern society.
12.00 – 1.00 p.m. Lunch (Available at the University Refectory)
1.00 p.m. Mrs. C. F. Cordell (Social Worker, Founder of ACCESS)
"Know Thyself"
1.45 p.m. Dr. E. Ferris (Gender Identity Research)
"Transvestism and Transsexualism: Their Origins and the Problems of coping with these conditions".
2.30 p.m. Feature Film: "The Queen"
Behind the scenes at an American 'Drag Contest' featuring Transvestite and Transsexual viewpoints.
4.00 p.m. Conference Workshops
to The Conference will divide up into a number of Discussion Groups, each
5.00 p.m. of which will be asked to examine some aspect of Transvestism and Transsexualism and its impact on Family and Social life. The results will be presented at the Sunday morning Conference Session.
-: Tea Break :-
7.30 p.m. Social Evening and Disco Dance for Delegates and Conference Visitors, at
to the Lipman Building (adjoining Leeds University Medical School)
12.00mdnt. Admission (on production of Conference Programme) 25p.
Lounge and Bar (Extension to 11.30 pm) Dancing to Top Discs.

34.

TRANS DIGITAL ACTIVISM

Trans-Inclusive Culture: Guidance on Advancing Trans Inclusion for Museums, Galleries, Archives and Heritage Organisations

'In the year ending March 2022, hate crimes recorded by police rose in England by 26%. Crimes against trans people showed the greatest growth of any category, up 56% from 2021. In Scotland, recorded violence against trans people doubled between 2014/15 and 2019/20.'

DEVASTATINGLY, on 11 February 2023, sixteen-year-old trans girl Brianna Ghey was lured into Culcheth Linear Park in Warrington, where she was fatally stabbed by two local teenage attackers. The horrific crime struck at the heart of the trans community, with social media channels flooded with outpourings of despair. In response, candlelit vigils were organised by trans activists right across the UK and Ireland.

The digitisation of trans activism proved to be an urgent and responsive tool for mass organising. Ironic, considering the devastating effect with which unregulated disinformation about the trans community is spread online. Using digital media to spread word of locations and timings, the direct actions went 'viral'. Tens of thousands attended the London vigil organised by Trans Activism UK and Trans Action Bloc, but local community mourners gathered as far afield as Orkney and the Cornish town of Redruth. In total, 124 vigils are known to have taken place, mapped

← All known public vigils for Brianna Ghey, a map created by Stonewall Was a Riot, 2023.

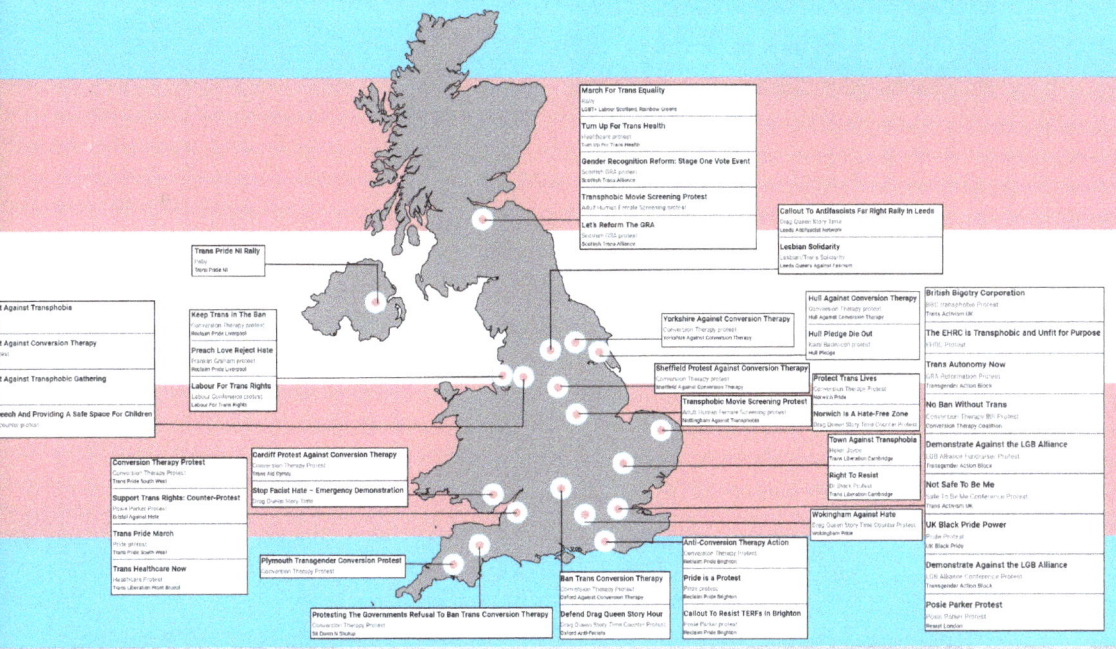

daily on Reddit by Stonewall Was a Riot (trackers of trans activism) and publicised on Instagram by the Museum of Transology, who received event details in direct messages from organisers. The final digital map of all locations reveals not only the way the vicious, senseless, premeditated murder reverberated throughout the trans community, but the way in which the trans community was alive, visible and united across the UK and Ireland and, moreover, supported by their local communities who showed up in in their tens of thousands in solidarity.

↑ A map of UK trans activism direct action in 2022, created by Stonewall Was a Riot.

Since these actions, several of these volunteer-run websites (including the seminal Stonewall Was a Riot) have disappeared. Not only does this reflect the ephemeral nature of queer digital activism but, ironically, it reveals the necessity of our determined efforts to historicise these events before the queer past repeats itself by slipping into yet another chasm of hidden history.

→ Sixteenth birthday candles and protest signs collected at the Vigil for Brianna Ghey, Department of Education, London, 15 February 2023, by the Museum of Transology.

4: ACTIVISM AND COMMUNITY | 193

CONCLUSION

THIS QUEER SCRAPBOOK originated before the pandemic in a project called 'Queer beyond London', which sought to offset the dominance of the capital in the UK's queer history. Justin, Matt and leading lesbian historian Alison Oram together explored the queer dimensions of Plymouth, Brighton, Leeds and Manchester to show how local economies, demographics, geographies, histories and traditions shaped queer lives, identities and communities in distinctive ways, and how queer people shaped their cities' histories. They worked with a mass of incredible material gathered by LGBTIQ+ community history projects in these places, with regional archives, and with the Lesbian and Gay Newsmedia Archive (LAGNA) at the Bishopsgate Institute in London.

This material was the basis for the historical narratives we wove in the resulting books – *Queer beyond London* (2022) and *Locating Queer Histories* (2022) – but these books couldn't do justice to the queer stories we encountered. First of all, despite the incredible range of sources we uncovered or that were shared with us by members of these communities, the books didn't give us the opportunity to sufficiently showcase these histories visually. And, second, we became increasingly aware in the course of the project that there was much, much more material relating to other parts of Britain and Ireland. We wanted to share some of this – and the idea for a queer scrapbook ranging across Britain and Ireland was born. We asked two more editors – Rebecca and E-J – to join us in creating it, and we have been energised by Manchester University Press's enthusiasm and creativity in building this scrapbook with us.

We've enjoyed working together closely in ways that reminded us of early collaborative queer experiments in history-making of the 1970s and 1980s. Those important projects were pragmatic in their commitment to the urgent need to preserve and bear witness to our history but also radical in imagining how to do it. Their work created anchor points to sustain and rethink identity and community in the present and for the future. We loved the idea of scrapbooking, of pulling together material which spoke of different experiences, places and people and formed a tapestry of queerness in Britain and Ireland. Its threads and loose ends show real diversity and possibility but also deep resonances in our queer island stories.

There is perhaps a queer drive to collect, born of cultural marginalisation, erasure and a historic lack of visibility. Accumulating queerly resonant 'stuff' allows us to fashion a sense of self, belonging and community; it fires our creative and historical imaginations in the present. For generations before our own, when social taboos and legal penalties forced queer people into isolation, scrapbooks built from newspaper clippings and similar evidence of other queer lives allowed individuals to imagine themselves part of a community. Early trans magazines and newsletters often drew on the format of scrapbooks to visualise possibilities for individuals and communities. The Lesbian and Gay Newsmedia Archive (LAGNA), meanwhile, holds over two hundred thousand newspaper cuttings about the LGBTIQ+ community, many of which have been collected by a network of volunteers from across the country. The clippings have been cut out with scissors and glued to pages with dates and sources handwritten above them. They are a collective effort in scrapbooking that has amassed a hugely significant community resource for envisaging the way queerness has been positioned socially, politically and culturally.

Scrapbooks and collections are rarely neat or coherent, but nor are our lives, and the materials collected here show in all their chaotic beauty how this messiness can in fact be a strategy for resilience. As with the scrapbooks our queer and trans forebears created, the lives and possibilities we have been able to represent have been constrained by what is more or less visible in the archives. Many inspiring people and experiences in the past went unrecorded or unpreserved; records of others were destroyed by family, friends or the individual themselves, either to erase the queerness of lives or to protect loved ones from hostile social judgement. These erasures are as much a part of our history as the stories which have survived. Similarly, there have always been challenges and controversies in LGBTIQ+ history. Scrapbooks are contingent and evolving and so too are the ways in which individuals and events in the past are interpreted. Our histories have been conceived in multiple and sometimes contradictory ways as we each try to make sense of our present by reaching out to those in our past. Working on our own scrapbook has brought home to us the opportunities collaborative history-making provides for coming together as a community and recognising the vibrant diversity within it.

We collected the material for this scrapbook in several ways. We began by putting out a call to archivists, community historians and others for sources or reflections on aspects of British and Irish local queer history. This yielded a wealth of fascinating material, and we are immensely grateful to everyone who responded. Inevitably, there were gaps, both in regional coverage and in the diversity of lives represented. In a second phase, therefore, we drew on our own networks and knowledge gained from previous work in queer and trans history to reach out to specific community history groups, individuals and archives that held material on other aspects of LGBTIQ+ history we wanted to cover – though still inevitably partially: this scrapbook is no exception to the genre in being eccentric and fragmentary. The images, clippings, documents and memories featured in the scrapbook will inevitably spark thoughts of all the things that are not included; that, we think, is part of the fun.

The task of selecting material and preparing it for the publisher has highlighted one of the many ways in which LGBTIQ+ forms of existence, community-building and activism have queered the society we live in. While legal frameworks around intellectual property and copyright insist that the creator of a piece of writing, image or other cultural artefact be contacted to obtain permission to reproduce it, feminist and queer practice has often actively challenged the social value accorded to the individual. Readers of homosexual and trans magazines in the 1960s typically shared stories, essays, sketches and cartoons freely and anonymously with other readers. In the 1970s and 1980s, many feminist publications were produced and filled with contributions by collectives as part of a political commitment to valuing collaboration and equality over individual recognition. These practices have enriched LGBTIQ+ culture and lives for the last half century and sit awkwardly – queerly – alongside copyright expectations. We have made our best endeavours to bring the two into alignment, but have not always been fully successful, and welcome anyone who can enlighten us on our unattributed sources to make contact so that we can include them in future works. Finally, we would like to thank all those who have so generously shared their work, memories and treasures with us as part of this project – it has been a joy and a privilege to scrapbook together.

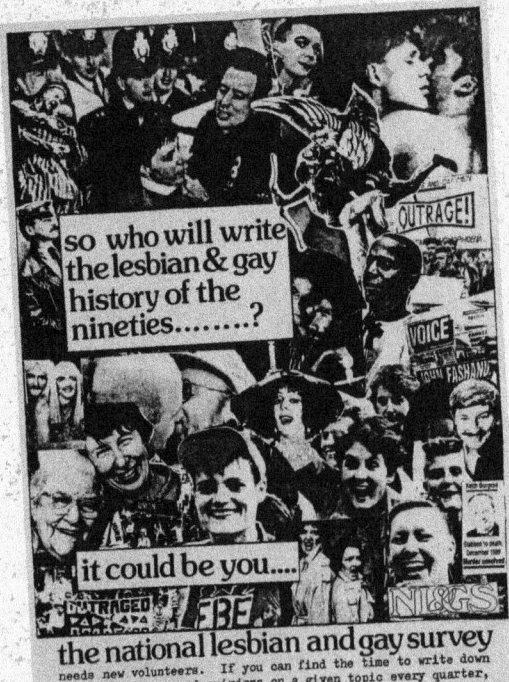

The National Lesbian and Gay survey (NLGS) was launched in 1986 by Kenneth Barrow, who was inspired by his membership of the Mass Observation national writing project (1937 to the 1960s; relaunched in 1981). The NLGS ran until 2004 and the autobiographical reports it gathered are available to consult at the Mass Observation Archive at The Keep, Brighton (www.massobs.org.uk).

LIST OF CONTRIBUTORS

Adams, Christopher 140-3
Asquith, Daisy 58-61
Bale, Anthony 16-17
Barlow, Clare 104-6
Beaumont, Kythé 170-1
Blachford, Gregg 92
Bossom, Kai 118-19
Brooks, Ross 65
Cant, Bob 80-2
Charlton, Beth 92
Crompton, Emily 68-71
Diamond, Caroline 148-50
Diggins, Rhian 54
Egan, Orla 139
Etheridge, Mark 159, 179
Fairweather, Paul 165
Figueiredo-Stow, Franko 148-50
Fountain, Daniel 166-7
Furness, Paul 112-13
Golding, Victoria 44-7

Hall, Charlotte 180-1
Heyam, Kit 190-1
Horsley, Ross 76-7
Jones, Kay 164
Le Flohic, Alf 88-9
McGraith, Peter 24-7
Malone, Andy 86
Massey, Ian 107-8
Montgomery, Idroma 114-15
Oram, Alison 22-3
Rathbone, Jaya 134-5
Scott, E-J 146-7
Sellers, Leila 40-1, 74-5
Severs, George 65, 172-3, 176-7
Walsh, Fintan 124-6
Waters, Ben 127-8
West, Khalil 83
Weston, Sally 170-1
Whittle, Stephen 30-1
Yockney, Jen 171

EDITORS

Justin Bengry is Senior Visiting Research Fellow at King's College London

Matt Cook is Jonathan Cooper Professor of the History of Sexuality at Mansfield College, University of Oxford

Rebecca Jennings is Professor of Modern Gender History at University College London

E-J Scott is a curator, Founder of the Museum of Transology and Senior Lecturer at Central Saint Martins, University of the Arts London

LIST OF ILLUSTRATIONS

Front cover, clockwise from top left: (1) Cardiff Gay Liberation Front, 10 November 1971. (2) Flyer for Transfabulous Strictly Bona Ballroom, London, 23 February 2008, designed by Jason Barker. Courtesy of Jason Barker and Serge Nicholson. (3) Black Trans Lives Matter London, Museum of Transology, June 2020. (4) Tilley with her pint. Photo © Robert Workman, June 1976. Courtesy of Bishopsgate Institute LGBTQIA+ Archives. (5) Save Sodomy from Ulster. Courtesy of Belfast *News Letter*, 22 October 1983, pictured: Tarlach Mac Niallais.

INTRODUCTION

Pages 4-5: 'This Is How We Got Here', a mural created by young people at the Manchester LGBT+ Centre. Courtesy of the Proud Trust, photo © Sally Ann Norman.

SECTION 1 HOME AND FAMILY

Page 7, top: Queer squat on Grand Parade, Brighton, 2013. Photo © Simon Dack / Alamy; **bottom left:** Kathy Sells and Daniel (her son) on a Positive Images march through Haringey in May 1987, protesting against the banning of educational books about homosexuality in schools. Courtesy of Bishopsgate Institute LGBTQIA+ Archives, photo © Brenda Prince; **bottom right:** Manchester Social Services poster advertising for lesbian and gay carers, probably circa late 1990s. Courtesy of Manchester City Council.
Page 8, top: Lesbian Mothers banner at the Lesbian Strength march, London, 27 June 1981. Courtesy of Bishopsgate Institute LGBTQIA+ Archives, photo © Robert Workman; **bottom right:** Scottish poet Jackie Kay with her son, Matt Kay, at her installation as Chancellor of the University of Salford in 2015. Courtesy of Jackie Kay; **bottom left:** Cover of Susanne Bösche's *Jenny Lives with Eric and Martin* (1983).
Page 9, top: Sketch of the FFLAG banner at Pride 1995, probably produced by a member of the Manchester Parents Group. Courtesy of Manchester Archives and Local Studies, and Sarah Furley, Chair of FFLAG. The FFLAG website (www.FFLAG.org.uk) contains links to resources and support services. FFLAG are unique in being a charity set up by and for parents of LGBT+ children, through which parents offer peer support to others with LGBT+ 'children' of any age; **centre:** Bryan Bale. Courtesy of Michael Hannah/John Harrison; **bottom:** Poster created by Out For Our Children. Courtesy of Out For Our Children.
Page 11: Cartoons by Jo Nesbitt, published together with Sue Cartledge and Susan Hemmings, 'How did we get this way?', *Spare Rib*, no. 86 (September 1979), p. 45. Courtesy of Jo Nesbitt.

Page 12: Cartoon sent in by a reader to the *Beaumont Bulletin*, vol. 2, no. 9 (May/June 1970). Courtesy of Wellcome Collection, PP/SUS/A/9.

Page 14: Two parents with placards from the Manchester Parents Group on the Clause 28 march in London, 30 April 1988. Courtesy of Bishopsgate Institute LGBTQIA+ Archives, photo © Brenda Prince.

Page 15: Undated letter sent by the mother of a gay man to FFLAG. Courtesy of Manchester Archives and Local Studies, and Sarah Furley, Chair of FFLAG.

Page 17: Bryan in Naples, 1970. Courtesy of Michael Hannah/John Harrison.

Page 18: Zenka Bartek and her girlfriend, Wyn Cooper, 1940s. Courtesy of Bishopsgate Institute LGBTQIA+ Archives.

Page 19, top: Band Jasmine.4.t after performing at BBC 6 live. Creative Commons CC-BY-4.0; **right:** Singer-songwriter Jasmine.4.t at the Green Man Festival. Photo © Rob Watkins/Alamy.

Page 20: *Beaumont Bulletin*, vol. 2, no. 8 (March/April 1970), p. 12. Courtesy of Wellcome Collection, PP/SUS/A/9.

Page 22, top: *News of the World*, 19 December 1954; **bottom:** *Daily Herald*, 14 December 1954.

Page 23, top: *Daily Express*, 14 December 1954; **bottom:** *The People*, 24 October 1954.

Page 24: A poster celebrating the history of human rights advocacy group LIBERTY. Photo © Peter McGraith.

Page 25: Royal Mail 'Smilers' stamps of McGraith and Cabreza moments after being married at Islington Town Hall. Photo © Peter McGraith.

Page 27: McGraith and his younger child, Ashley. Photo © Peter McGraith.

Page 28, top: Pauline Heap, Plymouth Campaign for Homosexual Equality's Women's Convenor, in her kitchen with children Joanne and Yvonne. Courtesy of Bishopsgate Institute LGBTQIA+ Archives, photo © Robert Workman; **bottom left:** *Daily Express*, 11 January 1978. Courtesy of Bishopsgate Institute LGBTQIA+ Archives; **bottom right:** *Evening News*, 5 January 1978. Courtesy of Bishopsgate Institute LGBTQIA+ Archives.

Page 29: *The Sun*, 19 August 1994. Courtesy of Bishopsgate Institute LGBTQIA+ Archives.

Page 30: Trans man Professor Stephen Whittle with his wife and their children (1996). Photo © Christopher Pillitz/Alamy.

Page 31: Freddy McConnell with his family in Spain. Photo © Freddy McConnell.

Page 32, left: *The Pink Paper*, 15 July 1994; **right:** Cover of 'Action for Lesbian Parents' leaflet, 1977.

Page 33: Cartoon by Lyn May, illustrating a Rights of Women 'Lesbian Custody Leaflet', c.1980. Cartoon © Lyn May.

Page 35: Collage of media headlines about lesbian and gay adoption in *Adoption and Fostering News*, no. 46 (January/February 1991).

Page 36: Vicky in the living room of her childhood home in Stockton-on-Tees. Courtesy of Rebecca Jennings.

Page 38: Maureen Duffy, *The Microcosm* (London: Virago Press, 1989).

Page 39: Andrée and Grace at home in Cornwall with a friend, 1960s. Courtesy of Rebecca Jennings.

Page 40: Photos of one of Martine Rose's parties in Sheffield. *Rose's Repartee*, no. 1 (September 1989), p. 2. Courtesy of Martine Rose and Bishopsgate Institute LGBTQIA+ Archives.

Page 41: An advert for a party held at Rose's House. *Rose's Repartee*, no. 1 (September 1989), p. 18. Courtesy of Martine Rose and Bishopsgate Institute LGBTQIA+ Archives.

Page 42: Cover of the Advisory Service for Squatters' 'Squatters Handbook' (6th edition, 1979).

Page 44: Moors above Todmorden. Photo © Victoria Golding.

Page 45: Lambeth Women's Workshop poster. Courtesy of Matrix Open feminist architecture archive, www.matrixfeministarchitecturearchive.co.uk.
Page 31, top: Doorstep of lesbian home in Hebden Bridge. Photo © Victoria Golding; **bottom:** Todmorden Cricket Club, location of the lesbian disco. Photo © Victoria Golding.
Page 48: Cartoon by David Shenton, *Roof*, no. 78 (November and December 1988). Cartoon © David Shenton.
Page 49: Flyer from Triangle Lesbian and Gay Tenants Association, Brighton, c.1990. Courtesy of Alf Le Flohic and The Keep.
Pages 50–51: LGBTIQ+ homeless charity, AKT banner at the Manchester Pride Parade, August 2022. Photo © John B Hewitt/Alamy.

SECTION 2 SOCIALISING AND SEX

Page 53: Nigel Young and Derek Cohen outside 267 Old Brompton Road, London. Photo © Gregg Blachford.
Pages 54–55: Older Lesbian Network stickers, Cardiff, 1990s. Courtesy of the Glamorgan Archives on behalf of the Women's Archive Wales, ref.: DWAW1.
Page 56: Joint membership card, Mary McIntosh and Elizabeth Wilson, Minorities Research Group, 1965. LSE Hall-Carpenter Archives.
Page 57, top left: Announcements, *Arena Three* (December 1967); **top right:** Cheshire Pen Club advert, *Arena Three* (January 1970); **centre:** Cover of *Films and Filming* (August 1958); **bottom:** Personal ads in *Films and Filming*.
Page 58: *This Week*: 'Homosexuals', ITV, October 1964. Courtesy of the BFI.
Page 59: *This Week*: 'Lesbians', ITV, January 1965. Courtesy of the BFI.
Page 60: *This Week*: 'Lesbians', ITV, January 1965. Courtesy of the BFI.
Page 61: *Man Alive*: 'Consenting Adults', BBC, June 1967. Courtesy of the BFI.
Page 62: 4 University Street, Belfast, home of Cara-Friend, 1984. Courtesy of Cara-Friend, photo © Doug Sobey.
Page 63, top: Cara-Friend Lesbian Line poster, 1980. Courtesy of Cara-Friend; **bottom:** Michael Workman answering the Cara-Friend helpline, mid-1970s. Courtesy of Cara-Friend, photo © Doug Sobey.
Page 64: Brighton Polytechnic Lesbian & Gay Society flyers c.1988. Courtesy of the Keep Archive Centre OUR123/3 and Melita Dennett.
Page 65, top: Cover of Oxford student magazine *Isis*, 19 May 1973; **bottom:** Cambridge Gay Group event, c.1985. Courtesy of Cambridgeshire Archives K2450/2/5/1.
Page 66: Black Lesbian and Gay Centre flyer, London 1998. Courtesy of Bishopsgate Institute LGBTQIA+ Archives.
Page 67: London Lesbian and Gay Centre, programme of events, August 1986. Creative commons CC BY-SA 3.0 / Alison Wheeler.
Page 68: Advert for the new Gay Centre in Manchester, published in *Gay Life*, July 1987. Courtesy of Manchester Public Libraries.
Page 69: The original interior and reception of the Manchester Gay Centre. Courtesy of Manchester Public Libraries.
Page 70: An Alcoholics Anonymous meeting held at the centre. Courtesy of the Proud Trust, photo © Sally Ann Norman.

Page 72, left: *Disabled Dykes Newsletter*, 2004. The Keep Archives Centre OUR46/1, courtesy of Jane Traies for Val Brown; **right:** *BLACKOUT: A Black Lesbian and Gay Magazine*, no. 1 (Summer 1986). Courtesy of London School of Economics (LSE) Hall-Carpenter Archives HCA/Ephemera/45.

Page 73, top left: *Older Lesbian Newsletter*, no. 1 (August 1984). Courtesy of LSE The Women's Library (TWL)/Journals; **top right:** *Gay Christian: Bulletin of the Gay Christian Movement*, no. 15 (November 1979). Courtesy of LSE Hall-Carpenter Archives HCA/Journals/34; **centre left:** *Campaign for Homosexual Equality Wigan Group* newsletter, no. 12 (January 1976). Courtesy of LSE Hall-Carpenter Archives HCA/CHE/7/125; **centre right:** *Gays in Mid Sussex*, no. 5 (August 1982). Courtesy of LSE Hall-Carpenter Archives HCA/CHE/7/146; **bottom:** *The Bi-Monthly: The Newsletter for Bisexuals*, no. 1 (January 1984). Courtesy of LSE Hall-Carpenter Archives HCA/Journals/240.

Page 74: *Gemini*, no. 2 (May 1975). Courtesy of LSE Hall-Carpenter Archives HCA/Ephemera/572.

Page 75, top: An advert for the Philbeach Hotel, *The Glad Rag: Journal of the TV/TS Group*, no. 14 (1984). Courtesy of the Wellcome Library; **bottom:** A map providing directions to the TV/TS Centre, French Place, *The Glad Rag: Journal of the TV/TS Group*, no. 36 (1987). Courtesy of Bishopsgate Institute LGBTQIA+ Archives.

Page 76: *Leeds Other Paper*, no. 19 (August 1975). Courtesy of West Yorkshire Queer Stories.

Page 77: 'Out in the North', *Leeds Other Paper* (10 November 1989). Courtesy of West Yorkshire Queer Stories.

Page 78: *Arena Three*, vol. 1, no. 1 (1964).

Page 79: Information about Esquire Clubs Limited, North-Western Homosexual Law Reform Committee, 1 July 1968. Courtesy of Manchester Archives.

Page 81: The Glass Bucket on St Andrews Street in 1977. Photo © DC Thomson.

Page 83, top: Multidisciplinary artist Vaginal Davis performing for Chew Disco at the Kazimier, Liverpool, November 2013. Courtesy of Khalil West, photo © Pete McConnell; **bottom:** Club Kali's longest serving Chutney Queen on stage celebrating the club's birthday in 2022. Courtesy of Club Kali, photo © KTB.

Page 85: Transfabulous poster designed by Jason Barker, 2011. Courtesy of the Bishopsgate Institute Archives, © Jason Barker and Serge Nicholson.

Page 86: Kremlin nightclub, Belfast.

Page 87: Birmingham Gay Festival programme in *Voice Magazine*, August 1984.

Page 88: Safari Bar flyer, designed by Barrie Appleyard and Ian Harding, 1983. Courtesy of Alf Le Flohic.

Page 89, top: MAGIC logo, designed by Chris Taylor, 1977. Courtesy of Alf Le Flohic; **bottom:** Tim Day and John Bruce at Hazelpits Farm, c.1978. Courtesy of Alf Le Flohic, photo © Nick Baines.

Page 90: Portway Picnic flyer, 7 August 1983. Courtesy of Bristol Archives, cat. ref. 45248.

Page 91: Header for 'Picnic Site Sex Scandal' excerpt. Courtesy of Bristol Archives, cat. ref. 45248.

Page 93, top: Tumulus, Hampstead Heath, London. Photo © Joe Passe / Flickr; **centre:** Chain Reaction poster, 1987. Courtesy of Bishopsgate Institute LGBTQIA+ Archives; **bottom:** Black Perverts Network invitation card, 1997. Illustration James Belasco. Courtesy of Ajamu X.

Page 95: *Thrilling Bits*, catalogue 2 (winter 1988/89). Courtesy of Bishopsgate Institute LGBTQIA+ Archives and Lisa Power.

Page 96: Defend the Bolton 7, Bolton 7 Defence Campaign flyer, Manchester, 1998. Courtesy of Manchester Archives.
Page 97, right: 'Wrap it up' stickers created by Alf Le Flohic, early 1990s. Courtesy of Alf Le Flohic; **bottom left:** Guide to Wellness poster, LIK:T, Manchester, 2004. Courtesy of Manchester Archives; **bottom right:** Sholay Love campaign poster. Courtesy of NAZ.
Page 98, top: Jason. Queer Pandemic Project; **bottom:** Kuljit. Queer Pandemic Project.
Page 99, top: Lalith. Queer Pandemic Project; **bottom:** Alison. Queer Pandemic Project.
Page 100: Brighton scene and club adverts. Courtesy of Alf Le Flohic, photo © Justin Bengry.
Page 101: Halloween Dance ticket, Brixton Fairies, London, ?1982. LSE Hall-Carpenter Archives HCA/Thornycroft/1.

SECTION 3 ARTS AND CULTURE

Page 103: Matt Cook, c.1976. Courtesy of Matt Cook.
Page 105: Interior of the Barn Theatre, Smallhythe Place, Kent, with Edith Craig (sitting), by Tony Atwood, 1939. Courtesy of the National Trust and Francesa and Michael Atwood. © The National Trust.
Page 106: Edith Craig, by Tony Atwood, 1943. Courtesy of the National Trust and Francesa and Michael Atwood. © The National Trust.
Page 107: Ian Massey at the Barbara Hepworth Museum, St Ives, 1976. Courtesy of Ian Massey.
Page 108: John Milne and Julian Nixon at Trewyn, St Ives, in June 1959. Courtesy of, and © Tom Sargant.
Page 109: Lesbian knits, c.1988. Courtesy of Leeds Museums and Galleries.
Page 110: Lesbian knits, c.1988. Courtesy of Leeds Museums and Galleries.
Page 111: Intentional Promotion badge and case. Courtesy of Leeds Museums and Galleries.
Page 114: Idroma Montgomery's illustration of Lilian Jemmott. Courtesy of Idroma Montgomery.
Page 115: St Mary's Church on Bute Street. Courtesy of, and © Jen Lund.
Page 116: The Rembrandt Hotel, c.1965. Courtesy of Manchester Digital Music Archive.
Page 118: Gay Bogies Simon Costin, Jane Wildgoose and Craig Sheppard. Courtesy of Marti Dean and to Hastings Museum & Art Gallery, 2022.
Page 119, top: Simon Costin and Marti Dean of the Gay Bogies, who have celebrated 'the release of the spirit of summer' in Hastings since the early 1990s. Courtesy of Marti Dean and Hastings Museum & Art Gallery, 2022; **bottom:** Logo of the Yorkshire Trans Choir. Courtesy of Claye Bowler.
Page 121: Poster for *Blood Green*. Courtesy of Bishopsgate Institute LGBTQIA+ Archives.
Page 122: The statue of Oscar Wilde in Dublin by Danny Osborne. Photograph by Holger Uwe Schmitt. Wikimedia Commons.
Page 123: National Theatre press release for Tony Kushner's *Angels in America*, 1991. Courtesy of the National Theatre.
Page 124: Tonie Walsh participating in the first Alternative Miss Ireland, 1 April 1987. Photograph by Seán Gilmartin. MS 46,006 /1. Courtesy of the Irish Queer Archive, National Library of Ireland.
Page 125: Poster for the final Alternative Miss Ireland in 2012, featuring a fragmented image of Panti Bliss. Designed by Pony. MS 46,006 /1. Courtesy of the Irish Queer Archive, National Library of Ireland.

Page 126: Poster for the first Alternative Miss Ireland in 1987. MS 46,006 /1. Courtesy of the Irish Queer Archive, National Library of Ireland.
Page 128: The Royal Vauxhall Tavern. Courtesy of and © Ben Tooke.
Page 129: Duckie on the road: Mods and Rockers night in Brighton, 2014. Courtesy of Simon Casson's Duckie archives, Bishopsgate Institute LGBTQIA+ Archives.
Page 130, top: *Victim*, Dirk Bogarde, 1961. Under licence from Everett Collection, inc. Alamy; **bottom:** ABC Cinema, Plymouth, c.1965.
Page 131, left: Notice for a 'movie party' at the gay nightclub Heaven. City Limits, June 1985; **right:** Poster for film workshop at Cork's 1981 gay conference. Courtesy of Orla Egan and Cork LGBT Archive.
Page 132, top left: Glasgay Arts and Culture festival flyer, 1999. Courtesy of Bishopsgate Institute LGBTQIA+ Archives; **top right:** Poster for the Second Irish Lesbian and Gay Film Festival, 1992. Courtesy of Orla Egan and Cork LGBT Archives; **bottom:** *Rebel Dykes* film showing at Dalston Superstore in London, 2023. Courtesy of the Rebel Dykes History Project.
Page 134: Still from *The Homecoming*. Courtesy of Topher Campbell.
Page 135: C. L. R. James plaque, Railton Road, London. Courtesy of Jaya Rathbone.
Page 136, top: Unicorn Bookshop, Brighton. Courtesy of QueenSpark Books; **bottom:** Gay's the Word badge. Courtesy of Gays the Word.
Page 137, top: Prudence and Gay at In Other Words bookshop on Mutley Plain, Plymouth, c.1982. Courtesy of Gay Jones, Alan Butler and the Plymouth LGBT Archive; **bottom:** Compendium Bookshop, Camden, c.1976. Photo © Claudio Araujo. Creative Commons.
Page 138: Lavender Menace signs. Photo © Alison Orr 1983. Courtesy of the Lavender Menace Archive.
Page 139, top: A clipping from West & Wilde's newsletter, 1991. Courtesy of the Lavender Menace Archive; **centre:** Books on display in Lavender Menace. Courtesy of the Lavender Menace Archive; **bottom:** The Women's Place (1982–90) was an inclusive social and arts initiative in Cork. Courtesy of Orla Egan and Cork LGBT Archive, photo © Josef Kovac.
Page 140: Cover of *The Hill* by H. A Vachell, 1905. Cover design by Percy Wadham.
Page 141: Cover of *A Chinese Garden* by Rosemary Manning, 1962. Jacket design by Germano Facetti.
Page 142: Cover of *The Heart in Exile* by Adam de Hegedus (London: W.H. Allen, 1953). Jacket design by Oliver Carson.
Page 143: Cover of *Aubade* by Kenneth Martin, 1957. Cover design by Lynton Lamb.
Page 144: The Museum of Transology, in Brighton and on tour from 2014. See museumoftransology.com. Photo courtesy of Katy Davies. Courtesy of the Museum of Transology, Bishopsgate Institute and by kind permission of Wellcome Institute.
Page 145, top: Logo of West Yorkshire Queer Stories. Courtesy of West Yorkshire Queer Stories; **centre:** Poster for the Cork LGBT Archive. Courtesy of Orla Egan, Josef Kovac and the Cork LGBT Archive; **bottom:** Nineteenth-century figurine of the 'Ladies of Llangollen'. Courtesy of Mark Etheridge and the National Museum of Wales.
Page 147: From the zine *The Kweens Haus: Kings Manor's Queer Heritages* by Fran Mahon. Courtesy of Fran Mahon.
Page 149: Out On An Island map of notable LGBTIQ+ figures on the Isle of Wight. Courtesy of Caroline Diamond and Franko Figueiredo. Copyright © StoneCrabs Theatre 2024
Page 151: Header, LGBTQ+ History Month 2025, Bodleian Library, Oxford. With permission of the Bodleian Library and courtesy of Evie Chandler.

SECTION 4 **ACTIVISM AND COMMUNITY**

Page 152: No Pride in War is a coalition of LGBTIQ+ and anti-war activists who were formed in response to the involvement of military presence and a flyover by the Red Arrows at London Pride in 2016. Designed by Matt Booner. Courtesy of Peace Museum, Shipley.

Page 153, top: Bisexual Action, Manchester. Flyer courtesy of Jen Yockney MBE; **bottom:** 'Free Sarah Jane Baker' protesters outside HM Prison Isle of Wight 5 December 2023. Photo © Talia Woodin.

Pages 154-155: Museum of Transology polaroids of trans activists and allies at the Black Trans Lives Matter protest, Parliament Square, London, 27 June, 2020. Photos by E-J Scott © Museum of Transology.

Page 156, top: Lady Phyll, Co-founder, UK Black Pride. Image by Wazaja, CC BY-SA 4.0 via Wikimedia Commons; **bottom:** Rainbow Noir at Manchester Pride in 2022. With thanks to Rainbow Noir, Manchester.

Page 157: Black Trans Lives Matter protest placard, London, 27 June 2020. Photos by E-J Scott © Museum of Transology.

Page 158: Gays Against Nazis badge, NMLH.2022.371.18. Courtesy of People's History Museum.

Page 159: Glitter Cymru banner, 2019. Courtesy of Amgueddfa Cymru - Museum Wales.

Page 160: Lesbian and Gay Men Support the Miners badges 1994 and 2014. Courtesy of Amgueddfa Cymru - Museum Wales.

Page 164: Liverpool Lesbian and Gay Action banner, 1990. Courtesy of National Museums Liverpool.

Page 165, top: Lesbian Liberation badge. Courtesy of the Bishopsgate Institute LGBTQIA+ Archives; **bottom:** 'YES, I'M HOMOSEXUAL TOO' badge, late 1970s. Courtesy of the Bishopsgate Institute LGBTQIA+ Archives.

Page 166: UK AIDS Memorial Quilt panel, created by Body Positive Devon and Body Positive Somerset, 1993. With thanks to Dr Daniel Fountain.

Page 167: UK AIDS Memorial Quilt in Tate Modern's Turbine Hall. Photo © Guy Bell/Alamy Live News.

Page 170: Poster for the Lancashire Lesbian and Gay Coalition's 'Never Going Underground' rally, 1991. Courtesy of Manchester Archives and Local Studies. With thanks to Sarah Furley, Chair of FFLAG.

Page 171, top: York Lesbian and Gay Solidarity (YLAGS) at the 'Stop the Clause' march in York, 1988. Photo © Kythé Beaumont and Sally Weston; **bottom:** Flyer addressed to Ben Summerskill of Stonewall. With thanks to Jen Yockney MBE.

Page 172: 'Jimmy's on the road', *Capital Gay*, 9 March 1990. Courtesy of the Bishopsgate Institute Archives, photo © Gordon Rainsford.

Page 173: 'What's on', *Capital Gay*, 18 April 1990. Courtesy of the Bishopsgate Institute LGBTQIA+Archives.

Page 177: left: GAY LIBERATION FRONT badge, 1995. Courtesy of Amgueddfa Cymru - Museum Wales; **right:** TEACHERS AGAINST SECTION 28 badge. Courtesy of Amgueddfa Cymru - Museum Wales.

Page 178, top: ACT-UP MARCH ON BRIGHTON flyer, 1989; **bottom:** A YEAR OF LESBIAN & GAY ACTION FIGHTING SECTION 28 EURO-TOUR flyer, 1988. With thanks to Melita Dennet for both.

Page 179: CYLCH banner, 1991. Courtesy of Amgueddfa Cymru - Museum Wales.

Page 181: 'We have a dream/Mae gennym freuddwyd'. Banner made for a march from Bath to Greenham in June 1983. Designed by Thalia Campbell Designs. Courtesy of the Peace Museum, Shipley.

Page 182: 'Campaign for Homosexual Equality' badge worn in the 1970s by the then group secretary of the CHE, Mike Ashdown. Courtesy of Amgueddfa Cymru – Museum Wales.

Page 184: Cover of *Trans-Inclusive Culture: Guidance on Advancing Trans Inclusion for Museums, Galleries, Archives and Heritage Organisations*. Courtesy of the Research Centre for Museums and Galleries.

Page 185: Transcestry: 10 years of the Museum of Transology (2025). Photo by Henri T. © Museum of Transology.

Page 186, top: Original rainbow plaque commemorating Anne Lister and Ann Walker's commitment at Holy Trinity Church, erected by York Civic Trust in July 2018. Photo by Phil Champion at Geograph. Licensed under a CC BY-SA 2.0 licence; **bottom right:** Replacement rainbow plaque erected at Holy in February 2019. Photo by Astronomyblog at English Wikipedia. Licensed under a CC BY-SA 4.0 licence.

Page 187: Huddersfield Pride march 1981. Courtesy of Bishopsgate Institute LGBTQIA+ Archives, photo © Robert Workman.

Page 188, top: 'Prisonopoly' cross-stitch by Sarah Jane Baker, completed while imprisoned in HMP (men's prison) Lewes. © Sarah Jane Baker; **bottom:** ACT UP activists catapult condoms over the boundary wall of Norwich Prison, 1994. With thanks to weRAGEon.com

Page 189: Trans Pride Collective UK & Ireland and the Museum of Transology centre trans heritage in trans protest. Graphic designed by TheyThem Studio.

Page 191: Conference programme, 'Transvestism and Transsexualism in Modern Society', University of Leeds and Leeds Beckett University (then Leeds Polytechnic), 15–17 March 1974. Courtesy of the Beaumont Society.

Page 192: All known public vigils in the UK and Ireland held in memory of Brianna Ghey, February 2023. With thanks to Stonewall Was a Riot.

Page 193, top: UK trans activism direct action in 2022. With thanks to Stonewall Was a Riot; **bottom:** Sixteenth birthday candles and protest sign collected at the Vigil for Brianna Ghey, Department of Education, London, 15 February 2023. Courtesy of the Museum of Transology.

Page 196: The National Lesbian and Gay survey (NLGS). Courtesy of the Mass Observation Archive, University of Sussex.

INDEX OF PLACES

Aberdeen 121
Aberystwyth 179

Banbury (Oxfordshire) 98
Bangor (Northern Ireland) 142–3
Barnstable 167
Bath 120
Belfast 62–3, 87, 133, 139, 184
Birmingham 13, 43, 87, 129, 153, 158, 189
Blackpool 129
Bognor Regis 88
Bolton 96
Bradford 77, 123, 131, 135
Brighton 7, 28, 49, 53, 64, 72, 86, 97, 100, 129, 136, 140, 144, 173, 178, 184, 189, 194
Bristol 13, 32, 57, 90–1, 123, 184
Burnley 165

Cambourne 175
Cambridge 28, 65, 109, 129
Cardiff 9, 16–17, 54, 114–15, 159, 182
Cheshire 20, 57, 153
Chester 120
Cork 116, 121, 139, 145
Cornwall 2, 39, 107, 174–5, 192
Coventry 189

Derby 120, 133
Devon 57, 140–1, 174
    see also Plymouth
Devonport 87
Dorset 15
Douglas (Isle of Man) 162–3, 168
Dublin 2, 120, 122, 131, 189
Dulais 136
Dundee 80–2

Eastbourne 129

Edinburgh 38, 109, 121, 123, 138–40, 173
Essex 14
Exeter 167

Glasgow 37, 48, 123, 132, 173
Greenham Common 44, 153, 181

Harrogate 112, 181
Hastings 118–19, 129, 189
Headcorn (Kent) 89
Hebden Bridge 44–5, 129
Huddersfield 134–5, 186–7
Hull 129, 140, 189

Ilkley (Yorkshire) 77
Ireland
    Northern Ireland 189
        see also Bangor; Belfast
    Republic of Ireland 56, 158, 184
        see also Cork; Dublin
Isle of Man 162, 168
Isle of Wight 12–13, 148–50, 153, 188

Kent 20, 104–5

Lancashire 162, 165, 170
Lancaster 120
Leeds 32, 37, 44, 72–3, 76–7, 97, 109, 110–13, 146, 158, 172, 189–91, 194
Leicester 99, 120
Liverpool 36–7, 83, 129, 183, 188
    see also Wirral
Llangollen 145
London 2, 8–9, 16–18, 27, 32, 35, 37–9, 42–3, 45–6, 48, 52, 56, 58, 66–7, 72, 74–5, 78, 83, 84–5, 93–5, 97, 99, 102–3, 111, 114, 120, 127–9, 131–2, 136–7, 141–2, 146, 153–5, 158, 176, 183–4, 188–9

206 | A QUEER SCRAPBOOK

Barnet 28
Bexleyheath 184
Bloomsbury 136
Brixton 42, 92-3, 101, 134-5, 172
Bromley 20
Camden 137
Catford 22-3
Dalston 132
Earl's Court 52-3, 92
Hackney 45
Haringey 7, 46
Hoxton 74
Islington 25, 66, 74
King's Cross 52
Lewisham 48
Old Compton Street 52
Peckham 66
Soho 52, 135, 141
Vauxhall 92-3, 127-9
Lothian 109

Manchester 6, 7, 14, 30-2, 34, 44, 51, 66, 68-71, 78-9, 86, 96-7, 116-17, 133, 138, 158, 165, 173, 176-7, 183-4, 189, 194
    Canal Street 53, 69, 116
Margate 12
Medway 89
Menwith Hill 181
Middlesex 160
Midlands 59-60, 176-7

Newcastle 120, 129, 131
Norwich 188-9
Nottingham 177

Oldham 133
Orkney 2, 192
Oxford 60-1, 65

Penzance 167
Plymouth 19, 87, 120, 130, 137, 167, 174, 189, 194
Portsmouth 189
Preston 170

Ramsgate 129

Reading 184
Redruth 192

Salford 8, 116
Scotland 58-9, 138-9, 160, 189, 192
    see also Aberdeen; Dundee; Edinburgh; Glasgow; Lothian; Orkney
Sheffield 2, 40-1, 87, 102-3, 121
    Millthorpe 121
Shipley 181
Shirehampton 90
Smallhythe (Kent) 104-6
Somerset 57
Southampton 189
South West (Region, England) 167, 189
Southampton 98, 120
Staffordshire 102-3, 176
St Ives 2, 107-8
Stockton-on-Tees 36, 120
Surrey 6, 72-3
Sussex 21, 72-3
    see also Brighton
Swansea 54-5
Swindon 110

Taunton 167
Todmorden 2, 44-7
Torbay 167

Wales 136
    see also Aberystwyth; Cardiff; Dulais; Llangollen; Swansea
Walsall 42
Warrington 192
Wigan 72-3
Winchester 189
The Wirral 183
Wolverhampton 176-7
Wombourne 176
Worcestershire 21

York 147, 170, 186
Yorkshire 12, 38, 111, 119, 134-5, 144, 146, 153, 159
    see also Leeds

INDEX OF SUBJECTS

Aaab-Richards, Dirg 161
activism and protest 4, 7, 8, 9, 14, 24–7, 32, 66, 106, 116–17, 125, 126, 132, 136, 145, 160–1
    ACT UP 76, 128, 172–3, 178, 188
    Black Trans Lives Matter 153–5
    Brighton Action Against the Clause 177
    Cambridge Scrap Section 28 65
    Homosexual Law Reform Society (HLRS) 183
    Lesbians and Gays Support the Miners 160, 180
    Lesbians and Gays Support the Printworkers 66
    Liverpool Lesbian and Gay Action 164
    North-Western Homosexual Law Reform Committee 78–9, 183
        see also community groups: Campaign for Homosexual Equality
    Outrage! 162
    peace activism 44, 180
    York Lesbian and Gay Solidarity (YLAGS) 170
    see also comminity groups; homes and housing: activism; Section 28; trade unions; Section 4: Activism and Community
Addy, John 187
adoption and foster care 33, 34–5
age of consent 64, 96, 122
Ajamu X 92–3, 134–5
archives and libraries 3, 126, 145, 157, 160, 165, 194–6
    rukus! Black LGBT cultural archive 134–5
    see also list of illustrations 198–205
art 104–11
Asri, Nadia 184
Atwood, Tony 104–6

Bale, Bryan 9, 16–17

Baker, Sarah Jane 188
BBC 176
bereavement 16–17
bisexuality 13, 60–1, 64, 72–3, 76–7, 134, 137, 140, 150, 153, 171
Black and Asian club nights 83, 150
Bolton Seven case 97
bookshops (Compendium, Gay's the Word, In Other Words, Lavender Menace/West and Wilde, Unicorn, Women's Place) 43, 136–9
Brixton Fairies 101
Brown, Ted 161

cabaret 116, 124–6, 127–9
    see also theatre and performance
Campbell, Topher 134
Cant, Bob 80–2, 160
Carpenter, Edward 102, 121
child custody 32–3
children's books 8
civil partnership 19, 27
    see also marriage
class 108, 121, 140, 145, 146
Clause 28 see Section 28
coming out 12–13, 80, 102–3, 144
community centres
    Black Lesbian and Gay Centre (London) 66, 72
    London Lesbian and Gay Centre 66–7
    London TV/TS Centre (French Place) 66, 74
    Manchester LGBT+ Centre 68–71
    Mutual Aid Centre 164
    Triangle LGBTQ+ Cultural Centre 189
community groups
    African Rainbow Family 158
    Beaumont Society 41, 190
    Bisexual Action 171
    Black Perverts Network 92–3, 134–5
    Body Positive (Devon, Somerset) 166–7

Brighton and Hove Disabled Dykes Club 72
Cambridge Gay Group 65
Cambridge Gay Outdoor Group 65
Campaign for Homosexual Equality (CHE) 28, 65, 68, 183, 72–3, 76–7, 174–5, 182–3
    see also Activism and protest: North-Western Homosexual Law Reform Society
Cara-Friend (Northern Ireland) 62–3
CYLCH (Aberystwyth) 179
East Anglia Bikers 65
Friend (London) 68, (Manchester) 74
Gay Black Group 66
Gay Health Education Group (Cambridge) 65
Gay Switchboard (Manchester) 68
Gay Teachers Group 66
Glitter Cymru 159
Is Rainbow Muid, We are Rainbow Support Group 158
Lancashire Lesbian and Gay Coalition 170
Leeds Bi Group 76–7
Leeds No Borders 159
Leeds Transvestite/Transsexual Social Group 72
Lesbian and Gay Teacher Support Group (Cambridge) 65
Lesbian Immigration Support (LISG) 158
Lesbian Line 63
Lesbian Link (Manchester) 68
Liverpool Homophile Society (Gaysoc) 161
London Bisexual Group 72
London TV/TS Group 74
Manchester Gay Alliance 68
Manchester Homophile Society 68
Manchester Lesbians Group 68
Medway Area Gay Independent Community (MAGIC) 89
MESMAC (Leeds) 77, 97
Micro Rainbow 158
Minorities Research Group 56
Naz (BAME sexual health charity) 97
Northwest Campaign for Lesbian and Gay Equality 70
Nottingham Dykes 177
Older Lesbian Network (Wales) 54–5

Positively (UK, East) 166
Rainbow Noir 156
Stonewall 95, 171
Stonewall Was a Riot 192–3
Trans Action Bloc 192
Trans Activism UK 192
Wolverhampton Lesbian and Gay Rights Group 176
    see also activism and protest; community centres; Pride; youth groups
community organising see activism and protest
conferences 32, 117, 131, 138, 145, 153, 162–3, 171, 190–1
COVID-19 pandemic 53, 98–9, 157
crafts 109–13
    see also HIV/AIDS: UK AIDS Memorial Quilt
Craig, Edy 104–6
cruising 61, 75, 80, 88, 89, 90–3

dance 117–19
    see also disco; theatre and performance
Dennett, Melita 64, 178
disability 7, 47, 48, 72, 164
disco 46, 65, 117
divorce 32, 36
drag 74, 88, 115, 124–6, 184
    see also theatre and performance
Duckie (performance) 127–9, 151

education 17, 31, 43, 193
employment 43, 58–9, 86, 98, 112
European Convention on Human Rights 168
European Court of Human Rights 96

family responses 13, 14–15, 40, 48, 49
Fani-Kayode, Rotimi 134
Fashanu, Justin 161
fashion and clothing 42–3, 46, 165
    see also leather
feminism 12, 83, 92, 116, 137–8
    see also Women's Liberation
fertility treatment 28, 30–1
film and cinema 102, 130–3, 134–5, 176–7
    Films and Filming magazine 56–57
    Get Your Clause Off Our Lives 176–7

INDEX OF SUBJECTS | 209

folk and folklore 146
    Gay Bogies 118–19
friendship 9, 13, 19, 21, 35, 39, 43, 56–7, 59, 61, 92, 98, 104–6, 118–19
    see also kinship

gay liberation 12, 62, 64–5, 111
Gay Liberation Front (GLF) 153, 190
Gay Sweatshop theatre company 102, 120–1
Gender Recognition Act (2004) 84
gentrification 52
Ghey, Brianna 2, 153, 192–3
Good Friday Agreement 86

hate crime 2, 19, 36–7, 153
health (and sexual health) 94–5, 97–9
    see also COVID-19 pandemic; fertility treatment; HIV/AIDS; medicalisation
heritage 122, 144–51, 184
    Arts Council 146, 151
    HLF (National Lottery Heritage Fund) 145, 146, 148, 151
    National Trust 90
    queer heritage projects
        From a Whisper to a Roar 94–5
        Millthorpe Project: Interviews with Lesbian, Gay, Bisexual and Trans Trade Unionists 160
        Out on an Island (Isle of Wight) 12–13, 148–50
        OutStories Bristol 13, 90–1
        Pride of Place (Historic England) 93
        Queer Beyond London 64, 86–7, 194
        Queer Pandemic 98–9
        West Yorkshire Queer Stories 37, 76–7, 135, 145, 159, 180
    Research Centre for Museums and Galleries 185
    Trans-Inclusive Culture: Guidance 184–5
HIV/AIDS 26–7, 89, 94–5, 97, 103, 124, 133, 174–5, 179
    support and campaigning groups 166–7
    UK AIDS Memorial Quilt 166–7
homes and housing 36–49, 104–6, 122, 150
    activism 48–9, 50–1
    council housing 6, 37
    house parties 40–1, 47, 134–5, 145
    neighbours 48
    safe houses 40–1
    see also squats
Homosexual Offences (Northern Ireland) Order 62

India 21, 26

Jacques, Juliet 84
jazz 114–15

Kay, Jackie 8
kinship, queer 9, 16–17, 18–19, 20, 24–7, 43, 46

Ladies of Llangollen 145
law and legislation 31, 129, 138, 168, 174–5
    see also Bolton Seven case; Gender Recognition Act; Good Friday Agreement; Homosexual Offences (Northern Ireland) Order; policing; prison; Section 28; Sexual Offences Act; Wolfenden Report
leather 92
libraries *see* archives and libraries
Lister, Anne 186
literature 140–3, 171
    Carpenter, Edward 102, 121
    Duffy, Maureen 38
    Forster, E. M. 102
    Gale, Patrick 150
    Hall, Radclyffe 104, 106, 141
    Orton, Joe 102
    Wilde, Oscar 122, 138
    Woolf, Virginia 150

Magee, Bryan 10–11, 58–61
marriage 20–1, 22–3, 24–7
    see also civil partnership; divorce
McKellen, Ian 95, 103
media *see* photography; print media; television
medicalisation 10–11, 12, 13, 14, 21, 29, 58, 84, 112–13, 189
Melly, Rachel 180
museums 107, 144, 145, 146, 181, 184
    Museum of Transology 144, 154–5, 157, 189, 192

see also archives and libraries; heritage; list of illustrations 198-205
music 52, 83, 89, 112-29, 135, 172
    Bell, Andy (Erasure) 173
    Boy George 42-43
    DJ Ritu 83
    Gaynor, Gloria 173
    Jemmott, Lillian 114-15
    Robinson, Tom 112-13
    Somerville, Jimmy 37, 44, 172-3
    see also disco; jazz

Naples 17
Nazi Germany 103, 176
newspapers and magazines see print media

oral history 12-15, 36-9, 56, 64, 76-7, 86-7, 90-1, 94-5, 116-17, 119, 130, 135, 137, 145, 159-60, 180

Palestine 153
parenting (gay, lesbian, trans) 7, 8, 9, 20-1, 27, 28-33, 43, 46, 82
Paris 26
Penny, Howarth 182
photography 63, 135
Phyll, Lady 156
policing 15, 36-7, 61, 96, 174, 176, 188
politics and local government 165, 183
    Greater London Council 27, 45, 66,
    Stringer, Graham 71
    see also Section 28
Power, Lisa 94-5
Pride
    BAME Pride (Cardiff) 159
    Gay 54-5 (Pride Cymru, Cardiff), 84, 119 (Hastings), 122, 150 (Rye), 127, 152, 153 (London) 164, 180 (Liverpool), 187 (Huddersfield)
    No Pride in War (Red Arrows, London) 152, 180-1
    Trans Pride 188-189
    UK Black Pride 156, 161
print media
    alternative 196
        Feminaxe 43
        Isis (Oxford) 65

        Leeds Other Paper 76-7
        Mukti 21
        Spare Rib 11, 13
        The Voice 161
    LGBTIQ+ 195-6
        Arena Three 20-1, 56-7, 78
        Beaumont Bulletin 12, 20
        Bi Community News 171
        Bi-Monthly 72-3
        BLACKOUT: A Black Lesbian & Gay Magazine 72
        Capital Gay 172
        Come Together 43, 183
        Disabled Dykes newsletter 72
        Gay Christian 72-3
        Gay Left 92
        Gay Life 68, 70
        Gay Manifesto 183
        Gay News 8, 89, 183
        Gay Sock 183
        Gemini 72, 74
        GIMS: Gays in Mid Sussex 73-3
        Glad Rag: Journal of the TV/TS Group 75
        Older Lesbian Newsletter 72-3
        Pink Paper 176
        Rose's Repartee 40, 41
        Y Ddraig Binc (The Pink Dragon) 179
    mainstream 16, 19, 22-3, 25, 27, 28-9, 30, 33, 34, 47, 57, 87, 91, 109, 110, 121, 122-3, 131, 133, 161, 162, 165, 168, 169, 174, 175, 182, 183, 187, 195
prison 146, 117, 153, 188
    see also law and legislation; policing
pubs, clubs and other venues
    The Anchor (Cambridge) 65
    Casino (Manchester) 86
    Caves (Brighton) 86
    Chew Disco (Liverpool) 83
    Club Kali (London) 83, 150
    The Coleherne (London) 92
    The Crown (Devonport) 87
    The Dome (London) 83
    Esquire Clubs 78-9
    The Fridge (Brixton) 172
    The Gauger (Dundee) 81
    The Glass Bucket (Dundee) 80-2
    The Haçienda (Manchester) 173

pubs, clubs and other venues (cont.)
    Halfway to Heaven (London) 52
    Heaven (London) 52, 173
    The Kazimier (Liverpool) 83
    Kremlin (Belfast) 86
    Longbranch (Brighton) 86
    Manto (Manchester) 69
    Market Tavern (London) 92-3
    Millionaire's Club (Manchester) 86
    The New Imperial Hotel (Birmingham) 178
    The New Union (Manchester) 116-17
    The Penrose (Plymouth) 87
    Philbeach Hotel (London) 74-5
    Porchester Hall (London) 74
    The Rembrandt (Manchester) 116
    Royal Vauxhall Tavern (London) 127, 128
    Safari Bar (Bognor Regis) 88
    Sheffield City Hall 87
    SNAX (Manchester) 69
    Speakeasy (Plymouth) 87
    The Swallow (Plymouth) 87
    The York Arms (York) 170
    see also homes and housing: house parties

Redgrave, Vanessa 165
refugees 158-9
relationships 37, 38, 39, 43, 98-9
    see also civil partnership; divorce; friendship; marriage
religion 69, 72-3, 81, 181, 183
Rose, Martine 40-1
Russia 26

Section 28/Clause 28 27, 34, 48, 65, 70-1, 160, 164, 170, 176-9
self-insemination 29, 35
sex and sex positivity 24, 97, 160
    lesbian sex wars 92, 94-5
    Rebel Dykes 132
    S&M 92-3, 94, 132
    Thrilling Bits 94-5
    see also age of consent; Bolton Seven case; cruising; leather
Sexual Offences Act (1967) 6, 39, 58, 62, 64, 96, 182-3
shame 14, 81, 127

Sinclair, Yvonne 74
squats 7, 37, 42-3, 44
suicide 161, 168-9

Tatchell, Peter 26
television 26, 58-61, 122
terminology 4, 36, 40, 64
theatre and performance 28-9, 32, 83, 84-5, 102, 120-9, 189
    Aida H Dee (Seb Samuel, performer) 184
    Alternative Miss Ireland 124-6
    Angels in America 123
    Bent (Martin Sherman) 102-3
    Birmingham Gay Festival 87
    International Festival of Transgender Arts 84
    Rebel Rebel (performer) 88
    Vaginal Davis (performer) 83
    see also cabaret; drag; Duckie; Gay Sweatshop theatre company
trade unions 66, 160-3
    Black trade union activists 160-1
    NALGAY 160
trans and non-binary 12, 20, 22-3, 30-1, 40-1, 66, 72, 74-5, 84-5, 86, 153-5, 157, 160, 185, 188-93, 195-6
    safe houses (Rose's House) 40-1
    Transfabulous 84-5
    Trans-Inclusive Culture: Guidance 184-5
    Transvestism and Transsexualism in Modern Society conference 190
Troubles (Northern Ireland) 86

Uganda 159
universities 26, 62, 64-5, 102, 111, 120, 167, 183, 190, 197

Winter, Mary 165
Wolfenden Report 183
Women's Liberation 116
    see also feminism

youth groups 4-5, 37, 77, 97
    LGBT Youth North West 71
    West Yorkshire Gay Bi Lesbian Youth Network 77

EU authorised representative for GPSR:
Easy Access System Europe, Mustamäe tee 50,
10621 Tallinn, Estonia
gpsr.requests@easproject.com

www.ingramcontent.com/pod-product-compliance
Lightning Source LLC
Chambersburg PA
CBHW051549220426
43671CB00022B/2982